ROCK STAR INTERVIEWS

Rock Star Interviews

Conversations with Leading Performers and Songwriters

by

PETRA ZEITZ

McFarland & Company, Inc., Publishers
Jefferson, North Carolina, and London

British Library Cataloguing-in-Publication data are available

Library of Congress Cataloguing-in-Publication Data

Zeitz, Petra, 1967–
  Rock star interviews : conversations with leading performers and
songwriters / by Petra Zeitz.
     p. cm.
  Includes index.
  ISBN 0-89950-898-7 (sewn softcover : 50# alk. paper) 
  1. Rock musicians—Interviews. I. Title.
ML385.Z39 1993
781.66′092′2—dc20   92-51105
                                                                 CIP
                                                                 MN

McFarland & Company, Inc., Publishers
  Box 611, Jefferson, North Carolina 28640

ACKNOWLEDGMENTS

Many thanks to Sabine Lewandowski for proofreading the original manuscript. Live long and prosper my friend!

Dankeschön to Corinne Ullrich for the Jack Bruce interview.

I would also like to thank all record companies and managements involved in organizing interviews throughout my career as a music journalist, especially: Chrysalis, EMI, Sony Music, MCA, Virgin Records, Phonogram, Electrola, Jive Records, BMG, RCA, WEA, and East West.

I wholeheartedly thank all the wonderful artists involved for their time, patience and interesting answers.

And to Emily Charette for her friendship and getting *The Writer's Market*.

CONTENTS

• Pop & Rock Music •

• Celtic Connection: Bands and Musicians from Ireland and Scotland •

• Blues Guitarists •

PREFACE

"This will be a (semi) scholarly work meant for serious researchers in rock history...," my editor told me. I agree—if you're crazy about music, this book offers a long and entertaining read, but moreover it is also a true and useful account of rock 'n' roll history. When rock stars talk to the press, for various reasons only a limited amount of what they actually say can be published, and many times their original words are changed to suit the style of the particular magazine that prints the story. I spent three years traveling through Europe interviewing bands and solo artists representing many different kinds of pop and rock music. I was mainly working for German music magazines, which published my articles regularly but were not able to print the entire interviews. This is the first time any of my interviews have been published in English (the language in which, in every case, the interview was conducted).

I was not interested in any sleazy stories nor in anybody's private life. In all my conversations, I made a point of sticking to music and other subjects the particular artist I was talking to was known for. This collection of interviews should be of interest to fellow musicians as well as to fans. Apart from the music itself, I also discussed recurring problems with record companies and other music-business related issues. I also wrote a short biography of each artist featured in this book. From the 120 interviews I conducted, I chose the following 39 because they were the most interesting and represented a diverse group of artists.

If I had to name the most important thing in my life, it would undoubtedly be music—all music. I would like to express my deepest thanks to all the artists who took the time to talk to me. I have enjoyed meeting them all.

—Petra Zeitz, March 1993

ROCK LEGENDS

JACK BRUCE

Jack Bruce was born to working-class parents in Glasgow, Scotland, in 1943. As a teenager, he studied bass and cello. At 17 he won a scholarship in cello composition to the Royal Scottish Academy of Music, but dropped out after three months to play jazz in Glasgow. Moving to London in his late teens, Bruce played with the British rhythm and blues pioneers Alexis Korner and Graham Bond. In 1965 he joined John Mayall's Bluesbreakers, whose guitarist at that time was Eric Clapton. Then, in 1966 Jack Bruce, Clapton and Ginger Baker joined forces and formed Cream—the first supergroup of the '60s. Tunes like "Strange Brew," "Tales of Brave Ulysses," "White Room" and "Sunshine of Your Love" defined the power trio. It wasn't to last long. In 1968 Cream played their final concert at London's Royal Albert Hall and released their "Goodbye" album.

Jack Bruce's first post–Cream group, Jack Bruce and Friends, featured jazz guitarist Larry Coryall and drummer Mitch Mitchell from the Experience. In 1970 and 1971, Jack propelled Tony Williams Lifetime, a band that distinguished guitarist John McLaughlin. He also formed a new trio with Leslie West on guitar and Corky Laing on drums and, after three albums with them, resurfaced in 1974 on Frank Zappa's "Apostrophe" album, for which he co-wrote the title track.

The late '70s and early '80s saw Jack Bruce playing with more acclaimed musicians such as Mick Taylor formerly of the Rolling Stones and Clem Clempson, formerly of Humble Pie.

In 1989 Bruce released a new solo album called "A Question of Time" and reunited with Gin-

Jack Bruce

ger Baker for a successful tour of the United States.

The following interview with Jack Bruce was conducted by Corinne Ullrich and myself in London in April 1990.

Petra Zeitz: Recently, I have noticed that you're going back to your musical roots, the jazz and the blues, that kind of thing.

Jack Bruce: Maybe. I'm just doing what I do. I do what I have always been doing and I don't think it's so different from anything I have done in the past. I just did some jazz things in New York a couple of weeks back. I like to play a lot of different kinds of music because otherwise I get bored doing just one thing. It's all music. I have always been trying to use the talents and whatever kinds of knowledge I have. I have many different influences.

Corinne Ullrich: You thank Jimi Hendrix, Spike Milligan and Malcolm Lowry in the credits of your new album. What influence did these people have on you?

Jack Bruce: Malcolm Lowry influenced my way of thinking because of his writing. I mentioned people who changed my life—hopefully for the better. Spike Milligan had a radio show called *The Goon Show* and as a child I grew up listening to that every week. It changed my sense of humor and, to me, Spike is the funniest person on the planet. I credited Jimi Hendrix because I was mixing the album in his studio, in Electric Lady. Also I loved Jimi and he was a friend of mine. I thought it was a kind of strange connection to be mixing an album at Electric Lady all these years later.

Petra Zeitz: Wasn't there a lot of competition between Cream and Hendrix in the sixties?

Jack Bruce: No, not at all. We were quite different. Although Jimi had a band, he was more like a solo player. He could have done it without anybody else, but Cream was very much a band. We covered different areas. We did quite a few shows together and I don't think there was any unhealthy competition between us. Maybe Eric [Clapton] felt a little bit different about that.

Petra Zeitz: You do have a new band now. Have you played with these musicians before?

Jack Bruce: Well, Ginger [Baker], I played with before. [*Laughs.*] I thought it would be nice to have him in the band because we played together on this record "A Question of Time." I also have another drummer because I play for up to three hours. So I need a couple of drummers—just like James Brown. I auditioned about 20 guitar players and this 17-year-old kid was the one I liked best. He's a great player and a great person. It's important to have people who are reasonably nice to travel with.

Corinne Ullrich: Is it not difficult to work with somebody who is so many years your junior?

Jack Bruce: No, it's necessary for me to have somebody so young, because I have a lot of energy on stage and I need somebody who can keep up with me.

Petra Zeitz: Do your own sons play with you?

Jack Bruce: They play on the record but not in the band. That would be difficult. I didn't stop them from becoming musicians but it would have been nice if they had done something else, too. They are both players now and there's nothing I can do about that. I wanted them to be doctors or lawyers. [*Laughs.*]

Petra Zeitz: You mentioned doing a three-hour set. What kind of material do you play?

Jack Bruce: I do everything from my new album and, of course, some old Cream things. There are people who really want to hear those old songs and I like playing them.

I also play some songs from my other solo albums and some blues. It's just a mixture of all the things I like to play.

Corinne Ullrich: How did you get back together with Ginger Baker again?

Jack Bruce: He was living in Los Angeles and I was recording in San Francisco. I had two tracks that were very much written with him in mind and I thought it would be nice to get him into the studio. He's a great drummer. Before that, the last time I saw him was when we played together at the Nice Festival. That turned out to be fairly disastrous, but I just wanted to see Ginger again. He used to live in Italy, but now that he'd moved to LA, it wasn't far for him to go to San Francisco. In the studio, it only took about 20 minutes to record Ginger.

Petra Zeitz: Has his playing changed over the years?

Jack Bruce: No, his playing is very much the same. I couldn't say he's changed at all—in any ways. He's still as horrible as ever. Well, he's mellowed out a little bit because he is getting married this month. So he's definitely settled down a little bit, but not too much.

Corinne Ullrich: In Cream, you and Ginger didn't get on too well. Was that due to musical differences or just a clash of personalities?

Jack Bruce: It was both— musically and personality-wise, too. We didn't see eye to eye on a lot of things. We're just like oil and water—we don't mix very well. But if you have that little friction, it makes the music a little bit more interesting.

Corinne Ullrich: You have now done 44 concerts with Ginger. Did they go well?

Jack Bruce: No, not at the beginning. It started off being very difficult, because I'm younger than he is and when I first knew him I was about seventeen years old, so he was like my big brother or something. All these years later, I'm the band leader and he couldn't take that from me in the beginning. He wouldn't play my tempos. He wouldn't play my endings. It was pretty much a struggle, but eventually he saw what was happening and he started to play properly. By the time we got to New York City it was okay.

Corinne Ullrich: Do you get on with him on a personal level now?

Jack Bruce: Well he got banned from the bus because he smoked this pipe which made everyone cough. So he got thrown off the bus and he had to drive everywhere with his girlfriend. They drove all over America following the bus. I did see him after the shows and we didn't have any problems at all. We actually became very good friends again.

Corinne Ullrich: Do you still have any contact with Eric Clapton?

Jack Bruce: Very little. He's doing his thing. He played with me in New York at the end of 1988. We did one show, but there's not really a lot of contact at the moment.

Corinne Ullrich: What about the rumors of a Cream reunion? Do you ever consider that at all?

Jack Bruce: If it was done in the right way, I would be happy to be part of it. I mean, I would certainly be happy to play with those guys again because there is a magic between the three of us that, I must say, I haven't found too often since those days. It would be interesting to see what would happen now. Who knows? Maybe the reunion will happen next year because that would be our 25th anniversary.

Corinne Ullrich: Is the atmosphere in the new band in any way comparable to Cream?

Jack Bruce: The energy on stage is very comparable to that. I think that is what people enjoyed in the shows. Although there are a lot of good bands around, they don't seem to have that feeling or that energy that we had. In fact, we like to take risks when we're playing. To me, it's pretty boring to just play the record. I like to go out a little bit and take chances.

Corinne Ullrich: You have

written this song called "Kwela," which was about a court case in South Africa. Have you been personally involved in that thing?

Jack Bruce: I wrote that song while I was recording the album. I am a member of an anti-apartheid organization and I give money to the ANC. But that's about it. I don't have any personal experience other than that. The song just seemed like a nice idea at the time. I'm very careful about charity things because a lot of artists use them in a selfish way, you know. I thought the worst example was the Live Aid thing.

Corinne Ullrich: You thought that was the *worst* example?

Jack Bruce: Yes, I did. A lot of people, whose careers were not doing too well, appeared on it and suddenly they were doing better. Okay, maybe the show did some good, so it was fine. But a lot of the things that people do, they don't do any good. In fact, I think, they do harm, because they take the attention away from what really matters. I mean, this is just my personal feeling. I've done a couple of things for charity and I wasn't happy with what afterwards happened to the money that was raised. Maybe they've raised a

couple of million dollars, but a million dollars go into the administration of the thing. Sting's got some problems at the moment. It's very difficult. People tend to jump on a bandwagon. I'm not against charity events if they do some good, but they sometimes raise the wrong kind of consciousness and trivialize the whole thing. I'm quite happy just to write my little song and hope the message gets across to people.

Corinne Ullrich: You were involved in a few political things in the seventies. What did you do?

Jack Bruce: The main thing I did was the UCS. Where I come from, in Glasgow, there was a lot of shipbuilding. And they wanted to close this shipyard down and the workers sat in. I helped to raise the money for them, but it was a failure in the end. The shipyard got sold off to an American company. But now the whole working class movement is dead anyway. That's life. Politicians would promise anything before an election and afterwards they say "Oh well, we can't quite manage to do that."

Corinne Ullrich: You have started to write with Pete Brown again, who, in the past, has collaborated with you on the Cream stuff. Why did you renew this partnership?

Jack Bruce: I didn't really ever stop working with him. We have always worked together. It's one of the longest running songwriting partnerships for this kind of music.

Corinne Ullrich: How does that collaboration work?

Jack Bruce: It varies a lot. I always write the music and sometimes he will just write the words. Most of the times I have the music and I also have definite ideas of what I want the song to be about. Then, we work on the words together. I'm writing more and more of my own lyrics, but I like to have Pete around to have somebody to work with. The music is something that I, very selfishly, protect. He might suggest something but I always say "no."

Petra Zeitz: You also recorded a version of the old Willie Dixon song "Blues You Can't Lose." Why did you decide to cover this track?

Jack Bruce: To me, Willie Dixon is the best American songwriter that I can think of. Years ago, we did this song of his called "Spoonful" and I was always looking for a new one of his that I could do. This is a great song and it's not too well known, so I had a shot at it.

Corinne Ullrich: The last thing I would like to mention is the royalty battle with Polygram over Cream records. Can you tell us something about that?

Jack Bruce: How did you find out about that?

Petra Zeitz: From the papers—we researched this interview, you know.

Jack Bruce: I didn't know it was in the papers. Well, basically what it's about, is, when Polygram started to re-release Cream CDs, they reduced the royalty rate from the very poor rate that we were having anyway. They said that it was more costly to make CDs, which, in fact, it isn't anymore. The whole thing is a rip-off. CDs are much too expensive. The royalty rate for Cream CDs is less than one percent, which is not too fair. I don't see why Polygram, which is a very large multi-national company, should be keeping my money. Our former manager, Robert Stigwood, was not too honest either and, like a lot of us in the sixties, we got ripped off. We were very keen to play, but we weren't business people. So now that our records are selling again, we shouldn't be ripped off again—not to that extent anyway. But I don't give up so easily. I think what they thought was that I would be dead by now. They assume those things because of the way we used to live in the old days.

Petra Zeitz: Do you think the music business has changed in that way—do people not get ripped off so much anymore?

Jack Bruce: No, it's just different people who do the ripping off. It used to be managers and now it's lawyers. Lawyers are pretty bad because they charge phenomenal sums of money to do very little. Record company contracts are this thick and it's all totally unnecessary. But it's true that, because of what happened to us in the past, people nowadays are more careful. We were pioneers. We were musicians more than pop stars, if you like. We were completely naive. So hopefully people of today are aware of the mistakes we have made. I'm sure they make different mistakes, though!

JIM CAPALDI

Traffic was formed in the mid–60s. The British rock group consisted of Steve Winwood, Dave Mason, Chris Wood and drummer Jim Capaldi. The band soon left its mark on the progressing rock scene of the time. They temporarily split up in 1969 and Winwood recorded an album with the so-called supergroup Blind Faith. In 1971 Traffic reunited and released their most successful and influential album "John Barleycorn Must Die." Bass player Rosko Gee joined the band and even though their lineup changed quite frequently, Traffic stayed together until 1974. All original members had subsequent successful solo careers.

Jim Capaldi went on to record several albums. His first solo effort was released as early as 1972 while Traffic was still going. The album was called "Oh How We Danced," but despite critical acceptance, failed to make the charts. In the mid–'70s Capaldi scored two UK hit singles and went on tour fronting his own band. The album "Let the Thunder Cry" appeared in 1981.

In 1988, Jim released what is to date his last album, "Some Come Running." It featured contributions from major acts such as Eric Clapton, George Harrison, Mel Collins, Mick Ralphs and former Traffic colleagues Steve Winwood and Rosko Gee.

In 1990, Capaldi and Winwood were once again united for the recording of Winwood's album, "Refugees of the Heart."

The following conversation with Jim Capaldi took place at his home in Marlow, England, in June 1990. Jim was one of the few artists to welcome me as a journalist to his house and I found him extremely friendly. We actually continued talking long after the tape recorders had been switched off. At his home studio Jim played me a new and yet unreleased song he had written and recorded with Steve Winwood. It was called "Living on the Edge of Grace" and was as great as anything the two of them had ever done. About a year later Jim called me at home to fill me in on the news. He was finalizing plans to do another solo record and had approached George Harrison to write some songs with him. He had also renewed his friendship with Paul and Linda Mc-Cartney.

Petra Zeitz: We were just talking about England and its role in the Common Market. Would you like England to be more open towards other countries in the world?

Jim Capaldi: Oh yes. That's what it needs. I came from a small town in Worcestershire and when you're young you get all the conditioning. Life looks through your eyes. They show the atmosphere you grow up in. This country has changed so much since the birth of rock'n'roll. When you get to travel and you see other people, there's so much misunderstanding because we usually don't experience other people's places and problems. There's a terri-ble lack of understanding. Everybody has a stereotypical attitude or image of other places, other people and other countries. But all that has been crashing down over the last 15 years, you know. Everyone is having to get together. All the old barriers and all the old problems seem very strange now. The environmental problem with the global warming, that's everyone's problem—from the Queen to the beggars in Calcutta. Nature doesn't draw any borders. So all the borders that have been drawn by mankind seem to get weaker every day. They have no real meaning. We all have to eat and we all have to live. I think the next 20 or 30 years are going to be a really important period. It's either going to be getting it together or complete chaos.

Petra Zeitz: Do you think we will get it together, though?

Jim Capaldi: The problem is money, money, money. Everybody wants money. We all struggle to survive. The very rich companies control countries. In America they are not cutting back on all the pollution and the gasses. They want to do it slowly, so the environment is dependent on those people.

Petra Zeitz: You're obviously a politically aware person.

You also did a video recently which was shown at a concert in aid of Nelson Mandela. Do you support the South African issue?

Jim Capaldi: Yes, that's why I did it. Apartheid has been an awful thing for a long time. I played with a lot of African musicians, so I've always had that connection with Africa. The song is called "Oh Lord Why Lord" and on the record I dedicated it to Steve Biko.

Petra Zeitz: Peter Gabriel and yourself are the only musicians I know to have written songs for Biko.

Jim Capaldi: That's right. I realized that he did that song, too. I didn't write the song—it's an old song—but, I think, it was so perfect. It is a black man's song written by an old black man. I've known it since 1969 and just suddenly thought I would do it. When the concert came up we said it would be perfect to put it in. Nobody asked us to play live, but they liked to have the video. Eric Clapton and George Harrison played on the record, but Eric was too busy to do the video. He was on tour in America.

Petra Zeitz: Do you believe it's important to write political songs?

Jim Capaldi: Yes, very. I think everything you do is political. You can't really get away from it. There is a political thing going on with everything that you do. Even spraying your hair is sort of a political act now. I do like music as entertainment. I love Michael Jackson because he's an incredible entertainer, you know. He dances and performs and it's pure traditional black American entertainment. When I grew up the people who did music performed in a real entertainment sense. They had groups that could sing and dance in harmony. That was a real show.

Petra Zeitz: Are you planning any live shows with your own band?

Jim Capaldi: No, and I don't really know when I'm going to make another record. Maybe I'm going to produce somebody else, but at the moment I'm writing with Steve Winwood. He's making his next record. He's got one more album to make for Virgin Records and, at the moment, he's in Nashville. I'm doing some lyrics for him. I'm probably going to work with Van Morrison in the next month or so. He was here yesterday. I want to work with people like that—people whom I know and whom I really like. I did a show last year in Holland where I played with Nicko from Iron Maiden. We had two drumkits and it was really good. But unless I have a record that sells a lot, it's not worth touring. I would have to pay my band and the guys I work with. And then to put in on the road I would have to have enough demand in the ticket sales. So I haven't toured a lot in the last few years. I want to make an album that really has a cutting edge. The time is coming to make a really strong statement. I think music is going to take a big turn.

Petra Zeitz: A turn in which direction?

Jim Capaldi: I think a lot of kids want to play again. Everything has a backlash to everything. I think the kids are going to get sick of a record, an artist and a package which is all separated. The producers and people with electronic ability lay the record down with electronic percussion and drums. Then they stick a bunch of kids on a video that dance around, but don't actually play. In the end you don't know what you're getting. You don't know what this thing is meant to represent. It's

a piece of product that is sold and played on the radio, but there is no feeling. But the kids will get fed up. When punk came it was a change from glam glitter rock. There will be a change towards bands really playing again. They will get rid of all this machine sounding stuff. It has to happen. There is a terrible kind of deafness to what is really special and to what has a meaning.

Petra Zeitz: Do you think it's going to be like it was in the sixties again?

Jim Capaldi: There was a program related to the sixties and television. Everybody really wanted to make music back then. If you made it and you were famous, of course, that was fantastic, because you wanted to be famous as well. But the music really mattered. Now you feel that is the second or third thing. You'd rather get publicity and get your face out there.

Petra Zeitz: How did Traffic get together?

Jim Capaldi: We first rehearsed in a cottage not far away from here. We started in Birmingham because we all lived in the city. Dave and myself had a band and we started to play at a popular nightclub in

Jim Capaldi

Birmingham. Steve used to come up and jam. We started to get together and we grew into a band. I came up with the name Traffic. Chris Blackwell who ran Island Records had a large piece of land in Berkshire. And there was this little cottage down a long lane. We rented it for two dollars a week or something like that. And then we all went out and lived there for a few years, through 1966, 1967 and 1968. It was fantastic. People would come down from all over the place. You could make as much noise as you possibly could because it was in the middle of no-where. We had some wild times there. We built a little hut where people could park their cars because there was just this muddy track. We had an old American Jeep. Denny Laine came up in a Jaguar sports car that got stuck in the mud. There were all kinds of people—Ginger Baker, Pete Townshend, Eric Clapton, Stephen Stills, Jimmy Page—there were loads of people. We would set up on the area for the parking and just play. It was magic for a few years. The summer of 1967 was fantastic.

Petra Zeitz: Would you say

the music of that era still has an influence on today's music?

Jim Capaldi: Oh yeah, definitely. My eldest daughter has music lessons at school and sometimes they show videos. The other day they saw Otis Redding, Muddy Waters, Jimi Hendrix, Janis Joplin, and the Rolling Stones. I said, "Well look, this was a fantastic period." It was a very influential period. The blues was what everyone was really trying to do. You wanted to be meaningful in a progressive way, but drawn from the blues, which is the strongest form of music, really. We were all so influenced by that. When I was a kid, the blues was the bottom line. That was the most real thing of everything. Now you've got today's kids and the most real thing to them is an electronic drumbox. But it's good to see John Lee Hooker again. And some of the commercials are good. They used that Muddy Waters track on a Levi's jeans commercial. We need anything to resurrect that music.

Petra Zeitz: Do you remember Traffic's first ever gig?

Jim Capaldi: Yeah, that was somewhere in Scandinavia. We went to Scandinavia to practice. Then we played at the Round-

house in London. Scandinavia got all the practice gigs; then you came back to London when it was good and tight. The Scandinavians should have filmed all those great bands in their first ever gigs. It would have been fantastic. It's a shame that there wasn't someone around who followed all these new bands and filmed them. He'd have such incredible footage.

Petra Zeitz: In 1967, Traffic went to America for the first time. How did the scene there compare to what you were used to in London?

Jim Capaldi: It was wild. I couldn't believe it! Haight Ashbury was incredible. San Francisco was really happening. They had psychedelic light shows everywhere. There's a lot more of the head-trip coming back in with bands now. There are a few bands like U2 and the Hothouse Flowers from Ireland.

Petra Zeitz: Has your attitude toward music changed since the sixties?

Jim Capaldi: No, Traffic just made statements about what we felt and what we saw. We made records to show how the world is and not just to make a few dollars. It would be nice to do that again.

Petra Zeitz: How did the

writing partnership in Traffic work?

Jim Capaldi: I wrote the lyrics and Steve wrote the music. You write in periods and Traffic was during a great period. I used to give Steve the lyrics and then we would make up the tune. Most musicians need a lyric to write. If you have something written on paper you've got half the thing there and you just have to find the sound to go with it. I think lyrics are probably the most important part of a song when they are good and powerful. The written word is such a powerful thing, because words have sound, but they have a meaning as well. Look at Bob Dylan's stuff: his music is nice, it works, but the words are just so powerful. You just gotta keep things coming. Steve and I still write together when he's up here. I wrote a track with him on the "Roll with It" album and we have been working together again since.

Petra Zeitz: How do you feel about other artists covering Traffic songs? Joe Cocker did it and also the Jackson Five.

Jim Capaldi: It's a great honor when somebody does your song. It's such a special thing, better than anything. You can't buy that, you know. Somebody likes what you have done and they want to do it—that's such a great compliment.

Petra Zeitz: So, what happened in the seventies that the music scene took a turn and developed in a different direction?

Jim Capaldi: It kind of splinted. It was around 1973 that it began to change. Hendrix and Joplin died. The Band and Bob Dylan made fantastic music, but, I guess, what happened then was glam rock like Gary Glitter, T-Rex and Bowie. Bowie was actually quite important in the seventies—he was good.

Now there are only a few people left that never sold out. Van Morrison and Neil Young are great. Their music survived all the changes and all the trends and when they play today, they still attract a large crowd. They've never done anything that had anything to do with jumping on a commercial bandwagon. And, of course, Dylan never compromises. That's what I liked about the Traveling Wilburys. I asked George if he had anything written for them and he said, "No, we just get together and knock it up."

Petra Zeitz: Would you like to make a record like that too?

Jim Capaldi: Oh, I'd love to.

You got to have a band, a collective unit. I've been on my own basically since Traffic. But working with Steve is nice—it's the same old thing again. We have been playing some of the old Traffic songs when we get together.

Petra Zeitz: Traffic's music had the same West Coast feeling that the Doors had, but you were a British band. How do you explain that?

Jim Capaldi: It's funny. The Beatles were never into that West Coast music. Traffic was the only English band that had that American feel of blues and jazz. The Who and the Stones were very British, and yet you would speak of Traffic with Jefferson Airplane, the Grateful Dead and the Doors. I think we all had such a strong sense of Latin music. We would have rhythms and conga drums. Not a lot of English bands had that feel. Traffic had this great producer called Jimmy Miller. He started to produce the Stones as well, which was their second great period after the very early hits. When Miller produced them they did "Jumpin' Jack Flash," "Sympathy for the Devil," "Honky Tonk Women." I mean, it was a really great period for them. And they started

using conga drums, which were directly out of the Traffic influence and all the African guys that used to hang around with us. Jimmy took that into the Stones. I've still got a demo of "Jumpin' Jack Flash" on my jukebox. Jimmy gave it to me. He would come home each day and tell us about the new songs the Stones had done in the studio.

Petra Zeitz: Many bands from the sixties are together again and go on the road. Do you go to see any of their shows?

Jim Capaldi: Yes, I'm going to see the Rolling Stones this year and Paul McCartney. I was talking to Marlon—Keith Richards' kid—at a Robert Plant gig in London. I was with some friends and this girl said to me, "Oh, my mum likes Traffic a lot and she plays your records." And she said something strange about some photographs, so I asked her who her mum was. And she said, "Linda McCartney." Then I realized that she looked just like her. It was Mary and she was great. She invited me to their show. I haven't seen Paul and Linda live—ever. I knew Linda very well. She took the first pictures of Traffic. When Linda first came to the cottage she brought a record of the Doors. She came all the way out to the country and no one else had ever photographed us.

Petra Zeitz: Was it difficult for you to win recognition after Traffic split up?

Jim Capaldi: Not really. I had already made three solo albums. I wanted Traffic to continue, but it didn't happen. For me, Traffic was the most important thing I've done in the music business. It was the most important contribution that I have made musically. There's a chance that we might get back together one day. It's not out of the question.

Petra Zeitz: Are you giving your fans hope for a Traffic reunion?

Jim Capaldi: We have lost one founding member which was Chris Wood, but there are still three of us around. Steve, Dave and myself would be very interested in a reunion. I speak to Dave a lot. He's in America playing clubs. He's in good shape.

ROGER DALTREY

Roger Daltrey has many facets to his career. His strong voice and flamboyant charisma has taken him to international fame as the lead singer of the Who, to screen star status with movies like *Tommy*, *Lisztomania*, and *McVicar*, and, ultimately, to film producer when he, along with other members of the Who, became executive producers for the movie *Quadrophenia* in 1978.

Daltrey was born in London, England, on March 1, 1944, and was educated locally. He formed his first band, the Detours, while still a pupil at Acton County Grammar School. In 1959, Pete Townshend and John Entwistle also joined the group. In the early sixties they changed their name to the Who, then to the High Numbers and eventually back to the Who. They soon attracted a loyal local following, especially with Mods and other teenagers. The Who were rebellious and loud. In late 1964 they dropped their existing drummer in favor of the wild Keith Moon. A few months later their first single "I Can't Explain" went to number 8 in the UK charts. Many more hit singles followed, but the early days of the Who were summed up in Pete Townshend's youth anthem, "My Generation."

Along with the Beatles and the Rolling Stones, the Who became one of the three most significant bands to emerge from England in the 1960s. The first ever rock opera "Tommy," written by Townshend but sung by Roger Daltrey, helped them to achieve superstar status in the United States and subsequently all over the world. They played the legendary festivals at Woodstock and Monterey, and in the early seventies became the best live rock'n'roll band of their era.

While the success story of the

Who expanded into new dimensions, Roger Daltrey landed his first acting role in Ken Russell's film of *Tommy*. It looked like nothing could stop the band, but in 1978, drummer Keith Moon died an untimely death as a result of the abuse of drugs and alcohol. He was briefly replaced by Kenney Jones of the Small Faces, but in 1982, Pete Townshend decided to quit. The Who disbanded after playing together for more than 18 years. Roger Daltrey was determined to pursue a solo musical and acting career. He released several albums, played leading roles in many television productions and dedicated time to his family and other business ventures.

In 1985, the Who reunited for Live Aid, but it was to be another four years before they were finally persuaded to tour the United States once again. In 1990, Roger Daltrey produced and starred in the film *Buddy's Song*, for which he discovered young singer Chesney Hawkes to play his son. Chesney subsequently had a US top ten hit with "The One and Only."

In 1992, Daltrey once again released a solo album which was called "Rock's in the Head." Another tour with the

Who was rumored to be in the cards.

My first interview with Roger Daltrey took place in May 1990 at Pinewood Studios in England. He was working on the final edits of his movie *Buddy's Song*. Added here are quotes from a second conversation I had with Daltrey in June 1991.

Petra Zeitz: Do you find it difficult to be accepted as an actor when everybody knows you as Roger Daltrey of the Who?

Roger Daltrey: Yes, it was difficult at first, but only because people had preconceptions. Once they realised that I was serious it was okay. It's like when I did the Shakespeare play for the BBC: I did *Comedy Of Errors* and I played the Dromio twins. All these really famous actors were biting their nails because it was Shakespeare. I was completely ignorant, you know, ignorance is bliss when it comes to Shakespeare. I just thought, "That's a bloody line, let's say it." It's just like a song, isn't it? I find the rhythm of that completely natural because it's just like singing. And once people realized that I could actually do it, they were nothing but helpful and wonderful. I always got on very well with actors, but at first they

Roger Daltrey

think, "Oh that bloody pop star is trying to act," you know, the usual thing. I don't think it's the fact that pop stars can't act, but it is very difficult for them to be given the opportunity. The trouble with pop stars is that they tend to think they have their image to protect. So they do roles they should never do and instead of pushing themselves into directions that they can cope with, they do things they shouldn't do. They think they have to live up to an image. So it kind of falls down 'round their ears, I think. I have done things that have been totally out of image and totally stupid, but then it teaches you not to be frightened. People start to accept you then. Once you lose that self-identity, then you're away and everything is a piece of cake. It's like stripping the paint off an old door and repainting it. That's the process, as simple as that.

Petra Zeitz: You started your acting career with movies like *Tommy* and *McVicar*, then you did a lot of television productions and now, you're trying to go back into movies. Is this a conscious development?

Roger Daltrey: I needed to learn how to act, basically. I knew I had the ability, but I didn't know any of the techniques. I needed to have freedom to develop and you can't have that making feature films. It's too naked. You're exposed too much. I feel what happens with people who are rushed into film is that they become too mannered in some ways. I'm talking about people who haven't been trained as professional actors like myself, like a lot of people from the pop business. I just fell in love with the process of acting. I thought, I'm not gonna learn it making feature films where I'm too exposed. You can't afford to take any risks. The only way to do it is to do all kinds of little things. Everything I picked, I did because I would learn something.

Petra Zeitz: You're a coproducer for *Buddy's Song*. Did you have any say in the casting as well?

Roger Daltrey: Well, the casting was very difficult because we could have never made the film without a very special person to play "Buddy." One of the prerequisites was that he had to sing all the songs live. I hate that thing in films where there's a band playing and they are really miming to a record. It makes everything sound wonderful, but music isn't like that, you know. Music has got rough edges and sometimes it sounds bloody awful—when it's live, that is! So we had to find this kid to play Buddy, and I did the usual rounds like stage schools and agents. There were some good people, but no one good enough. In the end, I went on a television show and said, "I've got a project and I have the money to do it. Is there anybody out there who can sing well and maybe act, who could possibly be my son?" Then I got a phone call from Chesney's dad who was in a band called the Tremeloes. We tested Chesney along with a few other people and he had this incredible charisma and he sang like an angel. He's a great Buddy because he's got a lot of soul, but his visual image is not stereotypical rock'n'roll.

Petra Zeitz: You also got a leading role in the film. Was Terry Clark a difficult character to play or were you playing yourself basically?

Roger Daltrey: The only way you can play anything well is always to use bits of yourself. You've always got to retain that. I'm not Terry at all, but he's great fun. He just refuses to grow up, but he is a very endearing character and, I think,

most blokes can see a bit of Terry in them.

Petra Zeitz: A very important part of this film—and of your whole life—is the music. What are you trying to say through this film?

Roger Daltrey: The film deals with where music comes from. It's not a music film, but the music that's there was actually written by somebody in the film. You see, it grows into what you eventually hear on the radio. I have always been intrigued to show on film where pop songs come from. They come from people having affairs, a bad time or a good time, going home and writing about it. I'm sure most kids listen to the radio and never give it a second thought where these songs come from.

Petra Zeitz: What do you think of musicals?

Roger Daltrey: I like them, but I don't think there are any good ones being written. I think all musicals are increasingly tedious at the moment. I still think a really good rock opera should be written and one of the few people who can write them is Pete Townshend. He could write the music, but whether he could write the story or not, is debatable. But if he teamed up with somebody with a great idea, some theatrical person, I think, he could write a great rock musical. But whether Pete would join forces with anyone is anybody's guess. I don't think he's got the ability to do it on his own. I think if he had someone with the story and a vehicle to write the songs for, then it could be amazing. I tried to team him up with Stephen Berkhoff, but if you take two megalomaniacs nothing is ever going to happen, is it?

Petra Zeitz: Would you like to get more involved in the production side of films?

Roger Daltrey: I think that's the way. I've always had that interest right to the days when we did *Quadrophenia*. I was the one in the Who who wanted to get into films. And then we started the company Who-Films. As soon as I've finished *Buddy's Song*, I'm going to be producing a film with Ken Russell on the private life of Keith Moon which I'm very excited about. I've got an idea about how to do it and it could be very, very interesting.

Petra Zeitz: Is that going to be a film to set the record straight about Keith?

Roger Daltrey: No, no, I'm not bloody setting anybody's rec-

ord straight! I think it could be a really great tragic comedy. His life was so surreal—it was unbelievable. And I think Ken would be the right director for it because there is no way Ken Russell would go any madder than Keith Moon was. I love Ken Russell. He needs controlling, but I think Ken and I will work very well together.

Petra Zeitz: You've worked with him before.

Roger Daltrey: We worked well together on *Tommy* and *Lisztomania*—another crazy film where no one understood what we were doing. But the one thing it isn't is boring. Lots of people make lots of films that are really boring and, at least, I have never done that. Criticize it as you like for other things, but it's not boring!

Petra Zeitz: Would you like to do more comedies? You have not done many yet.

Roger Daltrey: I love comedies! But see, that's because the producers don't see me as a comedian. People don't see that kind of humorous side of me. They all think I'm tough, I'm really hard, but I'm not like that at all!

Petra Zeitz: Yes, you've played a lot of villains.

Roger Daltrey: But I'm not

like that! That's what's so stupid, you see? That's what I'm saying about the image that people have. I'm not like that at all. But *The Comedy of Errors* was a comedy. One of those twins I played was incredibly stupid. He was like Stan Laurel. I loved him though. He was very nice and sweet. He would do anything for a peaceful life because he was beaten all his life.

Petra Zeitz: What keeps you going, trying to achieve success in films after what you already have achieved in music?

Roger Daltrey: Well, what would I do now? What would I do with the rest of my life? I'm working class. I was bred to work. In the early stages of our lives we were indoctrinated to believe that we had to work to put the bread on the table. I can't seem to give that up, I really can't. I could afford never to work again ever in my life, but, at the end of a week or a month, if I haven't done any work, I feel guilty. I'm being really honest, I do feel guilty. It's very strange.

Petra Zeitz: But you're lucky to be doing jobs that are kind of your hobbies as well.

Roger Daltrey: Very lucky! I actually have a line in this film where I say, "Fancy getting paid for something you like!" It's true that most of the working class people, and people lower down the wages thing, very rarely get to know what it means to get paid for doing something you'd really love to do. Most people are just working because they have to. That's wrong, but I don't know how to change it. I wish I did! Well maybe we should make everybody a millionaire tomorrow. That would solve so much! If you made everybody a millionaire tomorrow they would all realize that money doesn't buy them anything. They wouldn't be striving for it and maybe we would get back to some reality in this world. Do you know what I mean? It takes some thinking about.

Petra Zeitz: It would be some kind of rich communism, wouldn't it?

Roger Daltrey: Maybe yes, but it's the only way you can get to the real essence of communism, which is living in a more socially aware society. You can't do it in the progressive world in which we have got where we are. We are in a material situation all the time. We're bombarded with it. The only way you can do it is to supersaturate people with it. And the only way to supersaturate them with it is to make them able to have it all. Once they've got it all, they suddenly realize that the new Ferrari doesn't make you any happier. It doesn't do anything because then you start to think about polluting the ozone layer. My Ferrari sits out there and I drive it once a year. I drive an Audi usually—a really boring car, but it's less of a pollute. So anyway, what is really important in your life is the quality of it and all those other little things which really have nothing to do with money.

Petra Zeitz: Do you enjoy being famous?

Roger Daltrey: It's wonderful! The Who was very lucky. We were one of the top three bands in the world, but we never ever had that kind of distance between ourselves and our fans. It was a closeness. In the very early days we had some of that screaming and ripping clothes off, but that lasted for about six months. After that it was all on a different level, a more intellectual level. So, for me, it's like having many mates, you know. People come up and talk to me like they know me. They talk to me very honestly and it's nice. It's really like having lots of friends.

June 1991

Petra Zeitz: The Who is working on a tribute record for Elton John and Bernie Taupin at the moment. Which song did you choose to do?

Roger Daltrey: We're doing "Saturday Night's Alright for Fighting." It's coming up okay. The song is very Who-influenced anyway, but we're doing it a little differently than Elton did. It should be very interesting.

Petra Zeitz: There have been rumors around that you might be moving to the States. Is that true?

Roger Daltrey: There is not much work for me in England right now. The Who don't seem to be doing anything. I wouldn't be happy moving to the States, but I'm not happy not working either. I would probably move there for nine months of the year. Not that I have to work, but I get bored not doing it. I'm fed up with fish farms. That's like everything else—once you've done it, it's not a challenge anymore.

Petra Zeitz: How far along are you with your new album?

Roger Daltrey: I'm just finishing the demos. My solo career up until now has always been a hobby and it's always been experimental. Apart from my very first record ["Daltrey," 1973] which was an album of Leo Sayer songs, I have never ever gone into an album with the focus of what I wanted to do. I always wanted to do a bit of this and a bit of that, just to see what it was like to sing all these different styles. But this time I am focused on what I want to do and I know where I'm going. I've teamed up with an excellent songwriter who is actually producing the album as well. I'm very excited about it. It's sounding like something completely different which I'm pleased about. There is so much being done out there and people send me songs that they think I should be singing. But they don't realize I'm a 47-year-old guy and it's what I should have been singing 20 years ago—and it's what I was singing 20 years ago. So it's very difficult to find stuff that I should actually be singing at my age.

Petra Zeitz: What kind of styles do you like singing now?

Roger Daltrey: I still like rock'n'roll, but it has to have a certain vibe to it—a certain maturity which is hard to find in so much rock'n'roll.

Petra Zeitz: Would you like to play live again?

Roger Daltrey: Oh, I'd love to! I just love singing. I'm doing a couple of shows with the Chieftains, you know, the Irish band. I'm doing "Behind Blue Eyes" and an Irish folk song sung in a very heavy Cockney accent. [*Laughs*] I don't care where I play. I can play in a pub, it doesn't bother me. I played in a club in Greenwich Village and the drumkit was made of old watercans. It was great! I just want to play music. Music doesn't belong in newspapers and on videos. It should be out there with the people.

Petra Zeitz: What's the future of the Who going to be like?

Roger Daltrey: They haven't got a future! Talk to Pete Townshend—he's a boring guy. Of course, I would like to see the Who playing again. I'm proud of our past and it's great to still be able to play the music. I still think we play it well. It's not just any old rock music. No one has filled the hole that we left. The problem with the Who is that it's become so big that every-thing we do is on an enormous scale.

GENESIS

Genesis was founded in the late sixties while all members were still pupils at Charterhouse Public School near Godalming, England. The original line-up consisted of Tony Banks on keyboards, Mike Rutherford on bass, Anthony Phillips on guitar, Chris Stewart on drums plus lead vocalist Peter Gabriel. In 1967, the band was discovered by producer Jonathan King who took them into a studio to record their first single "The Silent Sun." Chris Stewart was replaced by John Silver. With the new line-up, Genesis recorded their first album a year later. It was released by Decca Records in 1969 and bore the title "From Genesis to Revelation." In 1970, the band signed with Charisma Records in London. In October, they released their second album "Trespass," this time with John Mayhew on drums. Later in the year Mayhew and Anthony

Phillips quit the band. Drummer Phil Collins—a former child actor and drummer in The Flaming Youth—joined Genesis, followed shortly by guitarist Steve Hackett.

The band began to establish itself as a leading avant-garde group in Britain. They recorded two more albums, "Nursery Cryme" and "Foxtrot." Their American debut took place at the Philharmonic Hall in New York in December 1971.

In 1973, Genesis released their first live album and recorded "Selling England by the Pound" which provided them with their first chart hit—the single "I Know What I Like." Their next project was a theatrical concept album conceived by Peter Gabriel and called "The Lamb Lies Down on Broadway." After performing the whole piece live 102 times, Gabriel announced that he was leaving the band in August

1975. Phil Collins took over on vocals and made the Genesis sound more accessible to general listeners. Three more albums were released before Steve Hackett left the band to pursue a solo career. Genesis' 1978 album "And Then There Were Three" marked the beginning of their current three-piece line-up and consisted mainly of intelligent pop songs. "Follow You Follow Me" became a worldwide hit.

The eighties saw Genesis dominating the charts every time an album was released. "Duke" and "Abacab" became their first million sellers in the United States. All three musicians embarked on separate solo careers with Phil Collins emerging as one of the most successful singers of the decade. In 1987, *Rolling Stone* magazine's readers' poll declared Genesis as "Band of the Year." After a worldwide tour in support of their album "Invisible Touch," the three musicians took more time off to dedicate to their solo careers. In 1991, they came together again to record the album "We Can't Dance" which was released in November of that year. The year 1992 was once again spent on the road.

Because Genesis received more requests for interviews than they could physically do, the following conversation took place in a round-table situation with several journalists present. Some of the questions were asked by myself, some were asked by my colleagues. I have therefore decided not to use my name for this interview. We met and talked to Phil Collins, Tony Banks and Mike Rutherford in Dortmund/Germany on November 16th, 1991.

Question: How do you celebrate the band's 25th anniversary?

Mike Rutherford: It's very hard to know when the 25th anniversary is. You take it from what? Maybe 1966? It's a very loose thing—between 23 and 26 years. We try to pretend the anniversary is already gone.

Question: All of your solo projects sound quite different. Is Genesis a compromise of three individuals or a real band?

Phil Collins: I think when you listen to solo records you hear what we do when we're left to our own devices. But Genesis is like a melting pot for all the areas we cover between the three of us. There is still a lot of common ground between the three of us when it comes to mu-

Genesis

sical taste and the kind of music we listen to. What ends up being Genesis is, I guess, the mixture of that common ground.

Question: Is it difficult for you to find the band's identity after a long break [4 years between albums]?

Tony Banks: I don't think so at all. When we're back together it's actually like we have never been apart. After working together for three or four days in the writing session—which is where all our ideas come from—you fit back into it very easily. We debate with each other in a natural kind of fashion, but once we've done that we're back into being a group again. By the time we get around to talking to the press we would have been together for six months now. So, it's very easy.

Question: Do you see each other during the years you're not working together?

Tony Banks: We see each other on a fairly regular basis really. Most of the time there are so many things relating to the group that need to be discussed. We see each other as friends sometimes too. Our children are kind of the same age. We all live within ten miles of each other.

Question: Do you go into the studio without having the basic ideas for any songs?

Mike Rutherford: Yes. With all the solo stuff we do, we actually keep the space we have with Genesis for going in and writing together. So although we do always have songs, we don't take any of them into a Genesis session. I think it's an actual process of writing from improvisation and messing around in the studio. To get the sound that we have is a very natural process.

Question: Are you aiming at any particular sound when you go into the studio to start writing an album?

Tony Banks: We really don't go about it like that. We don't go into the studio with any concept, apart from the fact that we want to write music that appeals to us. We don't have any particular urge to try and do something different from before. You go there and it's whatever comes to you. Your natural tendency is to try and look for things that you feel you haven't done before. That's the only motive we have, but what actually turns up in those improvising sessions is totally unpredictable. Even if you know what you're about to do, you don't know what the other guys are about to do and the two things can affect each other very dearly.

Question: What kind of music are you influenced by?

Mike Rutherford: I think you're influenced mainly when you first start listening to music. We listened to the same sort of things, going back to the Beatles and the stuff of the sixties—the English pop scene as it was then. I'm sure we all hear things now that have an effect on us, but I think the early days really tell you how you're going to go out musically.

Question: Whose idea was it to reunite Genesis?

Mike Rutherford: Everybody seems to have this impression that we stopped the band and then decided to reform it. When we finished the last tour in July 1987 we said to ourselves, we will do another album sometime in the future. At that stage we tried to avoid picking the date. And as the years went on we pencilled in 1990, but it got set back another six months. Anyway, in our minds, Genesis never stopped and reformed. It just went on hold for a bit until we finished our solo stuff.

Question: But five years between albums is a long time . . .

Phil Collins: It hasn't been

five years because we were on tour. It was only three and a half years which is not a very long time. When we finished the "Invisible Touch" tour we had been together for over one and a half years. So I think the fact that we go away and do other things has kept the group together. If we had nothing else to do, I think we would have driven each other nuts. It's actually good to go out and experience other things and play with other people. You have to be the dictator on your own records every now and again, so that when you're back with Genesis it's an enjoyable experience because you're not doing it all the time.

Question: What is the difference between a Genesis record and a Phil Collins record? They do sound very similar sometimes these days.

Phil Collins: As we said before, the Genesis albums are all group songs, which means, nothing had been written before we go into the studio. They're not my songs and they're not more by me. It's a true three person set-up. I think the idea that something sounds the same as the stuff on my albums is really the fact of my voice. I sing on my records and I sing on Genesis records. My voice is an identifiable instrument on both projects. Neither Mike nor Tony sing on their solo albums and they don't sing on Genesis records either. So that threat isn't there for them. If we all sang on our solo projects as well as on Genesis, the argument would never come up. I know for a fact that I'm not dominant in the Genesis writing sessions at all. You lower your ego when you come into a Genesis session and the three of us collaborate equally.

Question: Phil, do you prefer singing or playing the drums?

Phil Collins: I don't really know how to be honest. If I lose my voice I wish I was a drummer. When I'm singing I like singing. I like the responsibility of being out there singing.

Question: Have any one of you ever thought seriously about giving Genesis up to pursue solo projects?

Phil Collins: I don't think we ever had that situation come about. I'm forty years old and I should be able to do what I want to do. I don't really feel like I want to be trapped in a group doing nothing else. On the other hand, I think it's interesting to stand up and be counted as an individual and yet experiment with two other people to see what else you can do. The fact that people want you to do one thing and not the other bothers me. When I was doing Brand X people said I can't be in two groups at the same time. Most people can't deal with the fact that we can keep the group together and have successful lives outside Genesis. We developed this way of working and, I think, that's actually more healthy than three guys living together and playing together with nobody else for twenty years. Stamp it out—that's what I say.

Question: You changed the musical style of Genesis about ten years ago, maybe on the album "Abacab." What kind of relationship do you have to the old Genesis songs now?

Tony Banks: We like songs from throughout our career. I'm certainly quite pleased with some of the albums from the late seventies. On tour it's not a problem for us. We can easily find three or four songs out of the old material. It's not diffi-cult for us to find stuff we want to play. We might just stop play-ing some of the ones we played for ten years, you know. The reason for changing around the time of "Abacab" was much

more down to the fact that we felt we had explored that area of music as much as we could at the time. We tried to do things in a slightly different way. It doesn't mean we thought the stuff before was bad. It just meant that we thought we couldn't do it again.

Question: Some passages in your new songs are very much like the stuff you wrote in the late seventies, especially "Fading Lights." Is that a coin-cidence?

Tony Banks: I think, on this particular album ["We Can't Dance"] the main difference for us was that we were thinking in terms of CD length–which is 70 minutes. We reckoned we could get that much music on as op-posed to being restricted to the 50 minutes of "Invisible Touch" and albums before that. This meant we could let things run their natural course without feeling restricted. On "Invisible Touch" we left off a seven-minute instrumental piece which we would have put on def-initely had we had the room. So we're always doing these kinds of things. On this album two or three things came out which we felt were good. And that's why they are there.

Question: Why did you decide to work with a new producer on "We Can't Dance"?

Phil Collins: Well, we like the idea of putting little trick bars in front of each other, just to give us something new to work at. Obviously every time we come into the studio to write an album, that in itself is a challenge. But once you get past that stage, you have the same studio and there are not a lot of elements you can change. The co-producer until now was Hugh Padgham, but on this album we chose Nick Davis. We wanted to change basically because we wanted to see how it was working with somebody else. It turned out to be very successful. We had a great time with Nick. He has a very strong opinion which was useful and he made the thing sound a little bit different. Maybe it sounded fresher—who knows? It depends if you like the record or not.

Question: You released a new single ["No Son of Mine"] that runs for six and a half minutes. Don't you think this could create a problem for radio stations that want to play it?

Tony Banks: Who decided at some point that music has got to be three minutes long? It's irrelevant, you know. We're in the

sort of position that we will get played on the radio even with a six-and-one-half-minute song. Hopefully that helps to change the situation for other bands a bit. Over the years many of the classic pop songs that lasted 20 years have been songs that are over long. Whatever you like— "Bohemian Rhapsody," "Layla" and "Hey Jude" were all longer than the normal format. In fact, audiences like songs that are a bit longer so that they can get their teeth in them. I think radio stations could be a little bit more adventurous.

Question: Why do almost all Genesis love songs describe the sad side of love?

Phil Collins: Because it's easier to write that, really. I've come to the conclusion that most happy love songs are written by black artists. They have some kind of strange optimism in their lyrics which I find interesting. But, I personally find it a lot easier to write from the down side of it.

Question: Could you explain the title of the album "We Can't Dance"? Does it have to do with the huge influence that dance music has on the current market?

Mike Rutherford: No, not especially. Basically the idea came from the song title "I Can't Dance" and as the three of us recorded it we called it "We Can't Dance." We liked the phrase. It makes you smile a little bit. Once we had the title we found lots of justification for it. It's quite a nice dig on the fact that there is an awful lot of dance music around at the moment—and a lot of it is not wonderful. We don't play dance music. Phil is the best dancer in the group. He dances very fast for about two minutes!

Phil Collins: I do a lot of things very fast for two minutes!

Question: Do the lyrics of "I Can't Dance" show some kind of problem with your self-identity? It's all about "I can't dance, I can't do nothing right, but I make a lot of money by selling everything."

Phil Collins: True! [*Laughs*] No, the idea of the lyrics behind "I Can't Dance" is that in England we have commercials for blue jeans. And they have these fantastic looking hunks in them. We thought since the guitar riff sounded a bit like a jeans commercial guitar riff, we thought we would take it a bit further and write the lyrics around these jeans commercials. We're suggesting that maybe the hunks, whilst they look fantas-

tic, may only look fantastic. They probably find it hard to string a sentence together—a little like I am now. But it's a bit of a joke, really. We have nothing against male models. Some of my best friends are male models.

Question: How come Genesis songs have suddenly become so sarcastic?

Phil Collins: I think we've been witty and sarcastic before, but maybe it was not as obvious in some instances. Songs like "I Can't Dance" and "Jesus He Knows Me" are supposed to have a satirical side to them. I don't think that's anything new for us. We have been satirical before, but maybe people haven't noticed it.

Question: There was one other sarcastic title called "Selling England by the Pound." You are a very British band. What kind of relationship do you have to England?

Tony Banks: Countries have ups and downs in terms of the way society is and everything. Speaking personally, I have always felt very English. I don't feel terrifically comfortable anywhere else. Obviously, in places where they don't speak English that's a natural problem, but I don't feel comfortable in America either. I wouldn't want to live there. I just think it's the whole way of looking at things that you feel comfortable with, and I don't think that has changed in England. There are certain social problems at the moment, but that has happened before and it will happen again. We will get out of it.

Question: Is Genesis a band that needs to have theatrical shows, huge light effects and all that stuff?

Phil Collins: We would love to do small theatres with 2,000 seats. But then you get the other four million people who can't see you. That's the trouble, you know. We have done small gigs like the Roxy in Los Angeles and the Marquee in London for our own fun. We wanted to prove to ourselves that we can do it without the lights and the show elements. But ultimately you got to play to all the people who want to see you. And if you go into a stadium and you see three guitars, a keyboard, a drumkit and a microphone, people feel short-changed. They want to look at something. They can't really see the band so you have to give them something else. We try and give them as much as we can without detracting from the music. Hopefully we find a happy medium with that.

Question: Very often the music of Genesis does not correspond with the current trend in pop music. Where do you see your position in the music scene at this moment?

Tony Banks: We never see ourselves as being part of the mainstream. We have always been a kind of unfashionable group. We don't listen all that much. You switch on the radio and you hear two or three new songs. If you haven't liked any of them, then you stop listening. There are certain people I've liked for a long time and I'll carry on listening to them. It's much better to listen to things by recommendation than by what you hear in the charts.

Question: Phil, as a child you were an actor. Could you imagine acting professionally again?

Phil Collins: That's what I'm doing now. I did *Buster* which was a success in different parts of the world and I'm trying to do more. I'm doing a film in January/February of 1992 in Australia and I'm doing another film after the Genesis tour finishes sometime towards the end of the next year.

Question: There are many films about the history of a

band. Would you like to make a Genesis film?

Phil Collins: What an awful idea!

Question: A lot of the TV shows these days are done using playback. How do you feel as musicians miming to your own songs?

Tony Banks: I feel a lot better about it than trying to do it live to a TV situation. It's not the same as playing to a live audience. You are dependent on TV technicians being able to reproduce the sound. It took us two or three weeks to get it together in the studio and they have to get it together spontaneously. There's no way it's going to sound as good. The first time people hear a song it's nice if it has got all the atmosphere that you could get in it.

Phil Collins: When you go on the road you spend two months rehearsing with a sound engineer. So it's a lot easier to be in control. I have done a few TV shows with live vocals and I actually prefer that to miming. But there's so much that TV technicians can screw up that it's best to not let them have a chance.

Question: Is there any chance that Genesis will reunite with Peter Gabriel again?

Mike Rutherford: Who knows? Not unless there is a good reason to do it. The fact that we used to work with Peter isn't a good reason. I would imagine Peter feels the same as us. We have worked with him for many years and if the time became available we would rather work with somebody we haven't worked with. That's our attitude.

Phil Collins: We're all pally with Peter. We're all still friends. It's not like we've fallen out or anything.

Question: Why do you think older musicians like the Rolling Stones, the Beach Boys and Genesis are still so successful?

Tony Banks: We're young. We're certainly younger than that lot anyhow. I think with the particular groups you mentioned—I don't know how popular the Beach Boys are anymore as much as I used to like them—there has been no substitute. I'd prefer if you talked about people like Sting for example. There aren't any contemporary musicians doing that kind of thing. So you have no competition within your particular area. I think this has something to do with record companies. They'll sign up endless bands that look right, but people who decide on more ambitious music are much more difficult to promote.

Question: Would you say Genesis music is still progressive rock music like it was in the old days?

Mike Rutherford: I think it is as much as it ever was. Progressive rock is a phrase we never thought much about. All the descriptions of what our music is are basically written by you guys. There aren't that many people around who are doing slightly longer pieces. And I think that's an area of pop music that can still be explored.

IAN GILLAN

Born in London, England, on August 19, 1945, with musical blood already in his family (his grandfather was a professional opera singer), Ian Gillan was educated at Acton County Grammar School, and like fellow pupils Pete Townshend, Roger Daltrey and John Entwistle, later of The Who, was soon dabbling with the new rock'n'roll craze. By the age of 15 Ian had assumed the persona of Garth Rockett for his first band, The Moonshiners, a haphazard formation that played once a week at a youth club.

The following year, 1961, he changed his name to Jess Thunder after joining The Javelins, the band which took over the residency spot at the Station Hotel in Richmond. This spot had been vacated by The Rolling Stones when their first record made the charts.

After The Javelins split in 1964, Ian performed briefly with a couple of amateur bands, before eventually joining his first professional group, Episode Six, in May 1965. He quit his job at a supermarket, set off on a two-month session in Beirut, his first foreign trip as a musician, and never looked back.

Ian Gillan sang the lead role on the original Tim Rice/Andrew Lloyd Webber soundtrack of "Jesus Christ Superstar," but decided not to appear in the movie. Instead, he accepted an offer to join another London-based band. He also suggested that Episode Six's bass player should make the move with him, and thus the names Ian Gillan and Roger Glover became etched into the annals of rock'n'roll history as members of the best-loved line-up of Deep Purple.

Ian recorded six official albums with Deep Purple marshalling them to the summit of rock stardom in the early '70s. Hit singles such as "Black Night" and "Fireball," combined with anthems like "Smoke on the Water" and "Highway Star," placed Deep Purple alongside Led Zeppelin and Black Sabbath as rock's most innovative and influential bands.

By 1973, Gillan felt burnt out by the pressure of it all and quit Deep Purple to pursue a number of business ventures.

By December 1975, however, the singer had formed Ian Gillan's Shande Grenade with Roger Glover on bass. The project simply became the Ian Gillan Band and (without Glover) embarked on a five-album diversion into the realms of jazz rock. During the summer of 1978 Ian had his hard rock head on again and, shortening the band's name to Gillan, rode British heavy metal back to hit single prominence.

Gillan released five albums before disbanding in 1982. Ian returned to the rock scene within a year, now fronting the new-look Black Sabbath. After recording just one album ("Born Again"), he left to partake in one of the most clamored-for reunions in popular music history. In the spring of 1984 Deep Purple reformed.

Purple returned with the excellent "Perfect Strangers" album and enjoyed a triumphant comeback. They also released the albums "The House of the Blue Light" and "Nobody's Perfect," before asking Ian Gillan to leave the band. He was subsequently replaced by Joe Lynn Turner of Rainbow fame.

July 1990 saw the release of Ian's first ever solo album, entitled "Naked Thunder." He went on tour fronting his own band and recorded a second album, "Toolbox," in 1991.

The following conversation with Ian Gillan took place in London in June 1990 upon the release of "Naked Thunder."

Petra Zeitz: Surprisingly enough, "Naked Thunder" turns out to be your first-ever solo album. What made you do an album on your own after 25 years with various bands?

Ian Gillan: All the other albums I've made outside of Deep Purple, in the days of the Gillan band, etc., I was always part of a band. I've got a great deal of respect for musicians. So, we'd get into the studio and start recording and I'd have an idea of how I wanted the album to go. But then the bass player comes to say, "Let's try this idea, it's a bit off the wall, but it sounds

Ian Gillan

great." Then we do something a bit bluesy. Then somebody says, "Let's do some fusion stuff." And so we'd have a fantastic time in the studio over six weeks. We'd finish an album and everyone goes, "What is that? Let's re-mix it so that it all sounds the same." And so, working with musicians you get dragged—quite willingly—in different directions. It all depends on the dominant force of the time and other musical influences. It's an exciting business. So, this time I thought I'm not in Deep Purple anymore and I had a very clear idea in my mind of how I wanted the album to be. So I thought, well, I'll be a solo singer for now. I'll get a backing group for on the road with this guy Steve Morris, that I wrote all the songs with. We got session musicians in and we told them how we wanted them to play. Early in the writing sessions we decided that we didn't want many overdubs or anything like that. We wanted to have a very clean sound so that the power had to come from the songs, and not from studio effects. We got some great musicians who played with power and with enthusiasm. They gave it everything, but they didn't divert from the original intention all the way through. I ended up with something I'm very pleased with. I haven't made any changes at all because this album is exactly what I wanted.

That's why it's a solo record. I think, I should do this once in my life. I've been singing for 28 years and I've actually just made my first solo record.

Petra Zeitz: You have just come back from a six-week tour of the Soviet Union. How did it go?

Ian Gillan: It was the happiest tour I've ever done. It was absolutely fantastic! These guys in my band are so funny and so powerful on stage—just incredible! It was a very big tour. We started off with three nights in Moscow at the Olympic Hall. There were 25,000 people a night. I think the smallest audiences we had on this tour were about 10,000. We were playing in soccer stadiums and things like that. In some towns we were playing five nights in their stadiums, back to back. It was incredible. The people were kind, generous, friendly and critical. They understood about music and they weren't naïve. They were willing to listen to any new songs, which is something that can be difficult in some countries. I played four or five Deep

Purple songs because Purple has never been to the Soviet Union and I thought they would like to hear some of those songs. But at the same time, I was encouraged to play four or five songs from my new album. They went down equally well. People were appreciative and I was very honored by that. I think that these people have open minds. So it was a fantastic experience. It wasn't just Russia we went to, but we also played in Armenia, in Georgia, and in many other places.

Petra Zeitz: When you take your band on tour this time you play much smaller venues than you did with Purple. You even play some clubs in various places.

Ian Gillan: No, I don't think there are any clubs. Well, maybe there are some clubs—I don't mind. It's funny; we go from some countries where we're playing stadiums to other countries where we're playing small theatres. I think Purple made a lot of mistakes by not changing the material. They became a bit boring, I think. The last concert, Deep Purple playing in Germany for example, was in Bremen and 1,400 people came. So I'm very pleased to be starting again. I don't want to start up there. I've got to pay my dues. Just because I've been singing for a long time doesn't mean I can expect special treatment. I gotta go through the same as everyone else. On the norm, my favorite size venue is around about 5,000 people. I think that's ideal. It's big enough for it to be a big event, but it's small enough to be intimate. You know, us British musicians are not so fond of massive indoor concert halls.

Petra Zeitz: Do you like playing at festivals and big outdoor events?

Ian Gillan: Festivals are fantastic, because it's an event and people have traveled from all over the country. There's a good atmosphere and that sort of thing. And I like, of course, now and again to do places like Madison Square Garden. It's good to do one world tour of big venues, but then I think the next time around you should come back and do some slightly smaller ones again. It's no big deal for me to play in a club or in a soccer stadium. It's playing the music and to actually be there instead of sitting at a beach in Florida.

Petra Zeitz: Like many British musicians of the sixties, you went to work in Germany for a while. What did you do over there?

Ian Gillan: When I first started working in Germany I played in small places in Munich, Hamburg, Frankfurt and Cologne back in the sixties. A lot of British bands learned their trade there. Hamburg was the most famous one because of the Beatles, but there were lots of clubs in Frankfurt, Munich and Cologne. I was staying in a bed & breakfast right under the Cologne Cathedral. I remember it was my first gig ever in Germany. We used to walk to the club every day. We were each paid four Deutschmarks a day. This was in 1965 or something like that. The beer in the club was 75 Pfennigs—special rate for artists. But we drank a lot of beer, so there wasn't much money left for food. You could get a little Bockwurst [German sausage] for 1.75 DM at a stand there and the bread rolls were free. So, I took ten bread rolls with each sausage. And then hopefully, somebody would come up and say, "Oh, I like your music. May I take you out to dinner?" You don't forget those things.

Petra Zeitz: One thing that hasn't changed about you is that you're still working very hard. Don't you ever stop?

Ian Gillan: I like to do about 200 shows a year. That's a good number and I have achieved it before.

Petra Zeitz: Do you still have some respect for the past?

Ian Gillan: Of course I have. I do one or two Purple songs in every show, but not necessarily the same old songs that Purple was doing. Some unusual Purple songs. It depends where I'm playing. If I am in a place where Purple hasn't played before, then obviously people would like to hear some of the more well-known stuff, because they haven't heard it before. Maybe I would do "Smoke on the Water" and "Strange Kind of Woman" for them. In New York they've had it up to here. So I think with the Purple stuff I'll be doing some different songs in places like New York. I change the set a little bit every night anyway.

Petra Zeitz: You have said that you don't want to be a heavy metal singer anymore. Does it bother you that people still associate your name with heavy metal music?

Ian Gillan: I don't mind what people say. I mean, the wisest judges of all are the audiences.

But I would be foolish to myself if I wasn't honest and say that I'm basically a rock singer. If you want to say I'm heavy metal or whatever, that's fine. I've been called everything from progressive rock, underground rock, rock'n'roll, hard rock, heavy metal, punk rock, fusion rock to even the new wave of British metal. People like to have labels, but I'm just a rock singer. That's how I would describe myself.

Petra Zeitz: For most of your time as a songwriter you have been writing with collaborators. How do the different partnerships work?

Ian Gillan: It's very difficult, because for years I have been writing with my best friend Roger Glover. We just sit down and talk. When we write together we will be sitting at dinner and all of a sudden we develop an idea. Then it's forget the dinner, we take the guitar and we sit down and write words and music together. Mostly Roger was on the musical side and I wrote what the singer does. But it was a very close relationship and very inspirational because we knew each other so well. With Steve Morris, the guy I wrote most of the songs on "Naked Thunder"

with, a strange thing happened. First of all, he was sending me tapes of ideas just with backing tracks on them. They were so fantastic that the first time I heard the first track he sent me, I started singing to it straight away. By the time it got to the second verse I had the tune and by the time it got to the chorus I had the title. It was a thing called "Gut Reaction". With every other song Steve sent me, it was equally easy. Within the second playing I had the tune and an idea for the words. We're very excited about doing the next album now. I tend to work on what I sing—which is the tune and the words.

Petra Zeitz: Are you watching the current music scene?

Ian Gillan: Well, as much as I ever have done. I listen to the radio and I watch TV. I work so much that the only bands I get to see are when I get down to a club or meet somebody socially on the road. For years Pink Floyd and Deep Purple were leaving messages for each other and I've never seen Pink Floyd to this day. We were always working at the same time. We would be getting messages from airline check-in girls and hotel receptionists. It was really funny. But no, I'm not interested in fashion very much. In fact I'm very excited about the fact that, I think, I've reached a stage in my career now where I can hopefully be unfashionable. If you do what you believe in, and you're lucky enough every now and again to coincide with public taste, it means you haven't diverted in what you want to do. If you're very lucky you might have a hit record which is very handy because it pays the bills and it means that you can have a holiday and that sort of thing. That's about all it means. I have no idea about commerciality—I haven't got a clue what would make a hit record. If you asked me to choose a single from an album, I would probably choose the most obvious flop that would be there.

Petra Zeitz: In your opinion, what have been the biggest changes in the music business between the 1960s and now?

Ian Gillan: We were all boys in the '60s, but then again, there ain't no boys around anymore who understand about soul music and about jazz, blues, country rock and about those sorts of things. When the punk thing happened it destroyed pretty much everything that was bad about rock music. It had become self-indulgent and bloated with 30 minute solos. Punk music was a purely destructive force, but out of that came bands that were trying to be constructive and were playing rock music. So all the things that had been destroyed were gone forever. Heavy metal or thrash metal was born in '78 or '79 when magazines like *Kerrang* started. These magazines started as almost fanzines and that's why it became so segregated from all the other parts of music. Now it's very difficult to read about Eurythmics, the Pogues and Iron Maiden in the same magazine. Everyone has become channelled now. But the point is that the inspiration these young bands had was from around the time of Deep Purple, Black Sabbath and Led Zeppelin. So they think they are playing the roots of rock music—which for them it is— but for us it was much deeper than that. All the jazz and the blues that we have grown up on has gone from this form of heavy metal. All it has is the legacy of Deep Purple, Black Sabbath, etc. That's not a very broad base. There are some brilliant bands around, but I just wish that they would have had the chance to listen to some Chuck Berry records. So I'm happy to be saying this because it is important that it be said and I'm happy to be a little older.

Petra Zeitz: What do you think about the necessity to make videos these days?

Ian Gillan: If it's relevant, I think a video is a good idea. But I remember Deep Purple had a video of a song called "Knocking at Your Backdoor"—we weren't in it—made by this Australian producer. I fell off the bed laughing! I literally laughed so much because it was so unrepresentative of what the song was about. I would like to avoid the mistake of listening to music through my eyes. When you listen through your ears, then your imagination takes over. A similar thing is if you read a good book and you create all the images of the characters, but when you go to see the film made from the book you think: "No, he's not supposed to look like that!" Visual imagery is something totally different to deal with and, I think, compatibility is sometimes impossible. A lot of good creative work is sacrificed for the sake of a visual image. I think rock music isn't meant for that.

Petra Zeitz: Do you like live albums? I know Deep Purple was not pleased with their last live album "Nobody's Perfect."

Ian Gillan: No, but I love bootleg albums. I encourage people to bring their little tape recorders in. Take it away— that's included in the ticket price. Sell it to your friends and do what you want with it, that's great. I support bootlegs, but I don't like pirate albums where they take a studio album and copy it and sell it. We need the money from that. We're not wealthy people contrary to popular opinion. We don't make loads of bread. I hate live albums because for me a live show is an experience that can't be put onto vinyl. There have been a few successful live albums and a few successful live videos, but because there are so many of them that the good ones tend to be forgotten. I would rather live on the memory of a good concert.

Petra Zeitz: Did you go to see any of the other bands from the sixties like the Stones and the Who that re-united for tours recently?

Ian Gillan: No, as much as I love the Stones and as much as I love the Who, I must say that I thought the Deep Purple reunion was very valid because we wrote many new songs and it was very fresh. The Who—for me—are the same as the Swinging Blue Jeans, it's just like stadium cabaret. The Stones are an institution. I wouldn't like to level any criticism at them. They do write new songs, but they are so big that their legend is really their jailer. When you're that big—just like Elvis Presley or the Beatles—you become public property, which is something I've always tried to avoid. It's important not to be public property. It's important to be your own man and make your own judgment on things.

Petra Zeitz: Have you left Deep Purple for good this time?

Ian Gillan: I was fired. I don't know why. I have only spoken to Roger and he was so upset about it as well, he had nothing to do with it. It was just a call from their manager to my manager saying, "We will find another singer." I don't know why. Maybe they wanted somebody younger—I don't know. I hear all kinds of rumors, but I still have good memories of Deep Purple which I prefer to dwell on rather than the bad things. There have been enough bad things written about Purple. So I wish them good luck, particularly Roger. I love him very much. He's a very nice man and a great musician and extremely loyal to the idea of Purple. I don't understand why or what. Nobody even spoke to me about it. I've got over the shock now, but I don't think I'll ever get over the disappointment. It will stay with me forever.

Paul McCartney

PAUL McCARTNEY

Paul McCartney was born June 18, 1942, in Liverpool, England. As a member of the Beatles as well as being one half of the famous Lennon/McCartney songwriting partnership, he became the most successful pop musician of all time. The history of the Beatles is a legend. After they disbanded in 1970, Paul and his wife Linda formed the group Wings. During the seventies Paul continued touring and recording, but Wings came to an end in 1981—the year after John Lennon's untimely death.

Paul McCartney released several more successful solo records before once again going on a world tour in 1989–90. Highlights of these concerts were recorded and filmed.

Unfortunately, when Paul McCartney met the press at the world premiere of his concert movie *Get Back* on Hamburg's famous Reeperbahn, he was far too busy to grant personal face to face interviews. Instead a press conference was held at the Tivoli Theater on September 18th, 1991. Sitting in the front row I had a good view of the proceedings, but the general questions didn't cover as much ground as I had hoped. Some were nonsense and did not deserve a serious answer. Nevertheless there was deafening applause when Paul McCartney took the stage.

The following are the most interesting questions and answers from the press conference.

Question: How do you feel about being back in Hamburg?

Paul McCartney: I was here last year actually. So that spoiled your question right away, didn't it? It's wonderful to be back in Hamburg. I have so many memories of the Reeperbahn and Grosse Freiheit and other things, which I won't go into now. [*Smiles*]

Question: What would you like to do in Hamburg if you had more time?

Paul McCartney: I'd need more than time: I'd need some of the clubs to be re-opened. I would go to the Top Ten or to the Star Club if those are still open. Otherwise I couldn't do most of what I used to when I came here because it's not allowed now that I'm married. I couldn't go to some of the clubs I used to go to! Just kiddin', Linda.

Question: When you're on tour you play the old Beatles songs and then songs from "Flowers in the Dirt," but the reaction is not the same. Does this hurt you?

Paul McCartney: It's to be expected. The Beatles' songs are much more famous than my last album. It's okay, because there are many people who like to hear the new songs. If I just do the old ones, they would be disappointed. So I put in some new songs for them. But something like "Hey Jude" is more famous than "Flowers in the Dirt."

Question: Where would you like to go on "World Tour Two" and would you like to play a concert in China?

Paul McCartney: Well, it would be good to play in China and in all those places that people don't normally go to. If I was going to play in China, I wouldn't like to do a big technical trip. I would like to take some acoustic guitars 'round to the villages and talk to the people. That's what I'm interested in. Maybe on the tour next year we might finally get to Russia, which should be exciting.

Question: You composed the "Liverpool Oratorio" with Carl Davis. How firm are you in classical music?

Paul McCartney: I like classical music a lot, but I'm not very knowledgeable. I know the tunes, but I can never tell you who wrote it, when he lived, what he was trying to do. I don't really have much knowledge about it. But I don't really think in terms of pop music, classical music, African music, world music. I think of it all as the same thing—a collection of notes. I know the more popular classical music. My favorite composers would be Beethoven, Mozart, Debussy, people like that.

Question: Are you going to compose more classical music?

Paul McCartney: The thing is, with the Beatles, when we did things like "Yesterday" or more particularly "Eleanor Rigby," we were working with classical musicians. The fiddle players were all from classical orchestras. I always enjoyed working with them. I didn't really feel the snob barrier where they were more important than us. We just worked together like workers, you know. I enjoyed that and when I had the opportunity to work with the Liverpool Philharmonic Orchestra, I accepted it readily because it was a great thrill for me to do. It doesn't mean that I'm turning my back on rock'n'roll. I think the next thing I do will probably be a rock'n'roll album. But it is an interesting field. I really enjoyed making this oratorio. So, I'd like to do some more, but not exclusively that.

Question: In 1992 you're going to celebrate your 50th birthday?

Paul McCartney: I have no special plans for my 50th birthday—everybody else does! They are writing books because I'm 50. To me, it's just another birthday.

Question: The film *Get Back* seems like a flashback of your whole career. Do you plan to retire?

Paul McCartney: No, when I did the world tour last year, a lot of people asked me that question. "Is this your final tour?" I think when you get to my age people automatically think it's a farewell tour. I'm sure they ask the Rolling Stones that question at every press conference. It's a natural question, but I'm not intending on retiring. And the film is from Richard Lester's [director] point of view. So maybe he wants me to retire but I'm gonna refuse. I keep going because I like it.

Question: Why did you choose to show pictures of the Berlin Wall coming down in *Get Back*?

Paul McCartney: The film isn't my film—I didn't direct it. It's Richard Lester's film, so all the choices in the film are his. People somehow think I must have had a lot of say in that. I do in many projects, but not in this one. When you've got a real film director making a film, you don't tell him what to do. But I know Richard is very anti-war and very pro-humanitarian. That's why he put it in. Like for the rest of us, it was a great symbolic thing. Speaking for him, I think, that's why he put it in.

Question: What was it like working with Richard Lester again after all these year? [Lester directed the Beatles' films *A Hard Day's Night* and *Help!*]

Paul McCartney: It was great fun, actually, because we hadn't seen each other for quite a long time. It was strange because we picked up almost as if it had just been about a week, when in fact it was probably more than 20 years. It was very easy to work with Dick because I respect him and he's a good friend. So it was a great pleasure. He is a good filmmaker and we're still friends. I would like to work with him again if he will have me.

Question: With *Get Back* being completed now, do you still work on any other movie projects such as *Rupert The Bear* or *The Long And Winding Road?*

Paul McCartney: Well, the Rupert thing, I haven't got any plans to do anything further on. *The Long And Winding Road* is a Beatles compilation film about the story of the Beatles that we have been trying to work on for a long time to give our side of the story. You see so many of these other things where people are telling everybody how it went on. It would be good if we could correct some of the facts. We're still working on it—it's a long, long movie.

Question: Your last tour was presented by TDK. Why do you play for TDK and not for Greenpeace for example?

Paul McCartney: These days, most of the tours and things that people do have a sponsor. It's a modern phenomenon. We had the choice of just saying "No, we don't need a sponsor, we won't use them," but we decided there was nothing wrong with it. I think the problem is with the product. For instance, being a vegetarian, if I was asked to advertise McDonald's, I wouldn't do that. But someone like TDK is harmless enough. I don't mind that. I have nothing against limited sponsorship. I think that's okay. In my heart I'm playing for Greenpeace.

Question: You're a very rich man. Why do you still work that hard making records, movies and going on tour?

Paul McCartney: Normally I don't see my work as work. I'm just very lucky because it's more like play. Going on tour is not as bad as it used to be. Conditions are a lot better and I don't do it as much as I used to. The Beatles used to work nearly every day of the year. I don't work anywhere near that lot. So I do it 'cause I love it—certainly not for the money or the fame.

Paul and Linda McCartney

Question: How do you get your songs? Do you go out in the fields to get inspired? Where do you get your inspiration from?

Paul McCartney: I don't know where the inspiration comes from, maybe just ordinary life. It might just be something one of your kids says or something you see on TV. But I don't go out in the fields normally. I just sit in front of a piano and hope some inspiration comes. If I'm lucky something will come. Or I write with the guitar, but I don't go out in the fields to write music—I do other things in fields!

Question: Do you have any plans to collaborate with other songwriters like you did with Elvis Costello?

Paul McCartney: I haven't got any plans for any new collaborations, but I did write three more songs with Elvis this year. I'm writing some with Hamish Stuart out of our band for the new album, but no plans other than that.

Question: You have said that in the 1990s some of the ideas of the sixties are being resurrected. Could you explain that a little bit more?

Paul McCartney: A lot of what went on in the sixties was party-time for those of us who were young. I think it was easy to forget most of what was going on because you weren't always in full control, should we say. So I have forgotten a lot of specific things from the sixties. But the overall ideas that I was talking about were peace, ecology and a lot of other ideas which now seem to be coming through. There's no way to get rid of them without destroying the planet.

Question: Some people say that musicians can change the world. What would you like to have changed?

Paul McCartney: That's such a big question. I'd like to change everything that's wrong. I'm not sure that musicians themselves can change the world. I think they can write the songs that re-mind people that the world needs changing. I would like to change the world to a peaceful world—number one. I think that will be very difficult. I would like to see more equality. I would like to see famine not happening in Africa and things like that. There's so many things. I could go on—I would like to see animal rights. One animal with some rights would do me for the time being. I think there are many subjects that could be changed. I'm optimis-

tic. I think they may get changed, but maybe not until the next century. If music can help that, then that's great. My biggest example of it working was when John wrote "Give Peace a Chance." Towards the end of the Vietnam War there is this footage of people singing "Give Peace a Chance" at the White House. Shortly after-wards the war did collapse. So, you know, music can help.

Question: Can you explain the on-going success of many groups of the sixties like the Rolling Stones, the Who and your own group? They all enjoy amazing success although the music business today is much bigger than it used to be in the sixties.

Paul McCartney: It's surpris-ing, because nobody—including us—expected us to last this long. That's the first point. Peo-ple are just surprised at any success. I think they expect us to fail just because we're older. However I think the reason why we are successful is that we can play. I think a lot of the young acts of today can make records and can be produced, but they are not as used to playing in front of 60,000 people. So bands like the Grateful Dead have been doing it the whole time. We're not bad at it now, we know how to do it. The Rolling Stones are not frightened to play in front of 60,000 people, but I think Kylie Minogue probably would be.

Question: What does the success you had with the Beatles mean to you now?

Paul McCartney: They are great memories from my youth. I think the good thing about memories is that you forget the bad bits. So when I think about the Beatles now I just remember all the great bits. I don't really think there were that many bad bits because we were pretty good friends while we were doing it all. They are very special memories to me. I can actually think back—contrary to anybody else in this room—to what it was like to work with John Lennon, you know. That's very special.

THE MOODY BLUES

The Moody Blues were formed in Birmingham, England, in 1964. They soon secured a recording contract with Decca Records, the company that turned down the Beatles. This early incarnation of the Moody Blues included guitarist/singer Denny Laine, who sang lead vocal on their first British number one single "Go Now," a revival of the old Bessie Banks song. Denny Laine and Clint Warwick left the band shortly afterwards and were replaced by Justin Hayward and John Lodge. While Laine was later to find fame with Paul McCartney's Wings, The Moody Blues took off internationally. Hayward wrote their most classic single "Nights in White Satin" in 1967. This song made the band a household name even in the United States. Their success continued throughout the seventies and eighties with hits such as "The Story in Your Eyes" (1971), "Your Wildest Dreams" (1986), "The Voice" (1981) as well as "Ride My See-Saw" (1968) and "I'm Just a Singer in a Rock'n'Roll Band" (1971) written by John Lodge. The Moody Blues concentrated their touring activities in the United States, becoming a major concert attraction over the years. In 1991, they released the "Keys of the Kingdom" album which failed to meet expectations and didn't reach any notable chart positions. Nevertheless, the Moody Blues continued to tour and play in front of enthusiastic crowds.

The following conversation with Justin Hayward—one of the nicest guys I've ever talked to—took place in London in March 1991. Added is a shorter but more recent interview with John Lodge, whom I met during the band's European tour in October 1991.

Petra Zeitz: I heard you are working on the sleeve for the "Keys of the Kingdom" album at the moment. Are you designing it yourself?

Justin Hayward: I'm working with an art company in Chelsea. It's got a lot of the group's ideas—we all put ideas in. I don't do it myself, but I will one day. For a solo album I'm going to design the sleeve myself. Nowadays you have to try and get an image for a CD format that is just so small. So you have to have one strong symbol.

Petra Zeitz: You always seem to take great care with your videos to make them into little stories. I loved the video you did for "Your Wildest Dreams."

Justin Hayward: Oh thank you. I wish the record company thought like that. We did "I Know You're Out There Somewhere" as an extension of "Your Wildest Dreams," and I wanted to do a third one, like a soap opera video. I liked the idea of having another group in there that was like a younger version of us. I'd like to do that again. I think videos are vital. The power of the video is tremendous because a great video can make an average song so much better, but a terrible video can spoil a great song. You have to work just as hard on the video as on the record. It's probably more expensive as well.

Petra Zeitz: Where do you get all your inspirations to write songs from?

Justin Hayward: Well, really from personal experience. I think I'm quite an emotional person. Sometimes I write a song and I don't even find out what it's about until years later. Years later I play it and I realize what I was going through at a particular time and why I wrote the song. It's not clear at the time—it's only later that you find out why. I write about things that have happened to me and things that I would like to have happened to me, imaginings, romantic fantasies, things like that.

Petra Zeitz: Many of your songs have that mysterious, romantic image to them. Is that the way you are?

Justin Hayward: I think it is the way I am, yes. I get very emotionally involved with a song. When I'm singing it I feel that it's a real part of me. I'm expressing something that's very deep. That's the one way I can feel sincere about it. If I don't really feel that a song means something personal to me, then I have great difficulty bringing it

Moody Blues

over or performing it and it doesn't have the sincerity that it should have.

Petra Zeitz: When did you start writing songs?

Justin Hayward: I wrote the first songs when I was fifteen or sixteen, only they were rubbish. When I was sixteen I got a job as a guitar player for a rock'n'roll singer called Marty Wilde [the father of Kim Wilde] and I was in his backing group for two and a half years. I was really able to watch Marty and see how he worked an audience and how he made the whole evening work for the people watching. I started writing songs then. When I came to the Moody Blues we weren't doing any of our own songs. Our songs didn't fit in with what the group was doing because we were an R&B group. It was only after I had been in the band for about a year that we decided to do our own songs. We used to wear these very smart blue suits and we decided we didn't want them anymore. We wanted to wear our own clothes and play our own songs. That was a big turning point and after that the band took off. I'm the worst judge, though. I'm always wrong. I didn't think "Nights in White Satin" would be a hit, so here you go!

Petra Zeitz: Do you know

why you were more successful in the United States than you were at home?

Justin Hayward: We were very successful in England in the early seventies—from about 1972 to 1973. For about a year we were probably the biggest band in England because the Beatles didn't work together anymore and the Stones hardly worked together. Every album that we made went to number one. What happened in America was that we went there in 1967 and got caught up in that flower power/hippies thing and it just took off for us over there. It became sort of huge. From that time on Britain has always been our secondary market and America has been number one. That's why to this date we're signed by an American record company.

Petra Zeitz: Do you think the audiences are different in America than they are in Britain?

Justin Hayward: I find that they are very different! I think the American people are more used to going to concerts and they have better conditions and better venues. The places that we play in the summertime in America are usually outdoor amphitheatres. There's a cover over about 5,000 seats and then

there's a lawn at the back. People come for the whole day and make their barbecue. It's great! The crowds are very enthusiastic while the British are very reserved. You know what the British are like—they sit on their hands and are very quiet about the whole thing.

Petra Zeitz: How does your songwriting partnership with John Lodge work? The two of you are the main songwriters of the band.

Justin Hayward: We write separately and we always do things apart. But then we know that the things we do write together, we have a lot of fun over. Basically we have a lot of laughs and we enjoy each other's company. It's always done at my house because I've got a little studio there. John always comes over to my house and then we go into my writing room. Basically, one of us paces up and down while the other one sits and then the other one sits while the other one paces up and down. Usually we never come out without having done something. We're always guaranteed to do something.

Petra Zeitz: You must have a lot of song material lying around.

Justin Hayward: We have got

a lot of songs and a lot of bits and pieces of songs. We've got songs that we started and never finished and stuff we've recorded that didn't make it on the albums.

Petra Zeitz: Do you make any recordings at your home studio?

Justin Hayward: I make really good demos there. Often the things that I record there, I take into the studio and transfer them onto a bigger machine—still keeping the things that I've done at home. Sometimes you just capture something at home that is very special and you wouldn't want to re-create it again, 'cause you've already done it. There's a feeling you sometimes get at home that just works.

Petra Zeitz: Do you play any other instruments apart from guitar?

Justin Hayward: I play keyboards now. I've always played keyboards, but over the last few years I have become more involved. Some of my new songs are written on the keyboards and the guitar comes secondary. I tried playing keyboards and singing on stage, but I can't do both at the same time. I go mad.

Petra Zeitz: Would you consider the band a close unit?

Justin Hayward: No, I used to think that, but not anymore. The last few albums we used other musicians on and different kind of producers. We've used a different drummer on a lot of tracks this time. Although the band will always be the same, it's not as closed and as narrow-thinking as it used to be. I think that's better, you know. Music changes and styles change. The feeling and the sound of our music will always be the same because we have a particular identity that we can't get away from—whether we like it or we don't, we're stuck with it.

Petra Zeitz: Do you still enjoy touring although it's quite hard work?

Justin Hayward: I do! It is hard work, but I don't really know how to do anything else. I never had a proper job or anything. I literally woke up one morning on the road—it was about five or six years ago—and I thought, "This is great. This is wonderful. I'm in a lovely hotel. I've got a suitcase here with all my nice clothes and I don't have anything to worry about. There's somebody taking care of me, there's a tour manager looking after me, there's people who love me all around. I turn up and sing and people love the music." I kind of realized in my mind that all those people in the audience are on your side and they want you to do a good show. Before that I used to think: "What are they looking at?" and I used to resent being away from home, but I've got rid of a lot of those kind of ego things that I needed to dump. I see myself now as I really am, not as some fantasy person, you know? I know what I look like and it's not great, but that's okay. It doesn't matter anymore. As soon as I was free of that worry, I started to really enjoy myself. I realized how lucky I was.

Petra Zeitz: You were quite a hard-partying band in the early days. Have you calmed down now?

Justin Hayward: [*Laughs*] Yeah, we used to like big parties! In every hotel we used to have a room which we called the hospitality suite, with food and everything in it. After the gig I went in there and you'd have to be really quick to get your meal, because there are loads of other people that are already eating this stuff. You didn't know any of them—it was quite fantastic, really. The people didn't know who I was either, only that I was paying for everything. It was ri-

diculous! So we stopped all that. It went on for too many years, but it was fun.

Petra Zeitz: Do you have a favorite time to look back on?

Justin Hayward: Well I think probably the time from 1967 to 1970 was the best time. We were very young, we had no kind of responsibilities and we didn't really have any worries. The clothes were great, the fashions—it was like a big party. We had a lot of respect, but we hadn't really had great success. Big success came to us in about 1970 and it brought a lot of responsibilities with it. Money brings responsibilities trying to keep hold of it, for a start. We've lost a lot and have been robbed a lot of times. I played at a sixties night at the Royal Albert Hall the other night. People were wearing all the clothes and it took me back to how colorful it all was. Bright colors were everywhere in the late sixties and I miss that.

Petra Zeitz: Do you think those times could come back one day?

Justin Hayward: I don't know. It was a time when young people could do whatever they wanted. I don't think that will ever come 'round again— maybe in 50 or 100 years, but not in the next 10 or 20. The sixties were a time when even older people thought that young people had the answer. You weren't anybody unless you were young and I'm not sure whether that can happen again. I don't think so. But also, it was a time when there were a lot of wars happening in the world, like the Vietnam War. So there was a lot to rebel against. If this war in the gulf had gone on much longer, I think, a lot of young people would have stood up against it.

Petra Zeitz: Do you think music should be used to express political opinions?

Justin Hayward: There are no boundaries in music. It goes across any kind of country. It was very important to us in the sixties that we were very political about some of the things we were saying. Although some of it had a double meaning, there was still a political voice there. I think the only duty that music has is to reflect what the audience is thinking. Music is there to make the world a better place. That's why you and I can do that. We can share in that. Your magazine makes the world a happier and brighter place—it's fun, you know. As long as you are aware inside of yourself, that what you're doing is mak-

ing the world better, then that's all that matters really. I don't know many musicians who have very good political ideas, but I know a lot that make me happy.

Petra Zeitz: Do you enjoy doing all these interviews?

Justin Hayward: I do, because I meet people that I would never normally meet. I'm quite a private person, so I just tend to keep within the same circle of friends. I like people who are involved with the media because they are like a window to the world. You must get to meet so many different people—well, I don't, you see. People always think that musicians meet all the other musicians, but of course, they don't unless they do a television show together.

*   *   *

Petra Zeitz: Do your fans still expect you to play all your old hits?

John Lodge: It's interesting because you can only look at the audience to see their reaction when you're there. It's very easy to think that perhaps the audience will only come to hear and see "Nights in White Satin," but sometimes when you look at the audience they seem to know all our new songs as well. We hope to reach a cross-section of people. The only problem is that concert tickets are very expensive nowadays. I don't know what can be done about that—it's not the artist who is getting the fortune, it's just the cost of everything else, you know, the staging, the vari-lights and, I think, what happens is that young people see these huge stages on the TV and expect to see that in every concert.

Petra Zeitz: Has life on the road changed for you since the early seventies when you did those huge tours of the United States?

John Lodge: The venues have changed over the years and the amount of people involved is different now. When we were touring heavily in the seventies, there would be a minimum crew, perhaps three or four road managers, the tour manager and the band. But today you have personal road managers, you have stagehands, you have a lighting crew, you have a sound crew and a stage crew. Today we have three busses, two trucks, our own catering people who cook for everyone—it's like a circus, not a tour. In the old days there were maybe 10 people including the band.

Petra Zeitz: Would you mind

if your children went into the music business?

John Lodge: If they really enjoyed it, no. I'm doing what I do because I really wanted to do it from when I was 12 or 13 years of age. It's in my heart and in my soul and it's a way of life that I enjoy. But once again, with television you can make it very glamorous, while in reality it is a very hard occupation. People mustn't forget that. If my children ever wanted to be in this business, they would have to prove it to me. I wouldn't help them. I think when you're young you need some close friends around you. With the Moodies, we've been together for so long that we've grown up together. I wouldn't like to be on my own in this business.

Petra Zeitz: What advice do you give young bands that are starting off now?

John Lodge: The advice is: If they are starting off, I would learn to perform the music they like first—copy the record first—to understand how the record is made and to understand what makes a record. But then, arrange the same song yourself for your own band. You have to make that song your own song. Although it was a hit for somebody else, you can make it a hit for yourself. Then you can start writing your own material, but you have this experience and you can develop it into your own songwriting. Really, that's what we did. And also, I think for a new band it's very important to get a very good road manager. He's the guy who will get you out of all kinds of trouble—if he's good.

Petra Zeitz: For the Moody Blues you wrote most of the faster songs like "Singer in a Rock'n'Roll Band." Does that have something to do with your personality?

John Lodge: I really do like rock'n'roll. I'm a rock'n'roll person and all my heroes are American rock'n'roll heroes of the generation before us— Chuck Berry, Bo Diddley, Jerry Lee Lewis, Little Richard, Fats Domino. I mean, they are all people from the original rock'n'roll generation. One of the great things for me is that over the years I have managed to perform with a lot of them as well. It's been fantastic to be on stage with them. I did a concert last year with Jerry Lee Lewis, Chuck Berry and Bo Diddley. If I'm at a party with an acoustic guitar I sing and play all those songs. That's just me.

Petra Zeitz: Do you still listen to critics after all these years?

John Lodge: I think you always listen to critics— whether you believe them or not. If you believe the bad ones you've got to believe the good ones, too. Sometimes you can see the point of whatever they say. The most important thing is the audience reaction. If the audience has come to see an artist and they leave there in a great mood, then the artist has performed well and fulfilled the hopes of the audience.

Petra Zeitz: When I was living in England I had the feeling that all the bands from the sixties were still good friends with each other. It seemed like one big clique. Is that true?

John Lodge: I think so, because there were no artists really before us. We started the first wave, and you'd hope as the waves are breaking that all the other bands will come surfing in on a free ride, but unfortunately a lot of them are not doing it. I think that all the artists from the sixties period spent a lot of time on the road, playing night after night, and built up through that route. So today when we see everyone, we know we've all been there. There's nothing better than to have friendships and people that have had similar experiences.

Petra Zeitz: Did you ever regret having joined the Moody Blues?

John Lodge: No. [*Laughs*] I don't think I have ever regretted it. That's a good question, though. We go back a very, very long way.

COZY POWELL

Throughout his career powerhouse drummer Cozy Powell has worked with a number of the world's top acts. In the early 1970s he was a leading session drummer in Great Britain before joining Ritchie Blackmore's band Rainbow. He stayed with the former Deep Purple guitarist for five years. In 1973 Cozy Powell's solo single "Dance with the Devil" became an international million seller. Following this sudden success, Powell released two more singles, "The Man in Black" and "Na Na Na." His solo albums "Over the Top" (1979), "Tilt" (1981) and "Octopuss" (1983) featured such well known faces as Gary Moore, Jack Bruce, Don Airey and David Sancious.

Despite his own success, Cozy Powell kept playing many sessions. He did an album and a tour with ELP and helped guitar virtuoso Michael Schenker with several projects.

In the eighties he also got a job drumming for Whitesnake.

In 1989, Cozy Powell joined Black Sabbath. Tony Iommi had restructured the band and with Powell on drums they went through their most powerful incarnation. Powell could be heard on the albums "Headless Cross" and "Tyr" as well as playing on several Black Sabbath tours. Two years later a bad accident ended Powell's relationship with Sabbath. He fell off his horse and fractured his pelvis. His recovery took longer than Powell anticipated and Black Sabbath was not prepared to wait for him.

With a little help from his famous friends, Cozy Powell hit back with a solo album, released in May 1992. Entitled "The Drums Are Back" it featured Brian May of Queen, Steve Lukather of Toto, John Lord of Deep Purple, Billy Sheehan of Mr. Big as well as Don Airey on

Cozy Powell

keyboards. For Cozy Powell the album "The Drums Are Back" marked a new beginning.

The following conversation with Cozy Powell took place in April 1992 just prior to the release of "The Drums Are Back," a project the drummer was most eager to talk about.

Petra Zeitz: The drums are not a particularly melodic instrument and it's unusual that drummers pursue a solo career. How come you decided to go in that direction?

Cozy Powell: I was talking to some guys earlier and they said, "Why do you make an album?" Well, first of all, it's important because drums are being taken over by machines in the last few years. So many people have not really seen drummers in action for a long time. I think if you have the chance to make a record which is varied and got all sorts of musical styles on it and you can get it across to people, then it's a good thing to make it. It's coming from a drummer's point of view for a change. Usually the guitarist or the singer writes all the songs. So it's nice to get a record that comes from the other direction.

Petra Zeitz: Does your album mainly feature the drums then?

Cozy Powell: No, for exam-

ple, the guitar playing on it is just superb. It was good to get people to come and play with such passion. They did a great job on this album and it's worth it just to listen to the guitar playing—forget the drumming for a moment. Just the guitar playing is outstanding. It's very difficult to make an album and get people to listen to it. But once they do they will realize how high the musicianship is on this album and it might do very well. How this album does we'll see how we go from here. If nobody buys it I'll just jump in the river!

Petra Zeitz: Do you write all the guitar parts?

Cozy Powell: I write most of the tracks. On this album I got the arrangements. And then what I did was, I got the best people I could get that wanted to play on it to come along and put their personality on top of what I had already written. So you've got a complete mixture of tracks. Some I didn't write, but most of them I had something to do with. I think it's important to get good players to put their stamp on something that I've already done. It was nice because they didn't know what to expect. I just gave them the chord sequence, played them the tape, and said, "Look, this is what I've got. Would you like to do it?" They all said yes. Some people, for example Brian May, took it a step further. He actually wrote a song to go over the top of these tracks. So he was really inspired when he heard it. It was great because I got everybody to play on it. They really played very well. I mean, Steve Lukather has not played like that for a long time—even with Toto, although that's more or less his group. I think because he wasn't having to do a guitar solo towards a thing, he was able to just go for it. He was so excited that he had the level of this guitar so loud that people heard it in other studios.

Petra Zeitz: Did you work the same way when you recorded your solo albums in the 1970s and early '80s?

Cozy Powell: No, no. Most of the times I've been employed by a band to play. I made some solo records, but not with quite the amount of spirit I did this one with. I think before I had solo albums as a kind of sideline. When I finished working with the group I was with at the time, which was mainly Whitesnake and Michael Schenker, I was doing solo work as a sideline. This album was actually done with all my energy focused on it. I was also recovering from a very bad accident and I wanted to make sure that this album got 100 percent of my attention. I wanted to do it as a serious project. I didn't make any solo records since the ones before because I didn't have time to develop enough energy. I was always working and touring with all these other bands. You know, time goes so quickly you don't have enough time to do it properly. So I spent six months on this album getting it right. I flew to the States. I got all the different people involved. I spent a long time mixing it just to make sure that it was a good standard album and again, to make it a little bit different.

Petra Zeitz: Have you sat in the producer's chair before?

Cozy Powell: Yes, I have. I produced the "Headless Cross" and "Tyr" albums with Black Sabbath. I've coproduced quite a few things like the ELP album and one or two things before that. I've worked with some very unknown bands in Europe, but nothing really big. I want to develop out into production as well, because, I think, that's an area I have the experience for. It would be nice to branch out into something new.

Cozy Powell with Black Sabbath

Petra Zeitz: Even as a producer you are obviously worried by the use of drum-computers these days?

Cozy Powell: It bothers me to think that so many people use machines in the studio now. As a matter of fact, they don't even think they should get a drummer to do it. It's changing slowly, but it's not changing fast enough. I started off my life as a session drummer. A lot of bands have drummers that are okay for playing live, but when it comes to the record, they're not perfect enough to be right. I got a lot of work by doing that in the old days. I used to work three or four sessions a day and I worked five days a week. Now I get maybe three or four sessions a month! There isn't the work there. It doesn't matter how good you are; people don't think of using a drummer anymore. They use machines. This is my way of protesting that the drums should be used more. There is nothing better than a drummer when he's playing on stage and you can see that he's physically working. It's very exciting and I don't think anything can beat that. I'm sort of putting my flag out there, saying, "The drums are back!"

Petra Zeitz: You said you started as a session player. How did you get so involved in the *live* thing?

Cozy Powell: My whole career actually started in Germany. I went there in 1966 and I played in Hamburg, in Frankfurt and all over the place. I was there for two or three years playing every night in all the clubs. That was where I got my experience. I was in an unknown band called "The Sources." I also played with Casey Jones and the Engineers and a few other bands you don't wanna hear about. But that was how I learned my trade. When I went back to England I was discovered by Mickey Most and Jeff Beck and I ended up being the Mickey Most session drummer. I played on all the old Rak records with various people like Suzy Quattro and Hot Chocolate. I did lots of sessions for lots of different people. So I learned a bit of both—I had already learned how to play live—and then I went into studio work. Then I wanted to play live again and the next big band I joined was Rainbow. I played with them for five years. I've had a lot of experience both from live and from the studio.

Petra Zeitz: Are you planning to go on tour headlining as Cozy Powell & Band?

Cozy Powell: Yes, I am. I'm just finalizing the line-up of the group. I've got several options open. Several musicians have said that they want to do it. I'm looking for the right singer. I have two or three in mind, but I might do some dates with selected musicians that are on the album first of all. And then do a proper tour later.

Petra Zeitz: Are you going to stay with your own group from now on or are you waiting to join another established band?

Cozy Powell: There aren't any bands left! I've joined them all. I've got no plans to join another band. I think it is time that I did something myself and really work hard on promoting myself. I want to get a band together that's going to stay together for some time. There aren't a lot of bands left that I could feel comfortable joining anyway. All the established groups have either broken up or they just don't tour anymore. I'm gonna carry on under my own steam now because it's important to have the chance to make good music. It means starting again and building it up, but I don't mind doing that. If the music is good enough and the musicians are good enough—which they certainly will be—then I think people will enjoy it. It's important to bring the drums back and get people to come out and see them again.

Petra Zeitz: Did you ever feel part of the groups you were playing with, or were you just a hired drummer?

Cozy Powell: I felt part of Rainbow. That was a situation I worked very hard at. With the Michael Schenker Group I was more or less an employee, I think, and possibly with Whitesnake. Although I tried very hard to become part of Whiteshake, David Coverdale wants to run everything himself. So that was very difficult. In ELP, I was just brought in to do the album and a tour. Black Sabbath was good because I worked very hard with Tony Iommi to build the band up. I felt part of that band, but they changed their line-up so many times. I'd like to think I played in one of the best line-ups they had. It was very strong and very powerful. But again, things change, unfortunately. As I said, I had a bad set-back and it took a lot longer to fix than I thought.

Black Sabbath had to make an album and they wouldn't wait. Their loss, I say.

Petra Zeitz: Your solo album sounds much more melodic and less heavy than Black Sabbath. Is that the kind of music you prefer to make?

Cozy Powell: Well, I think Sabbath is almost caught in its own image. It has to have that certain sound. "Headless Cross" and "Tyr" were whirring out a little bit into the more melodic area. It's difficult to know, but I think a lot of the fans really want to hear "Paranoid" and "Sabbath Bloody Sabbath" and they're not too interested in listening to the more melodic things. That's a bit of a shame. I like a good song and a good melody. I happen to play in a very hard-hitting way, but I still like to combine the two. Good melodies with good hard drums is a good formula. Led Zeppelin always had a very powerful rhythm section, and their melodies were very good. That was a fantastic combination and it didn't do them any harm. That's really the area where I think I will go next. In fact, from this album on, if I can get the right singer, it will be in that vein. Nobody has really done anything since Led Zeppelin, not in that style. I think there's a great void out there. A lot of bands have tried to do it, but they were just a very poor imitation. But that's the sort of style of music I would prefer to go along, because that is where I'm happiest at. Good melodies, good music, but very, very powerful.

Petra Zeitz: Where did you find the singer Gerry Lane, who is on two of the new tracks?

Cozy Powell: He's a guy I found in Ireland actually. I was asked to produce a group he was in. They had so many good songs and he's got such a great voice that I thought it would be good to use a couple of the tracks. I re-did them and got them on the album. People should hear Gerry's voice because he is very good. He's a completely unknown guy, but it's nice to have a mixture of unknown musicians and well known names as well. There are some very well-known faces on the album. There's Steve Lukather, Jon Lord, Brian May, so we've got a complete mixture of old and new, if you like.

Petra Zeitz: Are you now looking for a known singer to join your band or do you want to discover more new talent?

Cozy Powell: I'd like to discover somebody. I know there's a lot of good singers out there. They need some direction. I think if I can give them a bit of help and steer them in the right way, I can get them to come out. I've worked with so many different singers over the past years I think I can probably help them a little. I've worked with Ronnie James Dio, Graham Bonnet, David Coverdale and Tony Martin. The list goes on and on. Tony Martin was unknown before the Sabbath thing and he's really good. There are people out there—you just have to look for them. My next plan is to attempt to get the right blend, and then I'll go out on the road.

Petra Zeitz: You said you're always looking for new singers. Have you noticed any good drummers emerging lately?

Cozy Powell: I haven't noticed anybody lately. I'm always asked if I've seen any new drummers. There's such difficulty in seeing live bands now. The venues that used to be there in the seventies aren't there anymore. In London you either play in a pub or you play Hammersmith Odeon, so it's difficult to see live bands. And again, most people are using machines now. They may have a drummer live, but he's not being given the chance to develop. Young kids aren't learning the drums anymore. They see the TV shows and they don't see any drummers. There are guys playing keyboards or guitars and people think there is no point in learning the drums anymore. It's very sad, but I don't see a lot of young drummers around. A lot of the drummers that I've known who were very good have either given up or retired. That's very sad and, I think, the music business has got a lot to answer for with the fact of the machines. How can a machine create music? You can't recreate drums on a machine—not properly anyway.

Petra Zeitz: Don't you notice any general move towards live playing again? I talk to many bands who say they want to play live and record live as well.

Cozy Powell: Well, they're slowly coming 'round, but it's taking a long time. It's been five years of nothing—just these awful machines. I mean, if they are starting to play live again, then that's great. I'm very pleased. Let's see some drummers out there doing some work. Keep at it! We must have drums back in the business.

Petra Zeitz: How much importance do you put on the drums compared to the other instruments in a band?

Cozy Powell: If the drums—the rhythm section—is right, then the record sounds very good. I think it's important to get the rhythm section right no matter how you do it. People spend many hours programming machines to do what a drummer could do in half an hour. Eventually they get it to sound quite good, but why bother to go through all that trouble in the first place when you could actually use a real drummer? I think the drums are as important as the guitar playing. The drummer is not actually playing a solo as such, but he's the foundation of the song. If the foundation of a building is not strong then the building will fall down no matter how beautiful it looks.

Petra Zeitz: After all these years in the business, is there anybody left you would like to work with?

Cozy Powell: I think I've played with most of them now. There's a few people I'd like to work with. I've never worked with Jimmy Page and, I think, that would be interesting. I'd like to work with Paul Rodgers, although I've already done a show with him in Seville. There's a lot of people I would like to play with *again*. But I think music is always on-going. You have to try and find some new talents and get them going. There's a generation of musicians that have come up and done their thing. But now they have gone and we need another generation of musicians to come and take their place.

Petra Zeitz: The main interest is still in the bands of the late sixties, isn't it?

Cozy Powell: It seems to be. People keep saying to me that this is finished and no more. But I don't think so somehow. If you can make good music, it doesn't matter how old you are. But it would be nice to find some younger people coming up and that's what I'm looking for at the moment. I'm hoping that there's some people out there but I haven't found them yet. It has to be outstandingly good to stand the test of time.

ROGER TAYLOR

For 20 years—until the untimely death of lead singer Freddie Mercury—Roger Taylor has been a member of the hugely successful British rock band Queen. Queen was formed in 1972, consisting of Brian May (guitar), Freddie Mercury (vocals, keyboards), John Deacon (bass) and Roger Taylor (drums). The line-up remained unchanged throughout the years. Although Mercury and May were the main songwriters, Taylor and Deacon also provided material. The band's first album "Queen" was released in 1973 but showed no signs of their future glory. In 1974, the single "Killer Queen" became their first Top 20 single in the United States. Queen's ascending career reached a new point with the release of the classic "Bohemian Rhapsody" in 1975, a six-minute progressive rock track. Their soundtrack for the movie *Flash Gordon* in 1980 was the first major film score by a rock band. A year later the band was criticized for appearing in South Africa's Sun City, but nevertheless, by the early eighties Queen had established themselves as one of the world's biggest bands. Their timeless hits included "We Are the Champions," "Another One Bites the Dust," "We Will Rock You" and "Crazy Little Thing Called Love." The Queen/David Bowie duet "Under Pressure" was the result of an impromptu recording session in Montreaux and marked the band's first collaboration with another star. Queen's set at Live Aid was one of the most acclaimed acts at the legendary July 1985 concert. Roger Taylor wrote the worldwide hit singles "Radio Ga Ga" (1984) and "It's a Kind of Magic" (1986). He also formed his own band the Cross while still remaining part of Queen. The Cross released three al-

Roger Taylor (*second from right*) with Queen

bums, but interest in the band was mainly due to their famous drummer. In 1991, the line-up included Roger Taylor on vocals, Clayton Moss on guitar, Spike Edney on keyboards, Peter Noone on bass and Josh McCrae on drums.

The last Queen album was called "Innuendo" and appeared in early 1991. Only a few months later, on November 24, 1991, Freddie Mercury died of AIDS. On April 20, 1992, Queen played one last all-star concert in memory of their flamboyant frontman.

Roger Taylor was expected to continue his career with the Cross.

The following conversation with Roger Taylor took place in September 1991. Whilst he could not have foreseen the untimely end of Queen, Roger was most eager to promote his new venture with the Cross—an album called "Blue Rock."

Petra Zeitz: Are you going on tour with the Cross because Queen won't go out at the moment?

Roger Taylor: No, it's got nothing to do with that. Touring—for us—is the most fun. It's a very important thing. Any real group has to be good in live performance. So we attach a lot of importance to that.

Petra Zeitz: Do you feel very different when you go out with the Cross instead of with Queen?

Roger Taylor: The Cross has been on tour several times and I'm used to it now. I remember playing clubs from years ago. When I was a teenager I used to play in very small places and also at the beginning of Queen we played in small places. Queen went back one time in London and we did a tour of clubs just to remind us and to make it more interesting for us. So I like playing small places.

Petra Zeitz: It's not just a matter of playing small places, but this time you're also supporting another band.

Roger Taylor: We're going to play with a band called Magnum

I know very well. I think they write very good songs. They have a strange image. Like ours, it's difficult to define. But they write very energetic songs. I produced an album for them six years ago and I thought they had a great songwriter, Tony Clarkin. I think it will be a good mixture to play with Magnum. It will be a good show altogether. I think we share the same audience.

Petra Zeitz: What does your audience look like?

Roger Taylor: They are the people who like hard rock, but they're not stupid. They like people to be good musicians and also to have some intelligent songs. This is what I think. And they're real, you know. They don't use all this hair spray and stuff. I've just been to America and it's strange—it looks like 1973 over there. I grew up like that with Queen. We used to wear all these leather clothes and had long hair. So it's very strange to see all that happening again. We were the start of heavy metal, Queen, Led Zeppelin, and everybody. It was like glam heavy metal or whatever, but it's all coming back 'round again.

Petra Zeitz: What do you think of the current development in the music scene?

Roger Taylor: It's not good at the moment. There are not enough good things. I think in America you can actually hear more quality music than in Europe. It's too dance-orientated for my taste. Everything is dance, dance, dance. There are no new ideas. They are just ripping off the old ideas. All the old good songs are being recycled. I hear very little good music these days. I like EMF. They might be able to write more really good songs. A lot of it is just electronic crap with a shelf life of one week.

Petra Zeitz: You seem to be one of the original rock'n' rollers.

Roger Taylor: Absolutely, but the thing is, you see, it lasts. It's timeless. There are hits from the sixties still around. Some of the best Motown stuff is becoming popular again.

Petra Zeitz: I remember when the first album by the Cross was released. Everybody called it Roger Taylor's solo project. Did you ever intend for the band to last that long?

Roger Taylor: It was never meant to be a solo project, you see? It was always meant to be a group. This has been a big problem. I have never been able to convince people that this is a

real group where everybody writes and everybody shares the money equally. It really is not the Roger Taylor Solo Experience—it's the Cross and I'm just the singer.

Petra Zeitz: When did you want to become a singer?

Roger Taylor: Well I've always been a singer. In Queen, I have sung all of the harmonies, you know, with Freddie and Brian for many years. Before that I was a singer anyway and a drummer at the same time. When Queen appeared live I would sing in every song. I'd sing harmonies at least and sometimes even double-lead with Freddie. On some songs, like "I'm in Love With My Car," I would sing the lead anyway. So I'm used to singing. That was not new—the thing that was new was to be at the front, not playing an instrument.

Petra Zeitz: Why do you never play drums with the Cross—not even in the studio?

Roger Taylor: Because we have a drummer and I am the singer. This is what people won't understand. I'm the singer—I'm *not* the drummer.

Petra Zeitz: "Blue Rock" was recorded at Real World Studios in England, a place owned by Peter Gabriel. Did the atmosphere of world music and exotic rhythms have an influence on your music?

Roger Taylor: When you say world music, you mean music from other countries, right? WOMAD is based at the studio, but we picked it because we liked the look of it. Our music is like classic hard rock. Although I like the idea of the world music thing, it had nothing to do with why we chose the studio. Real World is a good studio in a good location and basically a nice place. We liked it very much indeed. I've known Peter [Gabriel] for years.

Petra Zeitz: Are you very pleased with the results of the Cross' sessions?

Roger Taylor: I don't know to be honest. I think the album is quite good. We had a good producer this time. It's difficult because I usually have to wait six months to find out how much I like something. You know, we worked hard and I hope people like it. I can't say a lot more than that. I hope that the music is real. It's quite grown-up rock music and it's not pretending to be anything else.

Petra Zeitz: You have mentioned the producer Mark Wallis already. He is only 31 years old. Isn't it strange to take directions from a guy younger than yourself?

Roger Taylor: No, he's not that young. Thirty-one is not that young. He's very experienced. He's worked on "The Joshua Tree" with U2 and he has worked with Jeff Beck. This is all stuff we like so he's great to work with. I mean, he's older than three members of the band. But it was fantastic. I really enjoyed him telling me what to do. I enjoyed that for a change. It's nicer to receive direction than give it.

Petra Zeitz: Did you produce any previous projects by the Cross yourself?

Roger Taylor: Really yes, but the other members of the band also. You need somebody from the outside to give you that outside direction. You're too closely involved and you can't give an objective view. We had about 25 songs and we sat down with the producer one day and asked him which ones he liked. So we let him choose the songs.

Petra Zeitz: You have written some famous Queen songs and now you also write for the Cross. Is it a different writing process?

Roger Taylor: No, I write by myself. I can't do it any other way. Sometimes if I write with somebody else it's just the lyrics. The songs I write by myself I write completely by myself and then I bring them in and work them out with the band.

Petra Zeitz: Where did you look for the other members of the Cross?

Roger Taylor: Spike was a friend of mine who had played the keyboards with Queen on the tours. When Freddie has to move and sing, somebody else has to play the keyboards. So I have known Spike for about 20 years. We decided to start this thing up together and we wanted to find three younger guys. Just so that it wasn't all older people. We wanted influence from what was happening and everything. And we found the guys and we made the band. It's been very hard, very tough.

Petra Zeitz: Is it tough because people still see it as Roger Taylor of Queen?

Roger Taylor: Yes, absolutely. You just can't get away from that. It's very difficult. It's frustrating, really. People like to put you in a drawer, you know, in a box, but this is a different thing. It's completely separate from the other.

SONGWRITERS

JONATHAN BUTLER

Jonathan Butler is an acclaimed singer/songwriter and master guitarist from Cape Town. He has been performing since he was six years old. He had chart topping records by the age of 12. He also received the South African equivalent of the Grammy award.

An artist in tune with his muse, Butler left South Africa a long time ago and now resides in London, England. His skills as a writer and player have not gone unnoticed amongst fellow professionals and Jonathan's talents are in constant demand. He has worked with Whitney Houston, Billy Ocean, George Benson, Hugh Masekela and Al Jarreau to name but a few. In 1988 he supported Eric Clapton on a British tour. In between all these activities Butler still finds the time to pursue his own career. In the early eighties he joined Jive Records and soon became an important part of the writing and production team. With the release of his instrumental album entitled, "Introducing Jonathan Butler," interest—especially in the United States—began to grow. In 1986 he recorded a jazz album which was to bring him to the attention of those who appreciate this musical form, but it also crossed over from the Jazz Top Ten to the mainstream album chart. This is a rare achievement.

Butler's 1991 EP "Deliverance" went to Number 1 in the US R&B chart. He has received gold disk awards in six countries including the United States and the United Kingdom.

The following conversation with Jonathan Butler took place while Jonathan was promoting his fourth vocal album "Heal Our Land" in 1990.

Petra Zeitz: You have been quoted as saying your new album [Heal Our Land] is your best so far. In what way does it differ from your previous releases?

Jonathan Butler: Well, apart from the fact that I don't think it is a commercial project, it is something I've wanted to do for a while. I think I've reached this certain level of maturity where it really matters to me what I am saying. Just the standard of compositions and the lyrical content of this album are better. Also, there were so many people that came in and out of the studio and worked on it; they were the finest musicians in America, and I worked with South Africans which made it even more special because I worked with friends. All of us felt that the message of "Heal Our Land" was so real to us, it was something we all felt, we all wanted to say to each other at the same time. Just the words "heal our land" mean so many things, you know.

Petra Zeitz: What exactly did they mean to you as an individual?

Jonathan Butler: They meant where I was from—a poverty-stricken family living in shanty houses. And living in South Africa under apartheid and knowing that the grass is green on the other side, and where I am it's a

nightmare. I felt I wanted to talk about that situation as far as where I was coming from and so it became a personal album, a personal project.

Petra Zeitz: In the past you have been criticized for sounding *"too* American." Has that changed, too?

Jonathan Butler: The president of my record company was quite in love with the fact that this album turned out to be more of a Jonathan Butler project than Jonathan Butler being Americanized. Still, most of the musicians were Americans but the album sounds more like me, and it's more what I kind of feel about things.

Petra Zeitz: Your musical history brings us back to South Africa. How did your career start there?

Jonathan Butler: I'm from a really large family of 17 kids and I'm the baby. We were all involved in music, my father was a singer, my mother was a piano player and a singer. So my parents were responsible for putting us on stage. Initially I was quite shy to sing for my family because I didn't really want them to know I could. My friends told me to sing and in the end I did and my mother then put me on stage with the

Jonathan Butler

rest of the guys. They were all impressed that there was a new young singer in the family and they felt that he would go far. I believed that too. What I dreamt of most in my childhood life was that I would go far, be happy, world famous. At six or seven I was thinking about that all the time. I played guitar when I was six and it was all very important to me. I got involved in a few competitions and actually won most of them. The final competition was to win and go on tour with a musical company. It was a cast of 60 people, caravans, buses and everything. I won and went on the road at the age of six and stayed on the road until I was 12. We went to Zimbabwe, Angola, Zambia, all over South Africa as well as East and West Africa. I gained all my knowledge and experience from the road, playing different kinds of music and playing to different people. It was kind of a hectic life for a six-year-old. I didn't have any parents with me; I just had a brother who was also involved with the musical play. So he became a father figure to me and he supported me. When I was 12 I left that musical and joined a band. I wanted to be in a band and play the clubs. I

guess, by then, I was a household name in South Africa.

Petra Zeitz: Did you have any records out by then?

Jonathan Butler: I hadn't made any recordings, but I got picked up by a record company and made my first record which went to Number 2 in the pop charts. So I became the first black singer to be in the pop charts.

Petra Zeitz: Did this fact make you feel more accepted by white people?

Jonathan Butler: I didn't know what it meant because I was this black kid living in Cape Town. As far as I know, I still went home to this ghetto area. I had hits for five years but I still lived in the same colored areas. I had a lot of fans all over the place. So on one hand, you have all the fun and joy that fame can bring, but on the other, you had the ghetto and the shanty house to go to. People took from me every day because I was the only one that could give. And of course I was a minor, I had no right to my own money. So all that was a struggle to deal with.

Petra Zeitz: Did you feel happy about being famous at an early age?

Jonathan Butler: Fame doesn't always have blessings

added to it. It's got many curses attached to it, I guess. But I learned a hell of a lot. I was involved with pop music in South Africa for a long time. I made several albums and singles and then I became somewhat disillusioned with pop music. I felt that there wasn't enough depth and substance to what I was singing and playing and I wanted to be a jazz musician. I told my record company that I wasn't going to make any more records, but was going to learn to play music for a change. I got together with a few jazz guys and stayed and studied eight or nine hours a day. Then I started to work with jazz groups, but after playing to 20,000 people, there I was playing to 15. It was an amazing contrast. But then along with the jazz music came the drugs and the drinking. I really became sort of out of it and every gig I did was just to get high.

Petra Zeitz: How did you manage to survive the vicious cycle of drink and drugs?

Jonathan Butler: Nine years ago I got born again and met my wife. Together we started a gospel ministry and I started playing gospel music. But I was encouraged to leave the gospel music scene and pursue my ca-

reer again. I tried to get a recording deal in England and eventually moved there.

So this is my career today.

Petra Zeitz: Do you prefer living in England now?

Jonathan Butler: I have a passion for England and I have just discovered that! The lifestyle suits me. It's much easier than living in South Africa, because right now I'm dealing with myself and I'm able to identify with me; what I like to be, what I like to say, and what I like to think. All these things play a very important role in my life. I would have never been able to do this in South Africa. I like the fact that I'm able to be an individual whose right it is to be whatever he wants to be. I have been going to America and I have contemplated living there. I might move there one day, but at the moment the passion hasn't gone away. That's why I'm still in England.

Petra Zeitz: Do your recent records still get released in South Africa?

Jonathan Butler: Apparently so. I received a gold record for one of my albums which is fantastic. They are quite proud of me back home. They support my career and it is good for them to know that there is a

South African out there that's doing well. It's wonderful for the people of the country, the people who know what we believe in and what we are about.

Petra Zeitz: Is it difficult for a South African musician to get a break in other parts of the world?

Jonathan Butler: Oh yes, the main problem is that nobody wants to deal with you because you're South African—not just white, but black too. You need a tunnel-vision outlook for yourself and say to yourself you keep trying. One thing that was good for me was that I didn't compromise. It's a long road and not an easy one.

Petra Zeitz: The musicians union has been boycotting South Africa for a long time. Do you agree with their actions?

Jonathan Butler: One has to stand for something. No free person is going to let somebody else mess with his freedom. South Africa isn't really free and in order to achieve that freedom we need to stand for something. I'm not going to play in Sun City even if you gave me five million dollars! I'd play in Sun City if you gave me five million dollars to give to the black community, you know. Give that money to the poor people and I will come! But in reality it's all take, take, take. Everybody is taking, everybody wants to make a quick buck. My personal commitment to my country is that I won't play in South Africa. People who accept to play there, whether it's sport, music or anything, accept money without looking at the situation: The blacks are deprived of citizenship, their kids are detained without trial, twelve-year-olds are sitting in jail. That can't be right! One has to know where one's priorities really are. So the boycott is important but, I think, individually people need to be able to understand this thing. I want to go and play in South Africa one day and raise so much money to help the urban areas. That's important to me because I come out of the slums myself. I come out of a family of alcoholics and drug addicts. I understand these things very well. I understand when a kid stands on a corner doped out and doesn't know left from right. I've sat on pavements looking like that! I was a star one moment and low down the next. That's why it is important to me to succeed. Eventually I will use this name to lift some kid out of a bad problem.

Petra Zeitz: There are a lot of musicians from America or England who campaign for the South African issue without having experienced the situation you described. How do you feel about their actions?

Jonathan Butler: I think it's great that people support the struggle. Anyone who stands up against apartheid is important. In a way music and these people play a very important role in making other people aware of the situation. For young people today everything has to be trendy and fast; it's a certain way of dressing, certain ways of speaking—it's all young stuff, but we have to worry about what people print into their minds. Kids in America today have more information than what we have had. So I think it's great that people can be made aware through these pop musicians and actors. We all have that role to play.

Petra Zeitz: Do you believe music alone could change anything?

Jonathan Butler: Well, it's like . . . you might have a problem telling the girl you're with that you love her, but a song that comes on the radio will do it. All you have to do is buy that record and give it to the person you love and it will say it all. Music can—in a way—say all of it. I think music is very important in that area.

BILLY FALCON

Born in a New York City suburb in the mid-50s, Billy Falcon is a man who has experienced life's ups and downs without losing his positive outlook. During the 70s he recorded four albums, was critically acclaimed and even played the famous Bottom Line Club in Manhattan. But he had to wait until 1991 to achieve commercial success. His resurrection was overseen by none other than Jon Bon Jovi, and finally, his fifth album, "Pretty Blue World" sold in large quantities on American soil.

Billy Falcon is a poetic songwriter who always knows what he is talking about.

The following in-depth interview with Billy Falcon took place in January 1992.

Petra Zeitz: Your fifth album was your break in the music world. What was the difference between "Pretty Blue World" and your previous releases?

Billy Falcon: They were as different as, say, when you look at a picture of yourself from ten years ago and you see the differences. So they were all me, but for each time there were different levels of maturity. Some of the old things I listen to and I'm proud of, but others I feel kind of embarrassed about. Again, it's just like seeing a picture of yourself with clothes that at the time you thought were terrific, and now you think, "Oh Gosh! I can't believe I wore that!" That happens with music, too. I can't believe I sang like that, but most of it I don't mind. It was pretty good—just different levels of maturity.

Petra Zeitz: You've been wanting to be a musician since you were only eight years old. Is this the only profession you pursued?

Billy Falcon: I have always been a musician. I started wanting to play music after seeing the Beatles on the *Ed Sullivan*

Show [1964]. I remember sitting at the dining table in my mother's living room. I was doing my homework on Sunday night and my older sister and all her friends would gather around the TV set. It was different because they weren't usually in the house and I didn't know why they were all excited and why all these people were in the house watching TV. Suddenly Ed Sullivan came on and when he announced the Beatles there was this scream! Up until that point I wanted to be a baseball player, but then, when I saw that I thought, "Girls don't scream like this for baseball players, this is what I want to do!" Nobody believed me. Money was in short supply and my folks didn't immediately buy me a guitar just because I said I wanted one. So I started making guitars out of old soap-boxes with strings and rubber bands and I'd play and sing. I used to put underwear on my head to make it look like I had long hair. And then, finally, I convinced my parents that I was very serious about music, that this wasn't some little fancy I had that was going to disappear. So I got a guitar and immediately started to write songs. I didn't want to wait to learn, so I'd learn a chord and I'd write a song with one chord. Then I'd learn two and I'd write a song with two chords. That's what I did my whole life. I really tried to write songs and now I think I finally can. But that was how I started anyway.

Petra Zeitz: Do you see yourself as a songwriter first and then as a musician?

Billy Falcon: Sometimes people say "musician" and I'm not sure what they mean. I'm a much better songwriter than I am a guitar player, although I can play okay. But I write the music also. A lot of people seem to think a songwriter just writes the lyrics. So before I'm a singer and before I'm a guitar player, I am a songwriter. I think if I was a businessman and someone like me walked into the room and I heard him sing and play and I heard his songs, if I had to pick one thing that I wanted from this guy, it would be the songs. So if people like my singing that is almost extra to me. It's like Bob Dylan—he has such a funny voice, if he didn't write great songs we would have never heard of Bob Dylan. I learned to love his voice, but I don't think we would have heard of him if he wasn't a great songwriter.

Petra Zeitz: Do you ever write songs for other people or do you think it's best to always perform them yourself?

Billy Falcon: No, when I have the opportunity to do so, I do write for other people. I love it when someone says that so and so is looking for a song, because I'll write it in three minutes! Recently I wrote the Stevie Nicks record "Sometimes It's a Bitch." Jon Bon Jovi and Danny Kortchmar were in the studio with me and they were talking about their next project which was Stevie Nicks. They said they were so busy with me they didn't have time to find Stevie's songs. So I was smart, I took my guitar and I went out in the alleyway and wrote "Sometimes It's a Bitch," thinking about Stevie. I don't know her life but I know the press coverage and I think she's been through some extreme highs and extreme lows and so have I. I could relate to her and I wrote the song about that. Me and Jon finished it together. It's a song I would have never written had somebody not mentioned Stevie Nicks, so I like that. I wrote a lot of songs. Once I have finished the tour this year I might just go and write for other people's records.

Petra Zeitz: Your lyrics are very poetic. Do you ever write straight poems without music?

Billy Falcon: I write the songs like poems. One of my tests for a song, after I've written it, is to write all the words down and if it isn't musical to my ears just reading it, it isn't good enough. Sometimes I read people's lyrics, and without the music I don't get it and I don't enjoy just reading the words. The lyric has to hold up all by itself—you don't need the guitar solo to understand the song. You can play any of my songs on the guitar without missing anything because I try very hard not to rely on the beat and on the arrangement to finish a song. It's a danger to suddenly have all this help around you with a band. You can write half a song and let the guys work it out—instead of a third verse you put in a guitar solo, but you'd need the third verse to tell the story. Does that answer your question?

Petra Zeitz: Yes, it does. Do you read many books in order to find inspiration for your lyrics?

Billy Falcon: I guess I do, but I probably read all the wrong things. I read novels and lots of fiction. I hate sitting still, and I hate wasting time, so I started reading a lot in the last year while I was traveling. I read one book a week, but they were all different types of books. One day I should start reading books that will educate me as opposed to just thrilling me. But having the words running through your mind helps you as a writer because you have to stay in touch with the language. I love words—it's my job!

Petra Zeitz: Does that mean you get your inspiration more from day to day things?

Billy Falcon: Thank God I get it from anywhere. My songwriting is not about a place. I don't have to be somewhere to be able to write, I just have to live and be peaceful. People say, "How do you write songs like these in New York?" They think I come from down South or out West, but I don't have to live in the country to write music that sounds big and has an open sky. I just have to have a clear mind in terms of not being frustrated or angry. So I get my inspiration from things that happen to me and things I observe. If it all had to be about me, I guess, it would get kind of boring because there is not something exciting enough in my life to write about every day. I don't like making up nonsense. I can't

sing about heartache if there isn't heartache because I would not be able to convince anybody with that. But I can see your're hurting and write about your pain without having to go through it all myself. I have a very strong opinion of everything. That can be good or bad in itself, but it makes all my songs rather personal. It makes me no fun to hang around with a lot of times, because I can be too critical and too hard on people. I think that has something to do with why I write songs and why I am able to pick up little details. If you hear my songs you kind of get to know what kind of person I am.

Petra Zeitz: You seem to be very critical of other songwriters. Whom do you actually like?

Billy Falcon: I like Crowded House a lot. They are very well respected and I think when they put the perfect record out, they will be huge! U2 is another band I like. I don't really like everything anybody does. I have to go song by song. I think some tracks on the new U2 record ["Achtung Baby"] sound too much like INXS, but when I hear that "Mysterious Ways" song, that is a great song. I'm doing reviews here . . . I like

Bonnie Raitt, John Hiatt, generally singer/songwriter stuff. If it's bands, I still want to know that they're trying to say something, like U2 is. I love particular songs by particular bands, but I don't buy their whole thing. I am not affected by their image. I am not a loyal fan.

Petra Zeitz: You have worked in Nashville recently. I have noticed more and more artists— even rock'n'roll bands—are going to Nashville to record. What is it about that place?

Billy Falcon: Everybody who loves music should go and see what Nashville is like. It's a great place! It's a Mecca for any songwriter. Jon Bon Jovi called me when I was in Nashville and he said, "What the hell are you doing there? Do I not know something about you that I need to know, are you wearing a cowboy hat now?" I told him that there is a big community of artists and musicians in Nashville. Everywhere you go, there are songwriters sitting in bars and anybody can go and join in. If you want to rub elbows with the best songwriters in the world, you go to Nashville. And you can talk to them about songwriting and go to lunch with them. In New York City, everybody is

there also but it's an elitist thing. They are somewhere in their towers and you don't see them and if you do, they won't talk to you because you're not at their level. In Nashville there is a real scene where musicians get together and have conversations about music. I can write a song there in the afternoon and that night go up on stage in a little club and everybody sits and listens and nobody talks. And even if you screw up everybody understands because they did the same thing the night before. There's also the country music business and there are country songwriters from whom you can learn so much. Country songwriters don't take anything for granted. When I finished my record, Jon Bon Jovi asked me to take him to Nashville and I showed him around the place. He later told me he had the absolute week of his life! And what hasn't he seen in terms of the world?

Petra Zeitz: How did your collaboration with Jon Bon Jovi come about in the first place?

Billy Falcon: That was some kind of miracle, I think. I was at home, taking care of my daughter who was five years old at the time. I had been widowed a couple of years before that. So I was now a single parent, trying to figure out how to be in the music business and have a baby. I was very emotionally messed up and I couldn't find a way of doing it, but my songs were getting better all the time. I was taking care of my baby and writing songs, but I couldn't leave the house or anything. So now I was in Long Island and I got a call from my old guitar player and he said to me that he run into a friend of his who had been working for Jon Bon Jovi. He was a handyman. He worked in the garden, polished the cars, stuff like that, but this guy told Jon Bon Jovi that he had run into Billy Falcon's old guitar player and Jon got all excited about it. He said he used to go and see my shows all the time and he started pulling my old records out. Jon wanted to find out where I had been and what I was doing. When my friend called to tell me that, I didn't believe him. I very much wanted to believe him because things hadn't been good for a long time. I sent him a tape of just me singing along to the guitar. "Power Windows" and "Pretty Blue World" were on that tape with a couple more songs. I didn't hear anything for eight months. Then I went to Nashville (I left my daughter with my parents) and another friend called me in Nashville saying Jon Bon Jovi wanted to get in touch with me. He said Jon had absolutely flipped over my music. So I spoke to Jon, sent him more songs which he thought were amazing and he asked me what I wanted to do. I said I wanted to make a record but I also told him the situation was that I had a baby, no band, and record companies were not tripping over themselves to sign me. I'd had four records out already and nobody ever understood why it didn't happen in the first place. Jon said, "I can do it! Billy, they can't fire me! I'll do it." We had dinner and he gave me a record contract. We started working on the record in January 1991.

Petra Zeitz: Were you pleased with the acceptance the record eventually received?

Billy Falcon: We have done very well, but 1991 wasn't a particularly great year for selling records because there is a terrible recession at the moment. Many tours did not happen and we were very fortunate to be working continuously. Every tour we were on did well, and when nobody else could get a tour we got tours. The first single did very well, but should have done even better. We are still at the beginning, but we are selling consistently.

Petra Zeitz: You said you don't care about the things that most people care about. What did you mean by that?

Billy Falcon: Anybody that does anything artistic has a different set of values than anybody else. When I tell people I'm a songwriter they look at me kind of funny. They don't understand me. Before I had this record contract I used to sit on my patio and write. I don't like to be in the house all day when the weather is nice. My daughter would be running around and the neighbors were wondering what the hell I was doing. They thought I was a little boy. Now that I'm on the TV and the radio all the time, they begin to understand. I would like to live in a place where culture is more important than buying the groceries.

Petra Zeitz: Are you a religious person?

Billy Falcon: To a degree. I mean I'm a rotten guy; I'm not holy. I really do believe in God. In terms of morality I know what's right, but I don't always do what's right. Everybody is like that. I'm a religious person in that I'm a Christian and I believe in God and I believe that He had a Son. I don't go to church; I don't try to make other people believe what I believe. But if I screw up I think someone can still help me. That's why I wrote some of the songs, like "Heaven's Highest Hill" and "Still Got a Prayer." I think the basis for everything is believing in something bigger than what we can taste, touch, feel or see. There's gotta be more to it because loneliness is horrifying.

Petra Zeitz: Do you want your songs to always have a happy or hopeful ending?

Billy Falcon: Yes, those songs are my life and I want my life to have a happy ending. Most times I write about something I feel or see. If I look at a bad situation I want it to have a hopeful ending and I believe it will. Sometimes I'm disappointed and it doesn't, but I will always be surprised when I'm disappointed. Take the worst thing in the world, when my wife passed away I was surprised, I was shocked and yet she had been sick for two years. Although doctors were telling me she was in a bad way, I always believed she would get better. During the

last days of her life I was surprised that she was actually
going to pass away. So that is the
extreme side of my optimism.
I'd rather be like that than
spend my whole life worrying.
There is only one song I
wrote, "Not Funny Anymore,"
that doesn't have a trace of
hope.

JOHN WESLEY HARDING

The name sounds more than familiar: Having turned to the title of a famous Bob Dylan album for his stage name, it is perhaps not surprising that John Wesley Harding has already been compared to the living legend himself: "He may well be the next Bob Dylan" wrote the *Santa Cruz Sentinel* in 1990 and the *L.A. Times* added: "His new release 'Here Comes the Groom' is the first great album of the 90s." A year later the same paper asked Harding to review the latest Dylan release for them.

Born to artsy parents in the British town of Hastings in 1965, Wesley Harding Stace grew up in a musical family. Two years after he first picked up a guitar, he had his first record contract. "Here Comes the Groom" (1990) and "The Name Above the Title" (1991) were produced by Andy Paley who also co-wrote and produced the *Dick Tracy* soundtrack.

Harding has extensively toured the United States on various occasions, supporting the Mighty Lemon Drops and Michelle Shocked, as well as headlining his own gigs. In 1991 he was part of the "Gathering of the Tribes" traveling music festival.

Besides a great sense of humor, Harding has an expert knowledge of rock'n'roll history and borrows titles and phrases from certain songs. One of his most famous lines is "Bob Dylan is my father, Joan Baez is my mother and I'm their bastard son."

The following conversation with John Wesley Harding took place in London in June 1990. Since I have met and talked to the singer two more times at later dates, parts of this

John Wesley Harding

interview are updated accordingly.

Petra Zeitz: How did your collaboration with the Attractions on both of your studio albums come about?

John Wesley Harding: I didn't write with the Attractions but I needed a band to record with. My first album was an acoustic live set, but obviously a big label like Sire/Warner Brothers wanted a full band recording. I thought my best crack was to get a good band. We got Pete and Bruce Thomas from the Attractions, and also Steve Donelly who is quite well known in England, and Kenny Craddock on piano. He has played with Van Morrison and is just fantastic. We did all the backing tracks within one week, then I went to LA and just phoned up Peter Case and asked him if he wanted to write a song with me and he did. We wrote a song called "Things Snowball."

Petra Zeitz: Do you usually have all your compositions finished before you go into the studio?

John Wesley Harding: Yes, I write my songs on an acoustic guitar and then play them to the band. I write everything myself, apart from a couple of tracks on which I collaborated with other writers. On stage I also do "Like a Prayer" by Madonna and "Personal Jesus" by Depeche Mode, although I sometimes sing "Personal Cheese With." Not that I particularly like these songs, but I do them anyway— just for the hell of it.

Petra Zeitz: Your music was described as "Country Rock." Is that what you want it to be?

John Wesley Harding: Country Rock! Who said that?

Petra Zeitz: *Time Out* Magazine in London printed it.

John Wesley Harding: No, I wouldn't describe my music as "Country Rock," I'd say it's "Power Folk." I can't believe they said this actually!

Petra Zeitz: Who are your main influences then?

John Wesley Harding: I'm influenced by a lot of pop music: Phil Spector, Abba, Tommy James and the Shondells, Hüsker Dü. Also a lot of folk people from the 70s who are very famous now: Tim Harding, Phil Oats, Eric Anderson, Steve Goodman, a lot of rock people like Bruce Springsteen, Elvis Costello, and a lot of punk bands I was into when I was young. But I always wanted to be a pop singer. I don't want to be a folk or a country singer. I want to make pop records.

Petra Zeitz: Why did you take your stage name from the title of an old Dylan album?

John Wesley Harding: My real name is Wesley Harding Stace, but it became quite a joke when I was touring with the Hothouse Flowers and they just liked the idea of calling me John Wesley Harding. It's a great stage name because people always think they've heard of you—even if they haven't! Most people expect me to be about 40 with a beard. So there you go!

Petra Zeitz: You also did some soundtrack work recently, namely for the Roger Daltrey film *Buddy's Song*.

John Wesley Harding: Who told you about that? I thought it was still a secret! A good friend of mine called Nigel Hinton wrote the book and the film-script for *Buddy's Song*. He phoned me in desperation and asked me to write some songs because the film people had come up with a lot of crap songs, real middle-of-the-road stuff. So I got together with Nigel and we turned out loads and loads of songs really quickly. The record company liked them all. They thought they were all hits which was funny to me because I don't write hits, unless I'll write some by mistake in the future. So they asked me to come up with some more and I just kept writing. Roger Daltrey really liked my songs too and said he would be interested in me doing some work on his next record. He really loved me!

Petra Zeitz: Are you involved in recording the *Buddy's Song* album?

John Wesley Harding: No, not yet, unless they ask me to make a guest appearance as a folk singer or something like that. A young guy called Chesney Hawkes is doing the vocals and he's really good. But they've done some pretty evil things to the songs. I wrote a song called "It's Gonna Be Tough" and it's just a simple acoustic pop song. I listened to their album version and it had these heavy industrial drums, I mean, not that it's bad, but it's music I can't understand. And this noise—I mean, I had nothing to do with the writing of it at all! As far as I can see, what they did was like getting a fish and taking all the meat off it, so that you're left with just the bones, and then dressing it up with some fancy clothes. It was really funny to listen to, because there was nothing left to it. It didn't sound like a good song arrangement to me, but that's fine, because I'm an old hippy. So who knows? It was probably brilliant!

Petra Zeitz: Are you worried about people taking your songs apart in the studio?

John Wesley Harding: No, not really. With *Buddy's Song* the music is good in the film. I did demos. I can't really play any instruments, but I played everything on these demos. I did the bass and the guitar solo, the piano and the drums, terrible computer drums, they're really funny. So in the film the songs sound really like what I wrote, but the soundtrack record is completely different.

Petra Zeitz: But you have taken your name off soundtrack recordings in the past, haven't you?

John Wesley Harding: I had a song in an American movie and I hated the movie so much that I took my name off. It was called *Wild Orchid* and it was a shit movie with Mickey Rourke in it, written by the idiot who wrote *9 1/2 Weeks*. I mean, it was a really poor piece of work. I don't know why I did the soundtrack in the first place. It was just disgusting, so I got my name off it

completely and put it under the name of the Rhythm Methodist. The soundtrack album is out now and it's a John Wesley Harding rarity. This guy came up to me in Seattle and said: "Man, I'm such a big fan of yours—I've got everything! I even had to go out and buy that stupid *Wild Orchid* soundtrack!" I suppose that's kind of a compliment.

Petra Zeitz: You don't seem to take your career very seriously, or always with a grain of salt. Is that so?

John Wesley Harding: I treat my career as a pop singer as a bit of a joke. The whole idea of it is funny to me, you know. I mean, selling a lot of records and knowing 50,000 people in the United States have a copy of my album is very funny to me. That's why I put a funny photo of me on the cover. But my career as a songwriter and earning money through writing songs is very important to me indeed. What I liked about the soundtrack work was that it was just the music. Normally I write lyrics and then just stick some music on it, but this was just music and a good thing for me to concentrate on.

Petra Zeitz: How do you feel about your *live* audience?

John Wesley Harding: I prefer playing live to working in a studio. My albums are recorded live anyway, that's why I do them so quickly. Only my voice was overdubbed the first time, because when I finished rehearsing I had no voice left. But tours are great! I once stopped a show in Seattle and made everybody with a tape recorder hold it in the air. There were 25 people with these Walkmans up in the air. It was really funny! But you know, you heard what my music is like and you know what music that makes the charts is like. If I ever have a hit single it will be because people think I'm a bit of an oddball, a big novelty.

Petra Zeitz: Is being successful important to you after all?

John Wesley Harding: I am successful in the United States, in that sense of success. In England the only way to be successful is to have a hit single and I'm not gonna try to do that. I'm not going to make any attempt at getting a hit single. I keep writing songs that I like. I'm an American signing. I was signed by the same guy who signed Madonna and Talking Heads. So the record company is mainly promoting me in the States where I had all these

great reviews. At home in England nobody has got any idea of who I am. And that's good because it means I can carry on living a really nice life. In the United States they love the fact that I went to Cambridge University because it is a place they have heard of, but for the British music press it's a bit of a bind. I studied English and worked for a Ph.D in social science, but I gave up to make music.

Petra Zeitz: "The Devil in Me" managed to be "Single of the Week" on BBC Radio 1 in England. Was that just a novelty, too?

John Wesley Harding: That was a great song. I'm actually trying to get that re-released! Lyrically it's kind of an update to the Rolling Stones' "Sympathy for the Devil." It's also about people making big money by advertising things they don't believe in. It's about political responsibility and how we are responsible for everything, which is far more of a protest song than "No-more Maggie" or "Bring Down the Government," you know what I mean? We are directly responsible for Oswald, Gaddafi, Saddam, for all those people. It's just a bad side of us, the Hitlers in all of us.

Petra Zeitz: How much importance do you put on your lyrics?

John Wesley Harding: Exactly 50 percent. I'm a hippy-dippy protest singer. I'm very influenced by that kind of music. Rather than make my songs sit as protest songs it would be better to infiltrate the pop charts with them and disguise them, so people just end up singing "…it was the devil in me," rather than "Oh electric you…" It would be even better if people said "Tear down the government" but that's stupid and naïve.

Petra Zeitz: What do you think makes your music so refreshing to listen to?

John Wesley Harding: I like pop music. I like music that starts and stops, begins, middles, bridges and ends. I'm very traditional about that. People said to me I make incredibly original albums, but they are really mostly old fashioned. Touch wood, I get some good songs, some good players, record it live and put it out on a record. That's the whole story, but that's how Robert Johnson and Phil Spector made records.

GARLAND JEFFREYS

Garland Jeffreys grew up in Brooklyn, New York. Neither black nor white skinned, it was difficult for him as a child to feel he belonged anywhere. He was called names like Buckwheat by other children.

Garland went to Abraham Lincoln High School and later studied at Syracuse University and spent time in the Italian town of Florence.

Between 1973 and 1983 he wrote and recorded seven solo albums of which the 1979 offering "American Boy and Girl" became most famous for the hit single "Matador." Four years later Garland Jeffreys retired from the music business only to re-emerge in 1991 with the "Don't Call Me Buckwheat" album, featuring 12 of his most personal songs about his experience with day-to-day racism. It also had a Frankie Lymon cover version.

The following conversation with Garland Jeffreys took place in late 1991 and centered around the songs and lyrics on "Don't Call Me Buckwheat."

Petra Zeitz: Everybody wants to know what you did in all these years between 1983 and 1991?

Garland Jeffreys: Gee, you're the first one who has asked me that question. This is actually the first question that everybody asks. It's a very simple question and a very simple answer, really. In 1983, my last record, the "Guts of Love" album, came out on Epic records and it was basically the end of a period for me. I had done six albums in seven years and I really didn't know what the feeling of this was, I mean, I was so exhausted. Six albums, the touring, the traveling around the world, doing everything that I was responsible for, just exhausted me and so I took a break. I took about two years

Garland Jeffreys

off, I went to Italy for a while, I produced a record for an Italian artist, I began to do a little touring, but very light. I went to Japan where I had never performed before, but basically I got away from the record company push for the work that you have to do. As you can see, I'm back doing it now, but this time with a totally different perspective.

Petra Zeitz: Which music did you listen to as a child and what made you decide to become a singer/songwriter yourself?

Garland Jeffreys: My parents listened to a lot of music and there was always music in my house. They weren't musicians themselves but they loved Charlie Parker, Billie Holiday, The Mills Brothers, Ray Charles, Sarah Vaughan, Nat King Cole, etc.—this kind of music. When I and the kids that I grew up with started listening to music, we liked the Drifters, Ben E. King, and Frankie Lymon and the Teenagers. When the sixties came I got into Motown and Bob Dylan, the English explosion, the early Rolling Stones, all that stuff. Later I listened to reggae. I actually became friends with Bob Marley in the seventies. He was a wonderful man and a wonderful musician. I basically always continued to be influenced by all music that I hear.

Petra Zeitz: Did you develop any new ideas before you started working on this new record?

Garland Jeffreys: I actually went back to certain ideas that were really strong that I had begun in the early seventies. When you begin to reach a certain success level sometimes you lose your focus. I can look back now and tell the story easily, but at the time I was going through a big thing. My life had become very one-dimensional. I don't think I could have gone on much longer, but I was obviously able to stop and I'm glad I did. I'm so glad I took so much time to make this next record, because it took a lot of time for me to figure out what I wanted to do and how I felt.

Petra Zeitz: For the first time one of your albums is fully dedicated to the subject of racism.

Garland Jeffreys: I started writing new songs, but these songs didn't hit the mark, they didn't do it for me until I came up with this idea. A friend of mine said to me: "Garland, your strength comes when you're not thinking in terms of commercial concepts and ideas. Go back to your source." I quite often think about my whole racial makeup because it's my life, my racial identity which I have much more come to terms with during the last few years. As a child, being a very light-skinned black kid, being part black, part white, part Puerto Rican, I had a lot of problems with knowing what my makeup is. My best friend is Italian. As children we were very close and he was very clear about his world. On Sundays he had macaroni with his family and I was often invited, but my world was very spread out even though I had a family. When it came to coming into the world and experiencing people outside of my immediate family, it was often very confusing. I was often rejected by whites and even by blacks who were darker than me. I did not fit in and this was a big struggle. I was very confused as a child. So what better thing to write about than this subject?

Petra Zeitz: Racism is a very extensive issue. How did you manage to translate it into just 12 songs?

Garland Jeffreys: I tried to portray the issue of racism in a personal way, so that it becomes something that people find interesting. I chose to make an album about racism in America as told through the eyes of this kid who moves from this street corner. In his innocence, his naive lack of understanding, he moves from boyhood to manhood. He goes from here to here. It's not a simple step, however. He doesn't just step off the corner into the world. He goes through the process of discovering that the world is not so friendly, they call him names, he tries to pass for white, and pretends that he's not black, he rejects his color, he rejects the people that he might be most close to, he has a lot of problems with his own family, he sees what other black people go through, he sees the racism that takes place in the world, he grows little by little, he is often rejected by white girls, and he doesn't understand all this. He's a very loving person underneath and he wants so much to fit in and be a part of society just like any child would. Eventually he matures and he grows up into the person he is today. It's a musical story, too. Lyrically this story takes place from this point in time right up to 1991. I'm talking about skinheads; I'm talking about the Klan. In "Hail Hail Rock'n'Roll" I say, "Pockets of hate, pockets of love, it's never too late for change in the color of you, the color of me, you can't judge a man by lookin' at the marquee." You can't judge a book by its cover, you can't look at things on the surface. Beauty is not skin deep, you know. These are some of the ideas and themes I'm interested in. I love people, regardless of their color. My problem with people comes when they're hurtful, not because of their color. I'm open to all people and I'm always working in that direction. I would like to see that being more of the attitude that people in the world of today have.

Petra Zeitz: Will people all over the world be able to identify with your ideas on this album?

Garland Jeffreys: Yes. It's not just an American story, it's also an Australian story, it's certainly an Oriental story—the problems in Japan, it's a story that's going on in Belgium, the UK has its problems, the French, the Algerians, the Arabs, the Africans and the Dutch all have them. I just came from Holland and I'm always learning about the way situations are in different places. Of course in Germany, where I am right now, it is just amazing. I visited Berlin and the place was very, very intense.

Petra Zeitz: Were you responsible for the cover design of "Don't Call Me Buckwheat" which shows an old childhood photograph of you?

Garland Jeffreys: Yes, I was pretty much in control of the design. My father took this picture when I was four or five years old and I went to my first baseball game with my mother and father because they were big baseball fans. They got me a little baseball suit and a Jackie Robinson button. Robinson played in this stadium. He was the first black player to play with white major leagues. I have always liked this photo of me and I wanted to use it on a cover previously but it really worked out at this point.

Petra Zeitz: All the songs on this album somehow belong together. Was it difficult for you to take one cut and release it as a single, as happened with "Hail Hail Rock'n'Roll"?

Garland Jeffreys: Not really. I tried to make the songs not interrelated. In other words, one song doesn't depend on the other to understand the song. It's not a concept album but an album with a concept— there's a little difference. Everybody felt that "Hail Hail Rock'n'Roll" could be a big hit and it's proving to be a big hit in some countries now.

Petra Zeitz: Would you say that a child of a mixed racial background today still experiences the same problems you have experienced?

Garland Jeffreys: It's all very dependent upon how the parents bring the child up, you know, the kind of love they give him. *Boyz N the Hood* was a very powerful movie that talked about not having mothers and fathers in a family these days. I think that if you get a certain kind of direction from your family, you have better support out there in the world. My wife is white and my child is going to be a mixed child, but it's going to get a lot of love from a father like me who knows the situation, who knows how to lead the child, love the child, and support the child. I think my child will be able to make it in the world.

Petra Zeitz: In the song "Spanish Blood" you talk about denying your own identity, your own color, by saying you were Spanish.

Garland Jeffreys: Well, being a very light skinned kid, by the age of ten, I realized it was a big disadvantage being black. I remember specifically a day at school when a white kid was going to have a party at his house that Saturday and I was standing with him and a darker kid. This fellow invited me to his party but said Bobby couldn't come because he was black. His mother wouldn't like to have a black person in the house. So Bobby asked him: "What about Garland? He's black, too!" and I said, "No, I'm Spanish, my mother and father come from Madrid." I wanted to be part of things, you see. If I would have said I was black, I would have been very limited. It was a very painful experience and when I think about it now it brings up feelings. That's what the song "Spanish Blood" is about.

Petra Zeitz: You wrote a song about Malcolm X. What's your relationship with the Nation Of Islam?

Garland Jeffreys: When Malcolm X came on the scene in the early sixties, he was a very interesting man. He was the number one speaker for the Nation Of Islam, the Black Muslims, as they're more commonly known. This was the group of people begun by Elijah Mohammed, strictly a black organization. And when Malcolm spoke it was a very frightening feeling. That's why the song is called "I Was Afraid of Malcolm." We know that whites were very frightened by his message because it said that the white man is the devil. My world was a multi-racial one; my friends were Jewish, Italian, black, and this Malcolm X really scared me. But then I discovered some things about him. I read his autobiography that was written with Alex Haley, the author of *Roots*. Alex did a very extensive interview period with Malcolm

X to get the facts of his life right. Malcolm X was from Kansas, he found his father was murdered by the Ku Klux Klan. They had tied his father to the railroad tracks and a train ran over his head—a brutal, brutal murder! And of course, it destroyed Malcolm on some level. Eventually he wound up in Harlem and became a drug dealer, a pimp, a hustler, and a thief. He was arrested and put in prison. In prison he learned about the Nation of Islam and Elijah Mohammed, and he also educated himself. My whole point is this: when Malcolm X came out of prison he joined the Nation of Islam and did a lot of work for them. As he did this work he discovered some things about them that did not jibe. He began to feel uncomfortable about some of the ways things were being done. He made two pilgrimages to Africa and discovered that there were white Muslims as well as black Muslims and that the Muslim world was not just a black organization. Allah was not just the God of black people, he was the God of white people, too. I'm not a religious person myself, but if I look at this situation, I can see Malcolm thinking that some white people must be devils, or

bad people. So he came back to the States to promote this idea and he was murdered by the Nation of Islam. In the last lyrics of the song I say, "Things got better each day, I landed on my own backbone. And when I think of all the hearsay, I'm standing in my own skin tone." I basically talk about my own life, that I am more comfortable with who I am. Then about Malcolm I say: "Pictured as a man of distortion, painted as a monster in monster proportion, changing up with every bit of information, painting like a master in God's creation where each and every body is equal, where you don't have to wait until you see the sequel." So the idea there is that Malcolm X was moving much closer to the point of view of Martin Luther King, that maybe we can bring the world together eventually. You can't change progress, you can't change the future of this world which, I believe, is eventually going to be a multi-cultural world.

Petra Zeitz: Do you believe music has the power to change things?

Garland Jeffreys: Yes, I do. Definitely. I don't know if it has the power to completely turn things around. I wouldn't suppose that, but I believe the people really look for messages in music. Music helps, I'd say. I get letters from people saying my music and my lyrics mean something to them. I'm inspired by my audience in a way.

Petra Zeitz: Did you write all these lyrics as poems and later put them to music?

Garland Jeffreys: It happened in different ways—sometimes it was the lyrics and the music together, sometimes the music came first. I also like to work from a title like "I Was Afraid of Malcolm" or "Bottle of Love." It makes me come up with images.

MICHELLE SHOCKED

Michelle Shocked was born in Dallas, Texas, in 1962 and spent her years traveling around Army bases until 1977. At 16, she went to live with her father and discovered an interest in playing music. Her dad was teaching himself to play the mandolin and also possessed a small record collection. Michelle listened to Guy Clark, songwriter Randy Newman, country bluesman Leadbelly, and living underground folk music.

Michelle left Texas in 1983 and joined ranks with Squatters. While she was an activist in the Squatters movement, she learned that she had an album in the UK independent charts. Pete Lawrence had recorded a few of her tunes with his Sony Walkman and released them on his Cooking Vinyl label as an album called "The Texas Campfire Tapes."

Upon the success of this first album Michelle decided to continue her career as a musician and was signed by Polygram Records. She came up with a trilogy concept which consisted of the albums "Short Sharp Shocked," "Captain Swing," and "Arkansas Traveler." The impact of all her records was strongly felt. "Short Sharp Shocked" was a number one college album, "Captain Swing" succeeded with an alternative Top Ten chart position and "Arkansas Traveler" included some of her finest work and became a "career album."

The following conversation with Michelle Shocked took place in March 1992. Supported by her fiancé Bart Bull, Michelle went on an extensive promotional tour. "Arkansas Traveler" had just hit the shops and features were being published by *Rolling Stone*, *Elle*, and *Interview* among others.

Petra Zeitz: How did the idea

Michelle Shocked

for the "Arkansas Traveler" start? [The album was made with a mobile recording unit while Michelle was traveling in the United States.]

Michelle Shocked: That started with a trip I took with my father. "Captain Swing" had just been released and I told my father that I would take him for his first time hitch-hiking. So we went from Dallas up to Arkansas to visit a friend of mine. It took us three rides to get the whole way, so that was no adventure. After a few days we found a man with a boat in Memphis who would take us down the river. It sounded like a good adventure, but he said: "You must be in Memphis by tonight." So we took a bus to Memphis. The boats that go along the Mississippi never dock, so the tugs go out to the boats as they're going in. They met us and took us out to the boat and for five days we traveled on this boat. My father and I both play the mandolin, so every day we would go up the wheelhouse where the pilot was and we would play these tunes. That gave me the idea of playing music while in motion, while traveling. I have taken many of these tunes that we played and put my own lyrics around them.

That was the first I did, that was two years ago. Then it took a whole year to make this record traveling. I always knew I wanted to call it the "Arkansas Traveler."

Petra Zeitz: Were your destinations pre-arranged or did you just stop where you wanted?

Michelle Shocked: It was pre-arranged because we used a very fine quality recording studio. It was built into an 18-wheeler. It costs maybe $2000 a day to have this equipment. So we planned the tour very much like a concert tour. There was no possibility for mistakes. The schedule was so firm that, if we got a flat tire or if we got lost and couldn't find where we were going, we would lose that time recording, and we would have to go on to the next place. It was in this period of six weeks that we did 80 percent of the songs on the record. Then we had to fly to Australia and fly to Dublin.

Petra Zeitz: In Dublin you recorded with the Hothouse Flowers using traditional Irish instruments. Is your family of Irish descent?

Michelle Shocked: My family is of Italian descent, actually. My grandmother was a nurse and she would spend her holidays traveling to Russia and to China. She did a lot of traveling, and she was an inspiration to me. But the greatest inspiration for this music, for me, was my father learning to play mandolin at 35 years of age. So this idea was put in my mind that it's not important to grow up playing this music, but that anybody can learn to play. But I learned from my father that only an interest like a hobby is enough to play music. He bought a book that gives the numbers that correspond to the strings. He would read and learn. He had a few records so he could hear what the music sounded like. Now I have this great enthusiasm to say to people: "You can play music, it's possible! Music is not only something you consume, but also something you make."

Petra Zeitz: Did you start playing music after your father taught himself how to play?

Michelle Shocked: It happened at the same time. He was 35 and I was 16. I first played the guitar while he was learning the mandolin. Then he taught me the things he had learned. My brother, who is 10 years younger than me, started taking lessons on the banjo. We would sit around playing music.

Petra Zeitz: How did the collaboration with the Hothouse Flowers in Dublin come about?

Michelle Shocked: First of all, I am on the same label as them. Because of this connection I was invited to see them play a concert in New York. I was very impressed with their live concert. There was a lot of emotion, and feeling, and soul. I remembered this. It would be very natural to think that this traditional music originates from Ireland, but when I selected the songs and the people for this album, I was trying to make an argument. I had an agenda to tell people my story is not that the music came from Ireland. My story is that Europeans immigrated to America, brought their traditional culture with them and created something different when they were in America. So I chose the Hothouse Flowers because I felt that if they were in this time period, say the eighteen hundreds, when blackface minstrelsy was most popular, they would have come to America and they would have understood about black American music and would have done a reasonable presentation of it.

Petra Zeitz: What makes the

Hothouse Flowers different from other Irish bands?

Michelle Shocked: For example, if you think of traditional Irish music there's maybe the Chieftains or the Pogues, but I felt that the Hothouse Flowers had the most sympathy for this music. Not because it's Irish, not because it's nationalistic traditional Irish music, but because they, also in their own music, create a mix of cultures. I mean, for European culture, which they are, there has always been that decision: Are you going to make something purely European, or are you going to make something that is like a cultural fusion.

Petra Zeitz: You mentioned blackface minstrelsy. Are you researching this ancient tradition?

Michelle Shocked: I think this tradition of blackface minstrelsy traveled all over the world. When I was touring in Australia I found posters and stories of very popular blackface minstrelsy entertainers. I think what was fantastic about Australia in this case was that for Europeans it was possible to go to America or to Africa and have contact with this culture. I think (I could be wrong) but for the most part Australians' only

introduction to blackface was from other blackface entertainers. It would be like seeing a second generation. Let's set an example: It would be like never hearing the Beatles, but only hearing the Beatles Revival Band. In Australia, a lot of the introduction to true black culture was by seeing white musicians wearing black makeup. And they thought this is what black people are like.

Petra Zeitz: Do you think there is still a difference made between black music and white music?

Michelle Shocked: I think there is no difference between the music if someone's black or if someone's white. The difference is a much larger idea about culture. I think that African culture has come to America and European culture has come to America, and people must make a decision of what culture they are attracted to. It's just a very natural attraction. If they are attracted more to the European culture then I think they end up participating in minstrelsy, because European culture has for the past hundred years been very influenced by minstrelsy. If they are attracted to African culture, I think that there is some influence of minstrelsy also, but maybe, it's like your pendant [Yin Yang Sign]— a little bit of white inside the black, or a little bit of black inside the white. The mistake that is being made is trying to define it as white or black, because it's been too much influenced by each other. There are some lies told about true culture.

Petra Zeitz: In what way?

Michelle Shocked: When this traditional music that I have made is discussed, very often people say it comes from Ireland or it comes from England, and that it was brought to America. That is not the real history. That's just an argument for purity which is a lie.

Petra Zeitz: Is the "Arkansas Traveler" a one-off project or are you going to carry on with traditional music?

Michelle Shocked: It's a one-off because it's the last one of a project of three albums. The emphasis was to focus on the traditional music of my father. With "Captain Swing" the emphasis was on the blues or swing, and the album before had an emphasis on the song-writing. Now that's all complete. I don't know what will be coming next.

Petra Zeitz: You began writing your own songs while you were living in Austin, Texas. What made you want to write your own material?

Michelle Shocked: I think it must be typical. I did not know other people's songs, so I wrote my own. It was nice to have both kinds of music: my own music which I end up thinking is pop music, and then the traditional music that my father taught me. My musical taste is very varied. I once told this story of having only space for one cassette tape while I was traveling. On one side was Pink Floyd's "Dark Side of the Moon" album, and on the other side was Doc Watson.

Petra Zeitz: What was it like playing with Doc Watson on the "Arkansas Traveler" album after you have listened to his music so much?

Michelle Shocked: That's it, you see. It would be your favorite record which you listen to again and again, and then you create a situation where you are playing on your favorite record. That's how I felt when I was playing with him, because he is my biggest hero. I was so nervous! The way we made this song was at a festival that Doc Watson hosted for three days. So, each day, one time a day, I would be invited to go on stage with him and play this song "Strawberry Jam." I ended up with three selections to choose from to put on the album. Maybe by the end I wasn't so nervous anymore. I chose the third day. It came out the best.

Petra Zeitz: Did you have all the songs ready before you started traveling or were some of them written along the way?

Michelle Shocked: Some along the way. There's a song [Shaking Hands—"The Arkansas Traveler" album] we recorded on a riverboat with a band called Uncle Tupelo. It was one of the best inspirations for this project. I was so confident of this traditional melody that I believed that when the time came it would be reaching and taking. So I only wrote the words to the song the night before we recorded it. I already explained that there was no room to make mistakes. If, for example, the night before I couldn't write the words, we wouldn't have been able to record the song. That's how confident I was to work with this traditional material.

Petra Zeitz: Can you explain why you were so confident?

Michelle Shocked: It was for two reasons: One is, that the melody inspires a mood, and

that's very important for writing songs. Also, these tunes already have titles to them. The title to this tune was "Soldier's Joy" and they explained to me what this meant. It's a term for morphine. During the war, if a soldier was injured, they would give him morphine and send him out to fight again, because he wouldn't feel the pain. Maybe from this injury he was going to die anyway, so they sent him out to fight until he was dead. Or he would get the morphine and recover from the injury, but he would be addicted to this drug and die from drug addiction. So even though this melody had no words to it, I could see the story in my mind very easily. I made a story of a man who fought and was very brave as a soldier, but then he was injured and taken to the hospital. He was in so much pain that he cried: "Give me morphine!" It didn't matter how brave he was on the field, because now, in his mind, he was a coward. So he died asking the question: "Am I a coward or am I brave?"

Petra Zeitz: Did you research the stories to all the traditional melodies you recorded?

Michelle Shocked: I didn't research it like a scholar or like an actor. I relied on oral history. My father would tell me this song was written by Woody Guthrie—OK! Or in Arkansas we recorded with these hillbillies and they told us these jokes that were 100 years old. It was like this, you know. I didn't research it by reading books, but my fiancé is a writer and he researches. He gave me some more academic history of some of the melodies. He wrote a book called *Does This Road Go to Little Rock?* about blackface minstrelsy.

Petra Zeitz: You have been a bit of a musical gypsy. Have you settled down now?

Michelle Shocked: I'm settled. It's quite an ironic situation to make a record called "The Traveler" and to be settled in Los Angeles. The song "Come a Long Way" tells the story. Now it's a different kind of travel, now it's the traveling of the heart. My feet stay in one place but my heart travels because I'm in a relationship and I have to grow and change. I have to open my mind to new possibilities. So my heart is constantly traveling to keep up with this relationship.

Petra Zeitz: Did you go to LA because of the music scene there?

Michelle Shocked: No, this was by accident. I went to LA to record my last album, and while I was there I met a man and we fell in love. Then I decided to live there. At first, I had a very harsh attitude about Los Angeles, but he showed me the beauty of this city and now, I like it very much.

Petra Zeitz: On "The Arkansas Traveler" you worked with a musical director. What was his task?

Michelle Shocked: He is a man best known for the work he did with the Eagles, but my inspiration for working with him is that he worked with Graham Parsons, who was very influential in putting together country music and rock music. The man's name is Bernie Leadon and he has many of the same traditional influences that I have. He traveled with me and he helped me to work with all the different musicians that I played with. He was like a co-producer in some ways.

Petra Zeitz: Do you have a regular band to go on tour with?

Michelle Shocked: For the first time I'm putting together a band that I hope will be a constant band. I could not put together a band before, because in my mind, I knew there was this trilogy and I knew it would be different styles. Now the trilogy is complete and for the first time I'm putting together my own band of musicians who can play all of these styles, the traditional, the R&B and the folk.

Petra Zeitz: Before you did the trilogy, you had an album called "The Texas Campfire Tapes." Did you know there was going to be a record when Pete Lawrence asked you to play some songs into his Sony Walkman?

Michelle Shocked: No, I didn't know. If I had known, I don't know what I would have done. Maybe I would have said yes but maybe I would have said no. I think I would have said no because if he was going to make an album he should have asked me to go into the studio. Or maybe I would have said: "No, I'm anti-capitalist and I won't be part of this system!" There's no way to tell.

Petra Zeitz: Did the success of this album convince you that you didn't have to work in a studio, that you can record anywhere?

Michelle Shocked: It's a good possibility that I learned from that, that the music, and not the production, is what people care about. If people could listen to

the Campfire Tapes—the music goes too fast because the batteries were weak, you can hear the trucks, and the microphone falling—and they still receive the spirit of the music, maybe it gave me the confidence to make the "Arkansas Traveler." From the beginning the challenge was: How can you travel to so many places and then have it sound like it all belongs together? That was one reason for having such good quality equipment—it was 48 track digital high quality equipment to record with.

Petra Zeitz: The track "Hold Me Back" was actually recorded at the legendary Sun Studios.

Michelle Shocked: Yes, but we didn't use their equipment. In Sun Studios we brought in the truck and set it up.

Petra Zeitz: Do they still have their original equipment?

Michelle Shocked: They do. Actually, no, they have equipment from about 10 or 15 years ago. A man bought Sun Studios and started to preserve it for tourism.

Petra Zeitz: Do you feel comfortable working in modern hi-tech studios?

Michelle Shocked: Yes and I have always worked with an engineer, but I did have to be involved in some technical decisions. For example, there's a debate now with engineers and technicians where they ask which system is colder, the Sony 48 track or the Mitsubishi? Maybe I was not good for this job, but to my mind it sounds ridiculous. It reminds me of philosophers asking how many angels can dance on the head of a pin, you know? But they really consider this question a lot. It's an ongoing discussion with engineers. Is analogue better than digital? I say, "I don't care!" Maybe this is my failure as a producer. The more satisfying part of the job was to record with musicians who had never worked in such a formal setting before. The personal side was a challenge.

Petra Zeitz: Did you always want to be a musician?

Michelle Shocked: Not always, no. I wanted to be a traveler. I always wanted to travel, to have adventures, and to be a very interesting person. But I did start to play music while I traveled.

HEAVY ROCK

THE BLACK CROWES

The Black Crowes sold nearly 4 million copies of their debut album "Shake Your Moneymaker" in the United States. Not surprisingly, three headline tours followed. Then, after 22 months on the road, they recorded and mixed their second album within just eight days. "The Southern Harmony and Musical Companion" was released in May 1992.

Chris Robinson and his younger brother Rich formed their first band in the mideighties and named it "Mr. Crowe's Garden." Chris was 18 years old at the time and Rich was a fresh faced 15-year-old. They played their first gig at a club in Chattanooga, Georgia. In the years that followed the band went through several line-up changes and by the time producer George Drakoulias came to Atlanta, the Black Crowes, as they called themselves by now, consisted of Chris Robinson (vo-cals, harmonica), Rich Robinson (guitars), Steve Gorman (drums), Johnny Colt (bass), and Jeff Cease (guitars). Drakoulias offered them a recording contract with his own label Def American and went on to produce their first album "Shake Your Moneymaker."

In 1991 the Black Crowes were honored with two "Elvis" awards for "Artist of the Year" and "Album of the Year" at the 3rd International Rock Awards.

Keyboarder Ed Harsh joined the band before the recording of the second album and shortly afterwards Jeff Cease was replaced by former Burning Tree guitarist Marc Ford.

The following interview with Rich Robinson took place in March 1992. Advance-tapes of "The Southern Harmony and Musical Companion" had already been supplied to journalists, and the album was awaiting its official release in May.

The Black Crowes

Petra Zeitz: Did recording your second album put a lot of pressure on the band because people expect too much of you after your huge success?

Rich Robinson: No, pressure is all subjective. It's something you put on yourself for whatever reason. I'm sure everyone wants us to sell 4 million records again. It would be good for everyone and it puts money in our pockets and this bullshit. I mean, it's nice to sell lots of records and I would love to sell millions again, but that's not the most important thing. It's not even a consideration when you get down to writing and recording an album. We never thought that we had to make this one better than the first to make more money. You obviously put pressure on yourself to have it better than the first one for artistic reasons. You want it to be better because you want to progress instead of regress. That was the only pressure. We pushed ourselves to do better.

Petra Zeitz: Were there any discussions in the band about how to follow "Shake Your Moneymaker"?

Rich Robinson: When it came down to doing the second album we wrote it in two weeks, other than the two songs that we had already performed on tour. During the last couple of months we had two songs called "Thorn in My Pride" and "Morning Song" which we had written. But by the time we got home and recorded them they turned out totally different. We just went in and recorded the whole album within eight days—*live*. I don't think you can really overthink that by any means.

Petra Zeitz: It's quite unusual in this day and age to record an album within eight days. Have you always been that quick?

Rich Robinson: This first album took about a month. It was our first record and we didn't play as well as we do now. We didn't have 350 shows and 20 months of playing with each other to back it up. This time we came in and, you know, we had been playing together for so long that it was just natural to play new songs. We would always introduce new songs in the set and go with it. That's what makes this record as special as it is because there's a spontaneity to it that most records lack. If you're in a studio for six months playing the same songs over and over again trying to get everything perfect, the recordings become stale. There's no spontaneity to it. Everything's perfect and boring. There are no mistakes and mistakes can turn out to be cool.

Petra Zeitz: Did you try out your new material on stage before you actually went to record it?

Rich Robinson: Just the two songs I mentioned. We wrote the other songs after we got home. We played them two or three times together before we went into the studio. The rest were all brand new. We just recorded them like that. The two songs we played live had changed a lot by the time we recorded them. And Marc Ford, our new guitar player, had never played them before. When he came in it was new for him, too. It turned out to be pretty cool.

Petra Zeitz: Did you work with a producer again?

Rich Robinson: Well, we had a producer but he really didn't do much. It was the same guy as on the first record—George Drakoulias. The credits read co-produced by the Black Crowes and George Drakoulias, but it was actually produced 90 percent by us. But George is the one who found us and signed us, so we owe something to him.

Petra Zeitz: How do producers and engineers react when somebody wants to finish a record within eight days in the studio?

Rich Robinson: A lot of times they were going: "Oh, you don't wanna do that . . ." They were a little strange about it, but we just said: "Why not? It's something different." George didn't have control, so he didn't have a choice. That's pretty much what it came down to on this record.

Petra Zeitz: How long had you been playing together in Atlanta before George discovered you?

Rich Robinson: Chris and I had been in a band since I was 15. We had played together for about two years and then we hooked up with A&M and started doing demos for them. That's where we met George and he took us to Def American and signed us there. So we have been playing seriously for about four years.

Petra Zeitz: Is Def American a major label?

Rich Robinson: No, it's small. But they are distributed through Warner Brothers so you get the full service. It's kind of cool to be on Def American because they let us do whatever we want musically and as far as videos go and things like that.

Petra Zeitz: Why did you fire Jeff Cease, your old guitar player?

Rich Robinson: We had been playing for so long and everyone came to this level. Just Jeff Cease was still down there. He didn't care about playing his instrument right. He didn't really try to do anything. On the first record I wrote all his second guitar parts and we sat down and wrote his solos. He didn't even play some of the solos he was supposed to play. For ten months we tried to push him to get it together. We tried to carry him along. We wanted him to get better, but he never would. I think he realized what was going to happen. He said he was expecting it. Maybe he's more happy doing his own thing. Maybe it gives him a new attitude toward things.

Petra Zeitz: Where did you meet Marc Ford?

Rich Robinson: The Burning Tree opened for us on tour. Chris was really good friends with them and we just asked Marc to join. I think he was relieved that he didn't have to write any songs. All he had to do was play. With the Burning Tree he had to sing and write all the songs, but he loved playing guitar and he couldn't really concentrate on that. He's happy playing with us because he can concentrate on his guitar work.

Petra Zeitz: Are you going to get Marc involved as a songwriter in the future?

Rich Robinson: I don't know. I don't think Chris and I are having a problem so far.

Petra Zeitz: If you read the information your record company gives out to the press, you're a "back to the roots/late Sixties" style rock 'n 'roll band. I don't see you as such.

Rich Robinson: For some reason people are so simple-minded that they can't make up their own mind as to what we sound like. They go: "Oh yes, someone told me you guys were kind of rootsy." Well, there's nothing to being rootsy. I'm 22 and I wasn't even old enough to walk when this music was being made. So what the hell do they know? You know what I'm saying? It's just record company gibberish trying to find a selling point—rootsy rock sells well. But that's bullshit. We appreciate music of the past and we appreciate good music in general. If there's good music today we appreciate it. If it sucks—it

sucks! If it sucked back then it still sucks.

Petra Zeitz: The Black Crowes do sound different from other bands. Where did you get that different edge?

Rich Robinson: Maybe we're concentrating on music as a whole instead of what's popular. A lot of bands go: "What's popular? Let's dress and act just like Guns'n'Roses or Metallica. They are just cool and they sell tons of records." Well, what was before Metallica? They are cool, but they obviously got it from somewhere. So why don't you think like that? Once you listen to music that's not two years old you discover that there's a lot more to it than that. You have to look at the big picture instead of what's really cool right now. Do you know what I'm saying?

Petra Zeitz: Have you noticed that young bands are now copying you like they copied Guns n'Roses a couple of years ago?

Rich Robinson: I don't know. I think they're scared to copy us. I mean what are you going to do? We record a record in eight days. How many other bands could do that? Not many, I think. Def Leppard is a huge band and they took five years to finish their album. I'm not saying that's good or bad—they can do whatever they want for them. That's cool, but I'd like to see them trying to make a record in eight days and see if they can do it. And if they could more power to them! That proves to me that you can play your instruments, you're spontaneous and you can do something without worrying about record sales.

Petra Zeitz: Did you have that same attitude when you made "Shake Your Moneymaker"?

Rich Robinson: Yes. It sounded like nothing that was out at the time. We went in and just recorded it on a 15-year-old board, 24-track—not 170 tracks with all these stacks of computer electronic bullshit. We plugged in a couple of amps and did it. That's how we did the second record too. We had maybe three amps, just plugged into them and recorded it *live.*

Petra Zeitz: You are obviously a true live band. Do you dislike working in recording studios?

Rich Robinson: No, it has nothing to do with being more of a live band. Playing live is great and being in a studio is great, too. When you're playing live you sometimes want to be in the studio. When you're in the studio you want to go out and play live. Our records are live because that's how we record them. If you want to capture something special you don't beat it into the ground—you just record it. If you're a photographer and you see a bird flying across, you instantly take the picture. You can't just sit there and keep on focusing and then make the bird sit there. When you catch the bird flying, then that's something special. But when you missed it, you missed the moment. That's the same thing with music.

Petra Zeitz: Is your stage performance different from your records? They are both live, aren't they?

Rich Robinson: A record is for buying and taking home to listen to. But when you go and see a band live, you don't want to see them just act out their video. Otherwise you could sit at home and watch the video—it's cheaper! When you come to see us we want you to get into it and see something that is different. We wrote about 20 songs while we were on tour and we would always interchange them. We would also turn around old songs and take them into long jams that would last for 14 minutes. That's how you do it. Wouldn't you want to go and watch a band to see them play their instruments and see their ability to change music? You have to be able to use music to make somebody feel a certain way. That's the reason why I'm in a band.

Petra Zeitz: Do you like making videos or are they just a necessary evil?

Rich Robinson: I like them. All of our videos are totally different and they don't have girls with big boobs in them. We don't have any 10 million dollar projects with complicated plots.

Petra Zeitz: I just watched the video for "Remedy" and it was basically a film of the Black Crowes playing.

Rich Robinson: Yeah, what a novel idea! Who's done that? When was the last time you saw something like that? I haven't seen it in America since MTV went on the air. For some reason, nobody else wants to capture that. They all want to have big sets and all this bullshit. If you're a creative person you make creative videos. There's something artistic about this video even though it's very simple. You can make ten thousand edits and make a boring band look exciting. We didn't use any edits. It just shows the band as they are.

Petra Zeitz: Do you think that during the past two years you've grown much as a band and as people?

Rich Robinson: Yes. If you write articles I'm sure the twentieth is better than the first one. That rule applies in all walks of life.

Petra Zeitz: Did you ever regret having left the club scene behind that quickly?

Rich Robinson: No, the more people the better! When you're a big band you have 100,000 people coming to see you and they're all focused on this one idea that is on stage. They all have that in common. They all like this band otherwise they wouldn't be there. That means people of all generations, all races, all colors, all religions and all creeds can come together and enjoy this one idea. It breaks down boundaries. The more people that get it, the more boundaries it breaks down. That's the point of playing to more people and being bigger. Bands like Led Zeppelin, the Rolling Stones or even U2 are larger than life; they can do anything. They are like heroes in a sense. People get into that and think it's really cool.

Petra Zeitz: When you play

in Atlanta these days, does it generate this feeling of "coming home"?

Rich Robinson: No, people in Atlanta don't give a shit about us. The fans are great and the people that buy our records are always cool, but the music scene resents us because we never catered to just Atlanta. Who cares? Atlanta is one city in a whole world. Why would you just concentrate on Atlanta? Atlanta likes to pat itself on the back when it suits it. If we did something huge worldwide, if we won the Nobel Prize or whatever, then it's possible that Atlanta would be proud of us. But for the most part, they're not.

Petra Zeitz: Did you start a musical movement in Atlanta?

Everybody is talking about the Seattle sound right now.

Rich Robinson: Well, the Seattle sound is bigger than the bands that come from Seattle. Who cares about fuckin' Seattle? Everyone thinks Nirvana is so huge, but no one ever says how good they are. They sold two million records, but who cares? We sold four million. Guns'n'Roses sold 12 million— who cares? Is the band good? That's the whole point of the matter. In Atlanta a lot of bands got signed because of us, but then they didn't do anything. There's still an air of mystery around us and that's what's cool. How many times do you have to see Nirvana on TV? We'll see what happens.

EUROPE

Europe is comprised of Joey Tempest (lead vocals), Kee Marcello (lead guitar), John Leven (bass), Mic Michaeli (keyboards) and Ian Haugland (drums). The band originated in Sweden, but became extremely popular in America when their single "The Final Countdown" went to number 1 in 1986. A year later the band went on a hugely successful tour of the United States. Europe soon relocated to Los Angeles where they recorded several albums. Although they maintained their presence in the hard rock business, they were unable to top their initial success with "The Final Countdown," still a favorite with live audiences. In 1991, Europe released their fourth album "Prisoners in Paradise."

The following conversation with founding members John Leven and Kee Marcello took place in late 1991. Europe was on a promotional tour in support of "Prisoners in Paradise" and they were announcing another worldwide tour for 1992.

Petra Zeitz: Why did you have such a long break between your last album and "Prisoners in Paradise"?

John Leven: We have been touring all over the world, so we have been out of sight for some audiences. The last world tour finished in mid–1989. After that we started writing new songs and last Christmas we did an Asian tour. We also went to South America touring and we did a big festival in Milton Keynes, England, with Bon Jovi and Skid Row. Besides that we had one gig in LA at the Whiskey-a-Gogo under a different name just to warm up.

Petra Zeitz: "Prisoners in Paradise" sounds a little bit more guitar-oriented than your previous albums. Did that happen on purpose?

Kee Marcello: Yes. For this

Europe

album we wanted it to be a little more guitar-oriented. This is exactly the same thing we said about the last album. But then last time we had a producer whom we couldn't really communicate with. He was an asshole, basically. We couldn't touch base with him on anything. He mixed the album exactly the way he wanted and he put a lot of keyboards on it. I liked the songs on the last album, but it was over produced. This time our producer Beau Hill became a very good friend of ours. After the session he went down to the Caribbean with us. He had the same ideas as we did. We had some meetings with other producers, but Beau Hill was the only one that showed his interest. He came down to rehearsals and listened to the music a couple of times. There was no doubt about using him for the album.

Petra Zeitz: Did you ever consider producing yourself?

John Leven: Maybe in the future, yes. You never know. It's kind of nice to have somebody from the outside giving you his point of view. It's especially good when you're friends with the man—or woman.

Petra Zeitz: There are not many female producers about, are there?

John Leven: No. I know Madonna is involved in her own productions. I think the music business is so sexist that it wouldn't work. In five years they will probably have women as producers. It's not going to take a long time. We have girl singers and girl bands already.

Petra Zeitz: What do you think of male/female mixed rock'n'roll bands?

Kee Marcello: Oh, that's great! I actually went to see Warlock. What's the girl's name?

Petra Zeitz: Doro Pesch.

Kee Marcello: That's right, I went to see Doro Pesch. She was pretty good actually. She has some nice melodies and her music sounds very European. She was playing at the Whiskey-a-Gogo and there was such a big difference between her and the other bands that play there. It's good, though.

Petra Zeitz: Which other bands do you like to listen to?

Kee Marcello: Deep Purple, Thin Lizzy, UFO and many more.

Petra Zeitz: Deep Purple is still touring after 20 years.

Would you like Europe to go on forever too?

Kee Marcello: Hopefully we'll do the same thing. We love touring 'til the end. Some people like to be in the studio and most of them hate touring. I can't see what that is. Touring is the main thing. As soon as the spotlight is on you, it's great!

John Leven: You get very spoiled on tour because you're always taken care of. Everything is taken care of. You don't have to do anything—just make sure you're at the show! It's a bit like being a mental patient because everyone is leading you around.

Petra Zeitz: You've frequently toured in Asia. Did you notice any difference in the audience's reaction to your music over there?

Kee Marcello: Surprisingly enough rock'n'roll is so international that it's the same thing to play for them as anywhere else. People go nuts. They know all the songs and everything. It's really international. You'd be amazed to see Headbanging Indians in Bombay. They do everything right. Sixty thousand people showed up in Bombay. We did the show in collaboration with "The Times of India," so the money went toward education and hospitals. The main thing is not to give cash to them because they have the caste-system. If you give them money they don't know what to do with it. They tried to give apartments to the poor people, but they believe when you're born in the streets you're bound to die in the streets. So they spend the money in a year and then they are poor again. The only key to this problem is education.

John Leven: It was amazing. When we came from the airport we had to drive through these large slum areas and then you suddenly see a big poster of us. It was terrible—people were lying there and dying in front of it.

Petra Zeitz: Are you based in Sweden or in America these days?

Kee Marcello: Neither. We're based in the West Indies. We got a house down there. We moved out of Sweden mainly for tax purposes four years ago. Since then we haven't been back. We bought a couple of houses and some property in the West Indies. We just go down there once in a while and bring some equipment down so that we will be able to work there too. The plan is to build a studio. We got a big garage which is perfect for that purpose. But that's a future plan.

Petra Zeitz: What are the living conditions like down there?

Kee Marcello: It is very primitive. I mean, we have bathrooms and stuff, but that's about it. There's not a lot of restaurants. Mainly what you can do there is a lot of water sports. John's a diving freak. He goes down and wrestles with the sharks. Actually one of the sharks was his girlfriend for a long time! Just kiddin'.

Petra Zeitz: You're still recording in Los Angeles, though. Why did you choose to work there?

John Leven: The main reason was that we used Beau Hill as a producer and he lives there. Also he has a studio there and he's very familiar with it.

Petra Zeitz: Do you like the rock'n'roll lifestyle in LA?

Kee Marcello: Yes and no. We chose to write for this album in lots of different places. We wrote in San Francisco, Los Angeles, in Canada, and in London. That's the way we are. We're just gypsies. We travel all over the place. We rented a beautiful house in San Francisco to write some songs there. We just lived together and rehearsed. We tried to get back to the good old days when we were amateur musicians and just lived for the music. Usually if you want to have an original sound you shouldn't go to LA. There are too many bands there and they are imitating each other which makes it kind of dull actually. If you go to a club and you listen to some of the new bands, they are all called something with "Angel" or "Gun." They all sound the same, you know. I think we came to LA to look for something different and we found ourselves. We realized why we were different from other bands.

Petra Zeitz: What is it that makes Europe different?

Kee Marcello: It's where we come from. After spending all this time in America, I can hear the difference between European and American bands much clearer. The Scorpions, UFO and Deep Purple sound European—you can hear it. I don't know what it is. Some melodies maybe that Americans don't have.

Petra Zeitz: Do you prefer European music?

Kee Marcello: No. Well, I prefer to play it, but I enjoy listening to both. We are very European. There's always a minor chord in the bottom of every song we write. If you're talking about theoretics, it's a minor chord and a minor dominant. That's very unusual in the States because classical music and folk music have that as well.

Petra Zeitz: Many rock bands don't put as much emphasis on melodies as you do. Do you try to write particularly strong melodies?

John Leven: Yes, we are trying to do that—or we are doing that. Many bands tend to lean more into an attitude thing and they forget about the melodies.

Petra Zeitz: Are you still in touch with other Swedish bands?

John Leven: It's kind of hard to stay in touch because we don't spend much time over there. We know a little bit about the Electric Boys, but that's about it. Roxette is doing really good now, but that's totally different music. There's another band that looks and sounds like Guns n'Roses.

Petra Zeitz: Was it a struggle for you to be accepted as a rock band in Sweden?

John Leven: There wasn't much of a rock scene there. I think it changed a bit after we had become successful. All of a sudden everyone started playing rock. Unfortunately not a lot of bands came out of that.

Petra Zeitz: Coming back to your album, is "Prisoners in Paradise" just a title or does it have a deeper meaning?

Kee Marcello: It's got a meaning. The island we live on is a very undeveloped island. When we moved there, there was only one flight a week. So, if you missed that flight or if it was fully booked, you were stuck on the island for another week. Our manager called us and said: "You guys are really prisoners in paradise, aren't you?" After that Nick Graham came up with the idea to name the album "Prisoners in Paradise." We thought it was kind of fun and Joey even wrote a song about it. We're also prisoners of the lifestyle we chose. After becoming successful and moving out of Sweden, it became very hard to keep in touch with our friends. It's a choice you're making when you do that.

Petra Zeitz: Do you still have your old friends?

Kee Marcello: Yes, we try to stay in touch with them. It's not too easy to get new friends, so you tend to stick with the old ones. You can divide them into two categories: pre- and post-"The Final Countdown." [*Laughs.*]

Petra Zeitz: Do you mind that most people still remember you for that song, "The Final Countdown"?

John Leven: It gets kind of hard sometimes because critics always compare all our new stuff to "The Final Countdown." But we'll never go out and do another song like that.

Petra Zeitz: Could you play a gig without doing that song?

John Leven: No, no way! We are gonna have to play that for the rest of our lives. That's the one song we will always have to play. When we first wrote it we had no idea what would become of it whatsoever. I don't think we even considered it as a single song. Then we released it and it just took off. It became number one in thirty countries— amazing.

GIANT

Giant came together in 1987 after years of individual studio experience and rock'n'roll roadwork primarily in Los Angeles. Brothers Dann and David Huff had played together since high school days, and moved to Los Angeles together in the early eighties. Dann worked with Michael Jackson on the "Bad" album and also played with Bob Seger, Whitesnake, Elton John and David Bowie. Completing Giant's lineup there were drummer Alan Pasqua (whose credits included record dates with Eddie Money, Sammy Hagar, Bob Dylan and Santana) and Mike Brignardello on bass. Mike grew up in Memphis and worked with local bands before graduating to session work with best-selling country-rock artists such as Alabama and Travis Tritt.

Giant's debut album "The Last of the Runaways" was recorded in England and sold 300,000 copies worldwide. In March 1990, the single "I'll See You in my Dreams" became their highest charting radio hit and rose to # 20 on Billboard's Hot 100. Giant had been signed to A&M Records, but the relationship turned sour after just one record release, resulting in a new contract with Epic.

In 1990, Giant toured the United States supporting Heart and played several festival dates with Whitesnake. In 1992, a headliner tour followed after the release of their second album "Time to Burn." The album cover showed a man on fire, jumping into a river. The following interview begins with Dann Huff and Mike Brignardello joking about this stunt shot.

I met Dann and Mike in Cologne, Germany, in March 1992. They had attended an international music fair in Frankfurt and were on their way back to the States. I found them to be extremely nice and talkative.

Dann Huff: This is our new CD cover ["Time to Burn"]. We had to pay Mike a lot of money to light himself on fire and jump from a diving board.

Mike Brignardello: I made the sacrifice for the band, though. Eventually I had to pay the guys off because they wanted me to do the photo over and over again. I burned off all my hair. I'm wearing a wig because I'm completely bald now. But I was willing to make the sacrifice. Anything for my band!

Petra Zeitz: I'm glad you're still sitting here then!

On your forthcoming tour you will play support to a yet unnamed band as well as headline some club dates. Do you feel much of a difference between audiences in clubs compared to support-gigs?

Mike Brignardello: Of course it's more fun when you headline because the people are there to see you. We toured the States opening up for Heart last summer and that was tough. The people were there to see Heart and we had 40 minutes to try to win them over as best we could, so that's a little bit hard. But every band has been through it and it makes you grow. As our

manager says, it builds character. Of course it's more fun to headline even if it's only a small club because people are there to hear your music and not somebody else's.

Dann Huff: I think you get a chance to play when you headline and relax a little bit. You can develop some communication, although it's not like we ask people to come on stage and sing with us. When you support, the idea is to get many songs done in a short space of time. You can present yourself. It's like giving somebody a card, you know. It's just a way of introduction. In the clubs, we are given a chance to be what we really are and that's a band that has fun playing on stage. It's not the same night after night, but you gotta have time to develop that.

Petra Zeitz: You played the Marquee Club in London several times. Was that something special to you because most legendary bands have performed there?

Mike Brignardello: Yes, it's funny you should bring that up because you talked about headlining or opening the bill. When we played the Marquee we headlined and that was fantastic. It was packed and a lot of the people who knew our music came. That was really, really great. About two nights before we had played the Town & Country Club as a support act for the Quireboys. The audience was there to see the Quireboys—they did not want to see Giant! There were a few pockets of our fans spread around, but the hardcore Quireboys fans were all right down front and that was tough! It was a real tough audience. We said, "Hey, how are you doin'?" and they just went: "Get off the stage!"

Dann Huff: You just wanted to get out alive, that's all! We were just a new band. I will never sing a ballad to a Quireboys audience again. The whole night I was looking at people and I was singing this song that was a big hit at the time. It is "I'll See You in My Dreams," and these people looked like they wanted to kill me. It was like: "Don't sing that pretty music!" One thing I learned was that I will never sing that ballad again. Next time I'll invite the people who want to hear it back to the hotel, and I'll sing it with an acoustic guitar. But no more in front of those guys.

Petra Zeitz: This is just your second album. Do you have enough material for a long headlining show?

Mike Brignardello: More than enough. This record is over an hour long. And we still play a lot of the material from the first record. If you put all that together, we got at least 90 minutes worth of stuff. Plus there were songs we actually cut for this record but there wasn't enough room on the record. We've got a ton of material. Also when we play live, we don't just do the record versions, but we stretch certain parts out and jam a little bit. Just depending on the night, we may do a guitar solo double length from what's on the record. We're very flexible; it just depends on the emotion of the moment.

Dann Huff: We also do two cover versions, too. One is particularly designed to give me a break from singing the whole night. It's a Jeff Beck song and being a guitar player, I wanted to do one of his songs in our show. It's a gorgeous song and it serves two purposes. It gives me a break from singing and the audience may want to hear some guitar playing. We're also doing an old Sam & Dave tune, an old R&B song called "Rap It Up." So we have more than enough material. People will have to bring their sleeping bags and spend the night there to hear the whole concert.

Petra Zeitz: Why did you change record companies after releasing just one album?

Mike Brignardello: Our experience with A&M was good and bad. They gave us our initial break and all of that. I don't want to spend a lot of time slagging the company, but I think two things made us look for a change. Number one, a couple of months after our first record was released, the company was sold to Polygram Records. So the key people that were some of the reasons why we signed with A&M to begin with began leaving the label. The second thing was that we had been frustrated a bit because A&M didn't seem like they totally understood what we were trying to do, what our music was about and all that. We had some difficult meetings with them, where they would suggest things from a marketing and image standpoint that was totally inappropriate for a rock band. So when it was time to do the second record, we thought rather than struggle and try to build a relationship with people we didn't really know, it would be better to make a switch. There was a lot of interest in the band from a lot of other record labels. We talked to a bunch of them and it seemed to make the most sense to go with Epic. We got along really well with the people and they instantly understood what we were about and what kind of music we wanted to make.

Petra Zeitz: Was your music affected by this switch or would you say it was only a natural development between the first and the second album?

Mike Brignardello: "Time to Burn" is a little bit harder edged than the first one. After being together for three years we became more of a band. The sound of the band focused and toughened up a bit. So I think it was just the next logical step.

Petra Zeitz: How are your songs written and composed?

Dann Huff: There's no set way. Usually I start the musical idea on my guitar because we're kind of a riff band. All our music is based around the guitar part and that's where the ideas usually originate, but after that it's anybody's guess. Whoever is together at the moment will develop the musical idea to the fullest extent and then fit the words in. Sometimes we go half and half and we meet together. Mike and I do this quite a bit nowadays. I may have a musical idea and he'll come over with his little recorder and tape it with fake lyrics. I just sing words that come out of my mouth to fill the space, so I can give him the melody. Sometimes something good will come out and we write a song around it. Mike usually writes all the lyrics. We're piecing together puzzles. It's like sculpting. Sculptors see something underneath a stone, they don't just see block, they see a statue. It's the same thing with songs. We take out this little thing, pull something out, move things around and eventually it takes shape. We are musicians first, as opposed to lyricists turned musicians. The band was born out of the desire to play music.

Petra Zeitz: You have all worked as studio musicians before and you played many different types of music from Kenny Rogers to Michael Jackson.

Dann Huff: Totally different. I mean, every type of music you can imagine. All I can say is that I haven't done any polka records.

Petra Zeitz: Why did you give up your career as a studio musician?

Dann Huff: It was a wonder-ful education, but it wasn't enough to work with those people because it was really their thing. I was just a sideman and that wasn't what I was going for originally. I had to ask myself: Is it enough to earn a lot of money and be in the presence of artists, or do I want to become an artist myself? That's what we all decided to do. It was mainly frustration that led us to start Giant.

Petra Zeitz: Had you been in bands before you started the Giant project?

Mike Brignardello: Just small, local bands. I also toured a bit with other people.

Dann Huff: I was only in the studio. That was my dream, so I turned down all the touring stuff. I just played on the records. You make much more money in the studio than on the road and you can sleep in your own bed every night. People don't understand this. They think when you go on tour as a sideman you must earn a lot of money, but most of the time the artists and their managers are making all the money. The band gets nothing.

Petra Zeitz: How can you actually go in a session and play music you're not familiar with or music you don't really appreciate?

Mike Brignardello: You just walk in, you hear the song, and you play it. That's what they're paying you the big bucks for. You have to be able to instantly digest the song, come up with a part, have a great sound in time and get out of there. It's a lot of pressure, but once you know how to do it and get known for doing it, it can be really financially rewarding. Part of the job is learning how to deal with the pressure of it. Sometimes they have a musical chart for you to look at, but sometimes they don't. You're just expected to learn it really quickly and execute it quickly. Being a studio musician is so much geared toward efficiency.

Petra Zeitz: So you definitely prefer being artists yourselves?

Mike Brignardello: Yes, we do. An artist can take his song and do a demo, then re-write it, and work on it until it gets exactly like he wants it. There are artists who sometimes cut the same song four or five times with four or five different sets of players, maybe even different studios, different producers and different engineers. They get it just as they want it. That's the beauty of being an artist. As a studio musician you sometimes think: "Gee, I wish I had another 30 minutes on that" but the producer thinks it's fine as it is.

Dann Huff: That's pop music, though. Pop music is not based around details—it's based around a song, selling it and making money. It's not good enough just making money. Maybe for some people it is, but for us it's not. Every time I play the guitar and Mike plays the bass, we want it to be our best work. It's very important to us to get it right and make it something special. Most artists don't hear it that way because for them it's just background music. See, we never looked at it like that. We were playing to get money. You fight for any side as long as they pay you. We took the hard road which means becoming an artist and starting right back at the beginning where everybody is. But it's a lot more satisfying. I'd rather do Giant records and make a lot less money, because it's not money that makes you happy. You can do with a lot less.

Petra Zeitz: Have you given up your session career for the satisfaction of being an artist?

Dann Huff: I told somebody else this the other day, the sacrifice that a lot of bands make when they're young and living in the same house, or even in the same room, is really great. But, I mean, we sacrificed a hell of a lot more than that, in a lot of ways. We had already gone up to this point and then left it. It's very hard to do that. All the money we get from Giant we put back into the band. We could take some money for ourselves and make the albums with less money, but it wouldn't ultimately be what we think is the best thing to do. We actually didn't take any album advances on this one. We got some publishing money to live on, but all the album advance we put back into making the record. Occasionally we have to do a few sessions to support what we call our band habit. But we keep it very low key now.

Mike Brignardello: Our lawyers could not understand that. All our friends thought we were crazy. They couldn't believe that we weren't putting at least some money in our own pockets. But the point of doing Giant was to do something the best that we could and we did not want to be limited by money. So it went all back into the band. If we were interested in putting money in our pocket, we wouldn't have done the band in the first place.

Petra Zeitz: But a good rec-

ord could make you even more money.

Dann Huff: You just said *it could*. There is no guarantee that it will and business people are very calculated. They don't want to take risks. We spent all of our time developing this band. We did a first album and now a second album and we want to continue doing the albums and in the end there's always the possibility that they won't sell. But that's not what matters to us. Of course, we do hope that Giant gets big and that we can spend the rest of our lives making this music— that's our dream. But the idea is that we do something we believe in and at least we're satisfied with it inside that way. That's what life should be about anyway.

Petra Zeitz: Why did you all leave LA and move back to Nashville, Tennessee?

Dann Huff: As I said, we still need to do some sessions to pay our bills. In LA we did pop records that everybody buys all around the world. In Nashville we can do little things here and there. It was really weird because I did a record for this girl named Doro. And now everybody in Germany goes: "Oh, you played on the Doro album!"

I didn't know she was so big. I didn't want people to know that I had to do that record to pay my bills. But what am I going to do? Robbing a bank is not the answer.

Petra Zeitz: Are there a lot of rock 'n' roll bands in Nashville these days?

Mike Brignardello: Yes, people think there's nothing there but country music, but there's everything. There's rock 'n' roll, jazz, folk, funk, classical, alternative um-pah music, and of course, there's still a lot of country. But even the country is changing. It's more like Southern rock now, a bit like the Allman Brothers used to be. People who are now making country music grew up listening to rock 'n' roll. When they get their shot now all this sweeps through. It's a pretty happening scene down there.

MSG (McAuley Schenker Group)

The German heavy metal band the Scorpions was formed in 1970 by the brothers Michael and Rudolph Schenker with vocalist Klaus Meine. Michael Schenker quit in 1973 to join UFO, a British hard rock band the Scorpions had been supporting on a tour. Schenker soon rose to the status of legendary rock guitarist. In the early eighties he re-united with the Scorpions for the album "Lovedrive" and then left again to pursue a career with his own band. The Michael Schenker Group was born. They recorded several albums with well known musicians such as Graham Bonnet, Ted McKenna and Cozy Powell. In 1986, Michael Schenker joined forces with platinum-throated Irish singer Robin McAuley. The band was re-named McAuley Schenker Group, which they later agreed to shorten to simply MSG. Robin McAuley had previously been a member of bands like Raw Deal, GMT and Grand Prix and toured with major acts such as Iron Maiden.

MSG released the two well-received heavy rock albums, "Perfect Timing" and "Save Yourself." They toured as headliners as well as supporting Whitesnake, Rush and Def Leppard. In 1992 a third album called "MSG" followed.

For the first time the band played some purely acoustic gigs in front of invited audiences around the world. Four tracks of the "MSG" album were re-recorded acoustically and released as a CD single.

The following conversation with Michael Schenker and Robin McAuley took place in November 1991.

Petra Zeitz: Is this the first

MSG (McAuley Schenker Group)

time you have done *unplugged* gigs?

Michael Schenker: The debut happened in Korea recently. This tour is the first time we've played acoustically in front of an audience. People think that we've been doing this forever, but this is really the first time we've ever done it.

Robin McAuley: It was the record company's idea. When we finished recording the album we were going to release it in September, but then we had delays with packaging and preparing everything for the release. Then the record company decided it might be better timing to wait until the new year. Suddenly we had all this time and they were putting together a promo tour for us. They suggested that it might be a good idea for us to go back to the studio, take some of the tracks from the album, and record them acoustically. At first we didn't want to do it because we had just come out of the studio. So we went in unprepared, but when we started it sounded great. Now it's one of our favorite things. Thanks to the record company something really good has come out of this. It definitely makes us think that we would like to do some more of this and also do the albums like we've always done them.

Petra Zeitz: Are your future albums going to be mixed—plugged and unplugged, if you want?

Robin McAuley: I don't know. That's what's so neat because this acoustic CD we've just released is completely different from the "MSG" album itself. If you're an MSG fan it has become an extra special bonus.

Petra Zeitz: Who is the guest guitarist helping you during the acoustic gigs? Is he on your record as well?

Robin McAuley: He's Spencer Sercomb from Shark Island and this is his first time in Europe. He's not on the album be-

cause Michael plays everything—all the guitars. When we go on tour we would like to take Spencer on as a second guitarist. He's very fast, he's very good and a lot of fun to work with. That's a rare quality.

Petra Zeitz: You're both Europeans, but you're based in Los Angeles now. Is it difficult to be accepted by the American music business?

Michael Schenker: We have only one problem—we're not allowed to anybody's food.

Robin McAuley: In Los Angeles alone, the amount of people that actually come from there is very few. The real Los Angeles people are very nice. It's the other people—like us—who create the problem. [*Laughs*] No, acceptance is pretty universal.

Petra Zeitz: Isn't the rock'n'roll scene in LA full of clichés?

Robin McAuley: There is a definite similarity in a lot of things that go on. I guess you could say the same for most big places. If there's a local band that suddenly makes it big, then all the other bands on the circuit are going to start sounding the same but it's a little late in the day, you know. Instead of having one Guns n'Roses, you suddenly have a hundred. That's just the way it goes and it's always been like that. I don't think it's just Los Angeles, but because it's a big place, the scale gets bigger there.

Petra Zeitz: Was MSG founded in America or did you settle there because that was where you had the most success?

Michael Schenker: The band started a long time ago. MSG was formed in England in 1980. We actually had a first go in 1979. You wanna know why we're living in California now? It's because our record company is there, our management is there, the sunshine in there, everything we need is there!

Robin McAuley: Yeah, and the best chicken fahitas!

Michael Schenker: Even if these things weren't there, it would be my choice to live there. I left Germany when I was 17 1/2 and went to London. When I saw all these different nationalities walking towards me, I felt at home immediately.

Robin McAuley: Funny enough, 17 1/2 was when I left Ireland, too! I went to Holland on vacation for about three weeks and I stopped off in London to visit one of my sisters on my way back home. And that was it, man. I never went back to Ireland and stayed in London for 17 years after that.

Petra Zeitz: Ireland is pretty conservative. Was there much of a rock scene when you lived there?

Robin McAuley: Absolutely. I remember sitting on the floor several times watching Thin Lizzy when they were just a three-piece. Eric Bell was still in the band—long before Gary Moore. People didn't know what was going on. Radio Luxembourg started playing "Whiskey in the Jar" which was an old rebel song. It was played completely different. I was totally taken and I wanted to check this stuff out! Suddenly it broke loose. Radio Luxembourg was definitely responsible for breaking Thin Lizzy. Suddenly there was no more sitting on the floor because they were playing big places. What also used to be really big in Ireland was what they call a *showband scene*, which was Top 40 music. There used to be 8 to 10 members in the band, everybody used to wear suits and travel in big tour buses. They earned a fortune—it was big, big business. I used to do all that stuff when I was playing drums and it was great fun.

Petra Zeitz: I think your new

album "MSG" is the best record the band has made so far.

Robin McAuley: Thank you!

Petra Zeitz: What was your initial intention when you went into the studio to record it?

Robin McAuley: I think we wrote the songs the same way as we did on previous albums. Most definitely I know that we wanted to keep it as raw as we could this time. I think having James Kottak on drums and Jeff Pilson on bass was a great energy boost for us. We had gone through management changes and record company changes and things had become a bit depressing for a while. So when we went into pre-production we were kind of fired up. I think it shows on a lot of the tracks— how we were feeling. It's got its emotional side too but I think every MSG album does.

Petra Zeitz: Did you notice any growth of interest in MSG after the Scorpions [with Rudolph Schenker] had their huge success with "Wind of Change"?

Michael Schenker: With the Schenkers—my brother and myself—one hand washes the other. People always ask who is older, me or my brother? I just recently found out why they're asking this. It's because I was famous before he was. So people always think I must be the older brother, but I'm actually younger than Rudolph. When I joined UFO it helped the Scorpions in gaining attention. The advantage went forward and backwards. I don't know if I expressed this completely, but you know what I'm saying. It does happen that people make a connection because of the Scorpions' success. I'm not really that business oriented, but I can imagine that that's the way it goes. It's a natural thing and of course it helps MSG.

Petra Zeitz: Do you still watch the German music scene?

Michael Schenker: When I was with the Scorpions in 1970 there was nothing happening in Germany. It was not even allowed to have a management. We had to do everything under the table. The difficulties we had there were part of the reason why I had to move. When I went to England, all of a sudden, people appreciated what I was doing. It seems like the Scorpions had to get out of Germany first to be accepted by the Germans. Who is coming out of Germany right now? There's Doro, there's Kraftwerk, there's Bonfire and Helloween. One of my favorite bands of the seventies was Frumpy. I auditioned for them when I was 15 and I really would have liked to join them.

Petra Zeitz: Do people in America still consider you and your brother as Germans or do they think you're one of them by now?

Michael Schenker: I wonder, I'm not sure. I have bumped into people who were surprised when I said that I was German. It has happened.

SLAUGHTER

In one of the most exciting stories ever in rock annals, Slaughter has gone from a band that had never played together live, to multi-platinum success. Their debut album "Stick It to Ya" sold over two million copies and a million singles. In 1990, Slaughter had four number one videos on MTV and the band topped countless "Readers' Polls" as the Best New Act of the Year.

Slaughter rose from the ashes of the Vinnie Vincent Invasion. Mark Slaughter and Dana Strum played with the ex–Kiss guitarist until 1988 when they went on to form their own band. Slaughter's lineup was completed by Tim Kelly on guitar and Blas Elias on drums. Their debut album "Stick It to Ya" was released in January 1990 on Chrysalis Records. The Las Vegas band became highly rated on the heavy metal scene. During the first eighteen months that followed their record release, Slaughter played more than 300 concerts and built a great live following.

In August 1991 they started writing and recording a second album to be called "The Wild Life." It was released in April 1992 and was, once again, welcomed by critics and fans. It entered the Billboard charts at number 13.

The following interview with Mark Slaughter and Dana Strum took place on April 13th, 1992.

Petra Zeitz: Your debut album was a huge success. What went through your mind when you started recording a follow up?

Mark Slaughter: After playing 300 plus dates on the road, we just wanted to take the *live* element directly into the record. We're always trying to be a better band and better musicians. On our first record we put the

Slaughter

band together in the studio and we didn't play live until we played with Kiss. After that we had a very good education by playing with such legends as Kiss and being on the road as much as we were. So we tried to bring that element directly into the record.

Dana Strum: There's a responsibility when you've sold that many records and you know that many people are getting to hear your music. All of a sudden you feel very responsible to deliver music back to your fans who delivered themselves and their heart to you. It was like: "Wait 'til you hear this!" That's what you want as a band—you want the fans to dig it and you want them to be favorably impressed. They've opened up their heart to you and they've gone out and supported you. So we have a responsibility to give that feeling back to our fans. Hopefully we give them even a stronger feeling. That's what we tried to do.

Petra Zeitz: Why did you decide to work in a small, unpretentious recording studio?

Mark Slaughter: A lot of bands think: "Oh yeah, we sold a million and more records, why don't we just go in this kill-place where they have hot pinball machines and stuff!" That's how a lot of bands think, but we're not like that. We like a really hard-working environment. It's very comfortable in Las Vegas where we live, but we're never there. I was living in an apartment that just had a bed and nothing else. It's a sense of that hunger we want to bring into the record as well. You try to bring that hard element directly into the record as opposed to trying to be comfortable.

Dana Strum: Also when you're in a studio you don't want a studio to run you. I started wrapping cables and sweeping floors and learning my way up in the studio. You don't want to go in a studio where you're not completely in control of the room. If you're scared and nervous because you don't know what all that stuff does, then the room becomes in control of you. You never want to make a record where you're not manipulating the room and you're bringing your band into that room, rather than that room making your band sound like that room. We made one record at Red Zone Recording Studios and we knew that there was this certain outcome and that we had become familiar with it. The second record for

us made us think, "Let's really take it beyond what anybody believed this room could do." It's a very small room, but it's a very hungry room. You're just in there with no windows, no pretty view, nothing. And you're thinking, "Remember Salt Lake City? Remember Denver, Colorado?" And I think that helped us to make a record that was a harder edged record, that had different types of material than we had ever done before. I think it made a big difference for us.

Petra Zeitz: Did you record the second album the same way you did the first?

Dana Strum: It was much more natural to record the second one because we had come off the road. Mark had been singing two gigs a night sometimes. We had been out there every day. Mark's guitar collection grew from two guitars he had since he was a teenager to about 20 guitars that were all for different purposes. There were things to choose from.

Mark Slaughter: For instance we did a song called "Days Gone By" where I played piano. We wanted to try something a little different. I'm not a great piano player but after being on the road, I became more comfortable with the instrument to where I could take it a step further and use it on a record.

Dana Strum: Again that was learned by playing. We always look forward to playing because that's how we prove ourselves. People hear the record and can make their decision by seeing us live.

Petra Zeitz: Since you've already mentioned "Days Gone By," why did you decide to release two versions—one regular, one acoustic—on the same album?

Mark Slaughter: As songwriters we wanted to show people that you can do two different versions of one song. The regular version was done first. We liked the way it sounded and as we were sitting around, I played it on the guitar. We thought it would be cool to re-record it acoustically and put it on the end of the album. So we played it with acoustic guitars, not putting vocals on it or anything.

Some people hate it—some people like it. But the point is that we did it because that was what we felt like doing.

Dana Strum: I think it's in the vein of trying to be different. I don't think the average metal band would ever do "Days

Gone By" acoustically at all. The stereotype that goes on if you're successful is that you'd never do a jazz-impromptu version of your own song. This is our way of saying, "Don't judge a book by its cover because you might often be wrong." There are many bands that, unfortunately, were misjudged by their covers.

Petra Zeitz: Do you have an example of a band that you think was misjudged by the public?

Dana Strum: The Scorpions is one of them. Nobody in the States knew the Scorpions had an album out until "Lovedrive." It's really sad to see that. There were many good records that the Scorpions did that were overlooked because America misjudged that band. And then, all of a sudden, America was told that the Scorpions were really happening in Europe and people started to check them out. Unfortunately, now that we are still music fans, but playing our own band, we know a little bit about what that's like: If you don't get the chance to expose what you do and talk to people, they can go only on rumors and pictures that they see. That's not very fair.

Petra Zeitz: As your fans already know you like to play parts of classic tunes in the middle of your own songs. Why do you do that?

Dana Strum: We did it during our first tour. We did a version of "Back in Black" in the middle of our song "Eye to Eye." We played it just for the hell of it because we love AC/DC. We also played "Hell's Bells" and "Lick It Up." We also tried out a version of Black Sabbath's "Sabbath Bloody Sabbath." Mark and I wanted to do that, but unfortunately the only two people that liked it were two Marines in the front row. People thought we were crazy but we had a lot of fun!

Mark Slaughter: We're not a band that uses samples or anything like that, so we do things live. If we decide to throw something in the middle of one of our songs, we just do it. It definitely went over the audience's heads, but it was fun.

Petra Zeitz: You wrote the songs for your second album during August 1991. Didn't you have any songs that were written on the road?

Dana Strum: When you're on tour as extensively as we were you might get inspired. Your mind might take snapshots. And when you're back at home you remember all these things and maybe transfer them into the music. But if you're on the road and as busy as our schedule was, it would be impossible to sit down and write an album. We did write one song on the road called "Shouted Out" which appeared on the Kiss single "God Gave Rock'n'Roll to You" because it was used in a soundtrack. It was the first new song we had done in a while and it gave us a good release from being out there and playing live all the time.

Mark Slaughter: We recorded it on the road too. Every day off was used to record this song.

Petra Zeitz: Is songwriting in general a difficult process for you?

Dana Strum: You need to concentrate and you need to think about it, but the writing comes very naturally. "Times They Change," which is probably one of the most different songs on our second album, was the third song we wrote. We kind of thought: "Wow—what's the rest of the album going to be like?" You never know when you write something like that. We like to write songs that people can shout back and get involved in. Queen is one of our favorite bands and they have songs you can sing.

Petra Zeitz: That means you welcome any kind of audience participation in your shows?

Mark Slaughter: Actually our favorite part of doing the music is when the audience becomes part of the show. That's what we do this for. We want the audience to be singing with us and having a good time.

Dana Strum: We're very proud that we make music for our fans. We make music for people that love music. I wouldn't enjoy making music for cynics, because they're going to be cynical about anything. They'll be cynical about Metallica making this new record until it's old and then they will love it. They'll be cynical about anybody that does anything until it sells. So you don't make music for those people— you make music for people that buy and like real music. All you ever want as a musician is a chance to let people hear your music and see you live. And let them make their decision from there. You can't force people to buy millions of records. It's their decision and people buy what they like to buy. If they go in a store there are 3000 things to buy and if they buy us we

consider ourselves lucky and fortunate. Now it's time to prove ourselves and play. And to prove to them that they have bought something that was the right thing to buy.

Petra Zeitz: Was it because of all this time spent on the road that you took over two years to record a second album?

Dana Strum: It was a long break between the two records, yes. But we were constantly in people's faces. Our videos were being played on MTV and we were on tour. For us, it was a two-week break and we went back in again. January 1990 to April of 1992 is a long time, but for us it went really quickly.

Petra Zeitz: Is getting a lot of air play the greatest factor of your success so far?

Dana Strum: Many people think that MTV or radio broke Slaughter. What broke Slaughter was playing live every night. Later MTV and radio played this band, but it was much less radio than people think. I think you owe it to yourself to see any band live because the truth comes out in that live performance. With us, people were often saying they didn't expect us to be so heavy and they were surprised. That's all we want. What helped us up was letting people make decisions. It's a big world out there, as we know, because we've traveled it.

Mark Slaughter: The fans put us where we are today. Like Dana said, the radio and MTV didn't even play the band in the beginning. In the end, they played us because our fans called up and just insisted on it.

Petra Zeitz: You're known to be very good to your fans . . .

Dana Strum: One thing for sure: our best education and our best assets are our fans. It was actually the people out in the audience that put us where we are. They have put every rock 'n' roll band where they are. But, you know, a lot of bands don't even take note of that. We found out that the demos of our last record were being sold for over $100. We had a discussion within the band and with this record we sent out tapes of our demos to everyone in the fan club. We sent out 32,000 cassettes for free and stamped them *bootleg*. So nobody has ever got to buy them. We felt we wanted to give back to the fans what they're giving us. We wanted to do something no other band has ever done which was to give to our fans our music in its demo stages. For us, it's worked like

there is no tomorrow, because people saw that we were the same people that were dedicated to them before. And we can do more for them now. If you have a fan club card and we're playing in your town, you get in backstage for free. You don't have to know anybody. You don't have to beg your way in. And we do that to everybody. There's no band that has sold millions of records that does that at all.

Petra Zeitz: Where did you get the ideas to do all that?

Dana Strum: We were music fans ourselves. We wanted to do something that we wish our favorite bands had done for us. Now that we were lucky enough to be in this position we wanted to show people that you don't have to be a heroin addict, you don't have to have your body covered with 15 tattoos just because you're a rock singer. You can be a regular person, make good music and have fun with people.

Petra Zeitz: Would you say this attitude also shows in your lyrics?

Dana Strum: When people go out on a Saturday night they want to have a good time. I don't believe people want to hear negative lyrics about how the earth is over. The earth is not over—there's good times everywhere in the world. I don't care where you live, but every country we traveled to, people have a fuckin' good time. We hope that our music inspires people to go on having a good time.

Petra Zeitz: Do you have a personal, friendly relationship with some of your fans?

Dana Strum: We meet a great deal of them. We certainly don't know 3 1/2 million of them, but we do know certain people in certain parts of the United States and Canada very well. They have traveled to different places and we know them by name. There's this guy called Ken who has been to over 40 gigs. He just shows up. We put him on MTV. They were looking for stories that made Slaughter unique and we insisted they talked to Ken. Let the people do the talking, you know. We originally wanted to call our first album "Let the Music Do the Talking," but unfortunately, Aerosmith had a song by that title and everybody felt it wouldn't be a good idea.

Petra Zeitz: Las Vegas is an unusual place for a rock band. But Albert Collins once told me it even has a blues scene. What opportunities does a rock 'n' roll band have in Las Vegas?

Mark Slaughter: It's actually very dismal. There is no rock 'n' roll scene. Vegas is a very nice town to live in 24 hours a day. It's a non-stop party.

Dana Strum: It's a place of temptation. There's no rock 'n' roll scene because the most scene it has is temptation, whether it's drugs, money, corruption, gambling, prostitution—it's all in front of your face for the taking. It is unlike any other town in the world. You can do anything at any time. You could lose your life savings in an hour. Is that rock 'n' roll? Probably yes, because rock 'n' roll is all about challenging that temptation. But our music is really not a product of where we live. Otherwise we would be copying other bands. There is a place at the Pacific in the northwest part of America where that is happening a great deal right now.

Petra Zeitz: I guess you're talking about Seattle and the so-called Seattle-sound.

Dana Strum: Yeah, and unfortunately, I think that they are destroying it for each other because one band that came from there is one thing. Two bands that came from there with the same sound is another, when three and four and five and ten do, somebody begins to wonder who started it. For us, our music is our music. It wouldn't matter where Queen or Iron Maiden wrote their records because they always sound like Queen or Iron Maiden. So it doesn't matter where you're from but Las Vegas is the most bizarre place in the United States as far as having to live around temptation at all times.

Petra Zeitz: Has it made a change for you that the record label [Chrysalis] you're on has been sold to EMI?

Mark Slaughter: It was a very positive change. We're very excited about it. We were on a label that had absolutely no idea of how to break a hard rock band. I mean, what do Sinead O'Connor and Slaughter have to do with each other?

Dana Strum: One has hair and one doesn't!

Mark Slaughter: For us, it was a very positive thing. EMI has some of our favorite bands and it makes a difference. They understand the music we make and they can expose us to people that like the kind of music we play. If you exposed MC Hammer to a thrash metal audi-

ence, he would never have sold one record. If you expose Metallica to people that like Sinead O'Connor, they'll say, "Who?" If you expose Slaughter to that same audience they will say the same. So, for us, having a new record company is a brand new start.

Petra Zeitz: You made one fresh start already by forming Slaughter after the Vinnie Vincent Invasion. What was the problem with that band?

Dana Strum: It wasn't a band—that was the problem. Many musicians work day jobs, but we were living by playing as side musicians to a guy that we learned what not to do from. It was far from easy. It was far from having good times, but we don't dwell on the bad time and the negativity.

Mark Slaughter: One thing we learned from that was when we were looking for Tim and Blas to put Slaughter together, we were looking for two other players that wanted to be in a band that didn't have an ego, that didn't have a drinking or drug problem, that wanted to be a band and work one for all and all for one. So we found two other guys that also knew— after the discussions that Dana and I had with them—that they had to be very fan oriented because that was something we wanted to do. We're a very positive band. We think what definitely comes from Slaughter is a positive attitude. We have heavy songs and stuff, but we're still saying: "Hey—have a good time in your life and live your dreams!" If you have a dream, then reach out and go for it.

STATUS QUO

Status Quo, UK rock group, was originally formed in 1962. Francis Rossi and Alan Lancaster called their band the Scorpions, but by 1964 the name had changed to the Spectres. A year later they played a gig at Butlin's holiday camp in England where they met their future guitarist Rick Parfitt. Their first four singles flopped, but in 1967 Parfitt joined and the band's name was changed one last time to Status Quo.

Rossi and Parfitt worked well together and by 1968 Status Quo had their first top ten hit in England. It was a single called "Pictures of Matchstick Men."

In 1970 the band started playing a more heavy rock sound and released their album "Ma Kelly's Greasy Spoon." It hailed two more hit singles. Status Quo went even more heavy and released their first true hard rock album in 1971. It was called "Dog of Two Heads" and became a massive seller in England. By the mid-seventies Status Quo had become a household name in the British and European rock scene. In 1977, they stormed the charts with the classic "Rockin' All Over the World" and were celebrated as England's No. 1 hard rock band. Status Quo toured the United States several times, but were far more successful at home. "Whatever You Want," "Just Supposin'" and "Something 'Bout You Baby I Like" were just some of the 23 hit singles the band landed in Britain. By 1981 they had sold over 12 million singles and almost 8 million albums. To celebrate their 20th anniversary Quo played a charity gig in the presence of Prince Charles. It was the first time a member of the British royal family had gone to watch a rock concert. In 1985 Status Quo opened the legendary "Live Aid" concert at London's

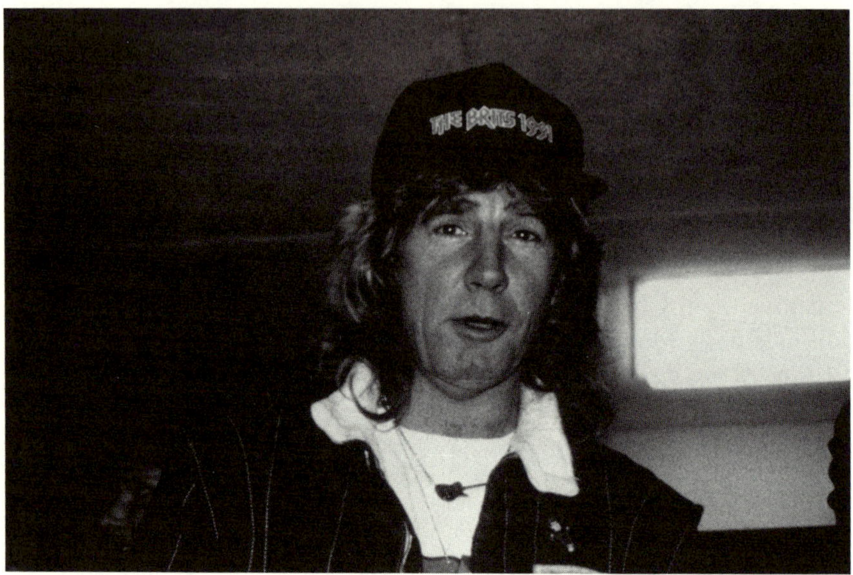

Rick Parfitt of Status Quo

Wembley Stadium. Three years later they sold out the Olympic Stadium in Moskow 14 times in a row.

So far, worldwide sales of Status Quo records have reached the 100 million mark. With 42 UK hit singles the band is third in line saleswise, behind only Elvis Presley and Cliff Richard.

The following interview with Rick Parfitt took place in February 1992. Status Quo was in the middle of promoting a tour as well as their latest album "Rock 'Til You Drop."

Petra Zeitz: I'm surprised that after 25 years in the business you still care to do interviews and talk to people.

Rick Parfitt: Well, this is what our business is all about. Everybody seems to get the impression that most of the time our business is all glamorous parties and awards ceremonies. To a point that is true, but it's maybe 15 percent. The rest of it is like anything else. If you want to get to the top of your profession and stay there, you've got to work hard. The fact that we're coming out here to do some shows, we want to let people know. So this is really part of what we do. I must say that sometimes I find it a bit of a slog traveling from one city to the next every day. Yesterday we spoke to 22 journalists—one after the other—and today is the same. But it has to be done. If you settle into it it's just another aspect of our business which is quite good fun. The reason why I'm sitting here talking to you is the fact that we play some shows and it would be nice if people came along to see us for the two hours we play on stage. That's really where it's all at. Everything revolves around that.

Petra Zeitz: Do you know why your career has taken off everywhere else in the world, while you haven't quite managed to win over American audiences?

Rick Parfitt: The whole American saga was because of mismanagement. When we first started looking towards America over ten years ago, the management we had at the time was ripping us off. They weren't working for us at all. In an organization like we have, you need a chain link and everybody must do their jobs properly. Otherwise it won't work. If you've got a management that behind your back is not really working for you, you have a

problem. We thought with the power of this band we would have no problem in the States at all, but it didn't seem to work. Live it was fantastic, but we didn't sell any records. We sold nothing. "Rockin' All Over the World" was a huge hit single everywhere except America. We felt very strange because we had already built a following in Europe. When we tried to build a following in America it just didn't work. It was all down to management. This time it's going to be different. Whether it's a bit late in the day to go for it again I don't know. But it would be nice to open America up. We've achieved an awful lot and the name is known very well in America. People wonder why they never see us in the States. We will go there later this year and talk to them. It's going to be very interesting to talk to them and tell them why we haven't been there. I know that we haven't given America our best shot yet. The band is better now than it was back then anyway, so I think we're still in with a chance.

Petra Zeitz: Is "Rock 'Til You Drop" the motto of Status Quo now?

Rick Parfitt: Yeah. When the title was first suggested to us by our manager David Walker, we thought it sounded a bit like thrash metal. We didn't particularly like it. Then Andrew, our keyboard player, came up with this ballad and set the lyrics with "Rock 'Til You Drop" to the song. We saw it in a different light then. It's becoming somewhat of a little anthem for the band. We'll just see how long physically these poor old bodies can take this battering that we give them every night.

Petra Zeitz: Are your live shows comprised mainly of all your hit songs?

Rick Parfitt: We would be on stage for two days if we played them all! We have a bit of a problem because with the Quo fans being like they are, they want to hear the songs they've known over the years and they like to sing along. I think this happens with most artists, but it seems that the Quo fans sing a little bit louder than other fans. They're quite an outrageous lot and very loyal. The problem we have is trying to put as many of the hits in as we can. We condense them all into a medley and do a verse and a chorus of this and a verse and a chorus of that. We link it all together. In, let's say, the space of 10 minutes, we can put in seven or eight of the hits. We try to put in as many of the big records as we can, combining that with our favorite album tracks. It seems to work quite well.

Petra Zeitz: Status Quo has played a lot of charity shows in England and, I know, you're very involved in the Nordoff Robbins Music Therapy Centre. Unfortunately it seems like the organizers of these shows can't get any bands to play there anymore. What's the problem charities are facing?

Rick Parfitt: It's a funny thing with charity gigs. I'm concerned about things like the Nordoff Robbins Centre. I actually went to the old school and saw a session going on. I came out crying because it's unbelievable to see these people and their dedication. They're getting bashed around by autistic children and slowly you see the child come out of itself and start to enjoy what is going on. Normally it's completely absorbed in itself and it won't talk. To see the child develop and come out, that is a charity I would work to the end of the earth for. It's a wonderful charity and we're all behind it. The one day we played at Knebworth in 1990 we made 9 million dollars. I've consequently been to the new center they built. That's the very essence of doing a charity—at the end of the day you can see the result. That makes me feel really good. Live Aid was another fantastic example of what charities can do. But in doing so you find yourself on worldwide television. Of course there's nothing wrong with that as long as your heart is behind the charity and not behind more exposure to further your career. That's where things start to go wrong.

Petra Zeitz: Have you turned down any charity shows yet?

Rick Parfitt: Yes, we have. You are probably aware of the Zeebrugge Ferry disaster that happened in 1987. There was a charity concert for that and we were asked to do it. We said no, because no amount of money can compensate these people for the loss of their loved ones. I have lost a child in my life. I lost one of my little daughters. That's something you can't buy with money. The boat was insured anyway and the people who lost family members were getting compensation anyway. That sort of charity I don't see, I'm afraid. I think people are doing that to further their career. Actually we do quite a lot which is not publicized, because

we don't seek publicity for charities.

Petra Zeitz: You have received so many gold albums and awards. Does it still mean anything to you?

Rick Parfitt: Oh, very much so. I love it! When I have one room full I fill another room. It's nice in as much as knowing that the record has done well. Status Quo is still alive and kickin'. So it's a way of letting us know that it's still happening. As you said earlier: It's 26 years now and are we still keen to do it? Yeah, we are! We now seem to get a little bit of acclaim as opposed to criticism. We were criticized for so many years, but we enjoy what we do and the fact that we're still around shows that there are a lot of people out there who enjoy it as well. We never conformed to any trends and we won't change our style for anybody. I don't think the fans want us to. And trends come and go anyway.

Petra Zeitz: I was just going to say that for 26 years you can always tell a Status Quo record when you hear one. How did you manage to keep your sound that recognizable without repeating yourself?

Rick Parfitt: That's another interesting point. I always compare it to Coca-Cola. They have a recipe which is locked away and it's a big secret. Look how successful that is and how successful it has been over the years. They obviously don't change Coca-Cola because they have a very successful product. It's the same with us. We have a successful sound, so why try and change it. It is what comes naturally. Even if what we play is simple, it is heartfelt. We put so much energy in it and we feel it from the heart, so that we always do it 100 percent. That's why it works. If you put any music under the umbrella of rock'n'roll, it must come from the heart, otherwise it's not real rock'n'roll. If you play it for the sake of it, it doesn't mean anything.

Petra Zeitz: How has the studio work changed for you over the years?

Rick Parfitt: Drastically! In fact, we don't even go into a studio anymore. I don't think we'll ever go into a recording studio again. We book a filmset, like a soundstage, and set all the gear up exactly as it is on stage. We get a mobile recording studio, park that outside, put the equipment up, rehearse the song and crank it up to full stage volume. Then we just play it and record it live. It feels so much more natural because it looks like I'm on stage. For us anyway it's important to have that eye contact. It's like being on stage without the audience. That should capture Status Quo as it is supposed to be captured. We said: "Sod all this technology—we don't need it." So recording studios are gone. I love the sense of freedom you get off a soundstage. It puts me into a better frame of mind.

Petra Zeitz: Do you see a time when Status Quo will be just recording, but not be able to play live anymore?

Rick Parfitt: I don't like to think of it. I suppose that time will come. No, I disagree with myself. I don't think that time will ever come. As long as we are recording we will be playing live. It may be in a slightly different fashion to what we do now, because I would like to try and make it 40 years which would be the year 2002. I think we will still be performing, but maybe we won't be dashing about like we do now. I don't know, I mean, look at Chuck Berry—he's still dashing around the stage! Anything is possible. No other band has ever done what we have done— not the Beatles nor the Stones.

Not in England anyway. We've had more hit singles than them and we're third in line only behind Cliff Richard and Elvis Presley. We're the top band, which is great. If you had said to me 25 years ago that in 20 odd years we'd still be touring, I would have laughed at you. So in the year 2000 I'm sure we'll still be around.

Petra Zeitz: How long does it take you to record an album that way?

Rick Parfitt: "Rock 'Til You Drop" took three months to do. We went off to play a couple of festivals in Europe between recording. I'm sure it could have been done in 10 weeks. We're not striving to be that quick because the music has got to be up to standard. That is only obtained by working from 11 A.M. to 4 P.M. every day because they are your most productive hours. You don't want to get into recording 30 or 40 takes and then listening back to the best ten. We were doing on average six takes per song, and by then we knew we had it. You close your eyes and listen to the band in its purest form and you know if a take is the final one. It's a very good way of working because it keeps you fresh. You're not confined within these four very

claustrophobic walls of a recording studio. I'm a claustrophobic—I don't like lifts or anything.

Petra Zeitz: Was there ever a time when you wanted to do something different and leave music behind?

Rick Parfitt: Never—not since I was ten years old. In fact, I got my first guitar for Christmas when I was ten years old. For some reason the first day I got it, I played it. I don't know how I played it, but I managed to play a song called "Mary's Boy Child" which was a favorite song of my mum. I sort of got this tune out of my guitar. I didn't know how to tune it or anything—I still don't know, to be honest. From then on I never ever wanted to do anything else because I had desires from the age of nine to be a pop star. I had all these pictures on my bedroom wall and dreamed that one day that could be me. So once I had played this guitar at Christmas, my academic studies went out of the window. From the age of ten I didn't want to know. I just messed about at school. I was one of the naughty boys but that didn't bother me at all. It does more now. Now I wish I had listened a bit. But my school was a pretty crappy school anyway and I wouldn't have learned much there. I concentrated on going into show business. That's all I wanted to do. As luck would have it, when I left school at 15 I could play quite well and I was offered a job at a holiday camp. Consequently this led to me meeting somebody else which led to me meeting up with Francis Rossi. I've been very lucky and very fortunate to have gotten to this position now and to still be doing something that I have always wanted to do. I consider myself very lucky. So when you ask me if I get sick of it, the answer is no. It's been very good to me and I have a duty to be good back. Like anybody, some days I don't fancy working, but I gotta do it anyway. I've never wanted to quit and I still don't.

Petra Zeitz: Has all the traveling affected your family life?

Rick Parfitt: Of course it has, but you have to learn how to cope with that, and so does your partner. It's hardest on the children because I'm away for such lengthy periods. I missed a lot of them growing up. Obviously you miss contact with them. My oldest son is 17 and he's a music student. He can read all these computer scores and program synthesizers. He can do all that, but I don't know what he's talking about. My youngest son is 2 1/2 and he likes Status Quo. He puts the tape of "Rock 'Til You Drop" on every day. So we have to see what happens there.

Petra Zeitz: You must have had so many highlights in your career, but are there any particular ones you care to mention?

Rick Parfitt: Opening "Live Aid" was quite a buzz, to be actually the first band on worldwide. That was quite a thrill. I don't know. Receiving the awards is always nice. The World Music Award and the Brits Award were very prestigious ones as was the Ivor Novello Award. These are great highlights. But generally I enjoy just being on the road. I know it sounds terrible and it's even going to look worse in print, but I get a buzz every night when the lights go down and the audience goes, "wow!" Ten minutes before, I'm trying to wind myself up to the gig, but it's not until the lights actually go down and the crowd hits you, then the adrenaline hits you too and the energy flows through you. I get that every night. I just generally enjoy it. As long as our mental attitude and our physical attitude is okay and we want to do it, then why stop?

Petra Zeitz: I thought you might mention a line of shows that got you into the *Guinness Book of World Records*. You played four cities all in one day.

Rick Parfitt: That nearly stopped us! Well, it was suggested to us to do it. Rather than put a poster on the wall of Status Quo's new album, we wanted to do something that gave the press a bit of fun and that had never been done before. So the logistics of it were horrendous. We use a lot of equipment on stage and it had to be duplicated four times, right down to the last button. Guitars had to be duplicated because we couldn't take them on the helicopters. There were 16 fixed-wing aircrafts and four or five helicopters involved. It was a nightmare, logistically. Four light rigs and four sound decks were needed. The crew members were overlapping on aircrafts, but they did it and they worked their asses off to get it together. All credit to them. Came the day, we started at 9 o'clock in the morning at the BBC in London. We played "Rockin' All Over the World" at the BBC. Then we went to the first helicopter that took us to Sheffield. We were on stage at 11:05AM. It felt really weird be-

ing on stage at 11 o'clock in the morning, but again, all credit to the people for coming out. It went fantastic and we thought: "Yeah, no problem!" We got onto the jet and went to Glasgow, Scotland. We literally had minutes to spare and went straight into the gig, took a fresh set of stage clothes, and went straight on stage. We did the gig, went straight back on the helicopter, back to the jet, and back down to Birmingham. At Birmingham we made up a bit of time; we had 12 minutes before we'd be due on stage. That gave us time to have a shower. I was in the shower for six minutes, dried my hair, put the stage clothes on and went on stage. We did the third gig. Then it was back to the jet and back to London. We were running on schedule. The crowd in London was amazing. The noise when we walked on stage was unbelievable. We were hurting physically by then, but we did the show one last time. The jubilation afterwards in the dressing room was fantastic. We just sat there and we were so knocked out that we had done it. All these months of planning and at last we had done it. Of course we were in the *Guinness Book of World Records* and we had certainly advertized the fact that we had an album out. The whole country knew about this event. Consequently we thought that we couldn't be earning money from advertising our album, so we charged a donation of six pounds [9 dollars] at the door and we raised one quarter million for children's charities all over the country. All in all it was a very good day. I suppose you could take it down as another highlight. But we'd never do it again—let's let somebody else have a go and they would have to do it quicker than us. If anybody can do it, then good luck!

TESLA

Tesla was founded in Sacramento, California by Frank Hannon (guitar), Jeff Keith (vocals), Troy Luccketta (drums), Brian Wheat (bass) and Tommy Skeoch (guitar). The five-piece band released their first album "Mechanical Resonance" in 1986. It marked the beginning of Tesla's "No Machines Campaigns" and went gold. For 14 months Tesla went on the road supporting major acts such as David Lee Roth, Alice Cooper and Def Leppard. Their "no gimmick" rock songs earned them critical acclaim and ever-growing audiences. In 1989 a second album, "The Great Radio Controversy," was released and did equally well selling over one million copies. "Love Song" was put out as a single and promptly made it into the US Top Ten.

A surprisingly different direction was taken with the acoustic album "Five Men Acoustical Jam" released in January 1991. In addition to acoustic arrangements of Tesla classics such as "Cumin Atcha Alive" and "Love Song," it featured versions of the Beatles' "We Can Work It Out" and the Rolling Stones' "Mother's Little Helper." Later on in 1991, Tesla went electric again and released their new studio album "Psychotic Supper."

The following interview with Tesla's bass player Brian Wheat took place in Cologne, Germany, in September 1991. Tesla was in town on a tour supporting the Scorpions.

Petra Zeitz: First of all, what does the name Tesla mean?

Brian Wheat: Oh come on—you know that, don't you? Okay, Tesla was an inventor. To make a long story short, he was an inventor who invented radio and electricity. You couldn't have rock'n'roll without those two. Tesla never got the credit

Tesla

he was supposed to get and not many people know of him, because he was kind of suppressed. That's what happened. We can associate with being suppressed, because rock'n'roll is suppressed. If you have long hair and you play rock'n'roll most people think you're a dirtbag. So we can identify with the connection there. Actually our manager came up with the name, but when he told us we really liked it. It gives some significant meaning to the band.

Petra Zeitz: Are you still playing parts of your acoustic set on stage?

Brian Wheat: No, we're not an acoustic band. I know we released an acoustic live album, but that was just a representation of what we can do. It was a one-off. We're not an acoustic band, so we're not going to do acoustic sets at all. Our first two albums weren't acoustic, so we're not meant to be an acoustic band. It's one of the things we do when we want to have a good time. Sometimes it can get a bit too much when people kind of expect that we're an acoustic band, because we're not. We mix it a little bit in our headline set, but when you only have 45 minutes to play and you've got to cover four albums, we tend to cover the three electric albums.

Petra Zeitz: Does your new album which was recorded after the acoustic one differ from the first two electric albums that you released?

Brian Wheat: No, they are all straight-ahead rock albums. I mean, hopefully people think the new one is better. It's a natural progression. The songs are better, the playing is better and the singing is better.

Petra Zeitz: You've said you are a "no-bullshit rock'n'roll band." Do you stand by that in your live performances?

Brian Wheat: Yes. We're as straight ahead as we can be. We're not going to blow up anything.

Petra Zeitz: Are your songs written in the studio, or do you have them ready before you start recording?

Brian Wheat: We usually have them before we go into the studio. We don't write much in the studio. We write them before and that way we don't waste a lot of money and a lot of time. That way you go in and it's really fresh—you just whip it out. If you tend to not have the songs when you go in the studio you can spend a year in there. You can lose the spontaneity. One thing we like about the new album is that it's very spontaneous and there is a lot of energy on it.

Petra Zeitz: You seem to have quite long gaps between albums . . .

Brian Wheat: Yeah, usually two years. We don't want to spit an album out every year. 'Cause you know what happens? The quality of your record goes down. We don't care if we take three years to do an album as long as we think it's the best record we could have made. In fact, no one has complained yet.

Petra Zeitz: How long does it take you to record an album?

Brian Wheat: Six weeks to record it, but it takes a lot longer to mix it. When we got signed and were trying to make our first record, no producer thought we were good enough. Then we found Steve Thompson and Michael Barbiero and we made the first record with them. It went gold and after that everybody wanted to produce us, but we stayed with Michael and Steve. But it was like a dream. You watch films on Elvis and on the Beatles and you think: "One day I'd like to have a gold record." Everyone wants to be accepted, don't they?

Petra Zeitz: Do you take your songs further in a live situation?

Brain Wheat: Some songs we play like they are on the record, some songs we take out and jam. It depends, because we never do the same set all the time. When we headline we play around 25 songs.

Petra Zeitz: Do you find it difficult coming to Europe and having to support other bands while you could do a headlining tour in the States?

Brian Wheat: Well when you've had four albums out and you headline everywhere else in the world but Europe, then to sit there and say it's not different, I would be lying. It is different because we've got only 45 minutes. You can only play a couple of songs off each album. If you see us in a headline situa-

tion we can present a whole spectrum of material.

Petra Zeitz: In a support situation the audience is really there to see another band. What do you do to win them over?

Brian Wheat: That's always the case when you're supporting, but I mean, last night in Stockholm it was fine. The audience was great. We're known a little bit, so it's not like we're starting from zero, but we're not starting from ten either. They know what "Signs" is and they know what "Love Song" is. It's a start. We have never toured Europe before. It will be interesting to see what happens.

Petra Zeitz: Are live gigs the most important part of your work with Tesla?

Brian Wheat: When it's that time, yes. When you're making a record, writing the songs is the most important bit. Once the record is made, the most important bit is the show and what it takes to make that show the best thing you can. The kids spend a lot of money and they want the best show they can get. It's up to us to make sure they do.

Petra Zeitz: Does your hometown of Sacramento have a healthy rock scene?

Brian Wheat: There isn't a good rock scene, no. There are

a few bands trying to get a record deal and I wish them the
best. It was better ten years ago
when we first played in the
clubs. But we're still based
there.

Petra Zeitz: Did you all know
each other before you formed
the band?

Brian Wheat: We were kind
of friends, yes. Frank and I
were friends and Jeff was very
like us. Now it's different than
friends. They are like my family. We have lived through so
many things together. I mean,
we have our personal lives separate from the band, but there is
definitely a bond between the
five of us that is very special.
No one is allowed in with the five
of us.

Petra Zeitz: The Californian
rock scene is based around Los
Angeles. Do you have to go down
there to work?

Brian Wheat: We don't go
there to record, but we've been
there to do videos a few times.
We've just been there twice during the last months and that's a
lot by our standards.

Petra Zeitz: Are videos important even for rock'n'roll
bands that don't rely on any
given image?

Brian Wheat: I think it has
become an important thing be-

cause of MTV and stuff. People
didn't use to have them, but I
would be stupid to say that the
videos for "Love Song" and
"Signs" didn't help to make
these singles Top Ten hits. They
got the shit played out of them!
But I can't think about videos
really. I'd like to think about
music, songs, records, but with
videos I can't be bothered. I
just show up and do my bit.

Petra Zeitz: Are videos, as
well as promotion, a burden to
you?

Brian Wheat: Well, we decided that next time we will do a
press tour right after the album
is done so that we don't have to
do it during shows. Like I said,
the main thing is the music.
We're trying to do too many
things at once. I'm up for a promotion tour because I love going
to different places. I enjoy the
food and I like different cultures. I'm very open-minded.

Petra Zeitz: Do you still enjoy
playing in small clubs like you
did in the early days?

Brian Wheat: Yes, sometimes. We did an acoustic set at
the Astoria Club in London and
that was a blast. It is fun, but we
like arenas, too. It's a real
charge when 20,000 people are
standing up singing your song.
We burst into a version of

"Rocky Raccoon" the other night. We just like music.

Petra Zeitz: Which bands had an influence on you when you first started Tesla?

Brian Wheat: You got four hours? Just music in general. It wasn't just any particular band, because we drew it from anything. Once it comes, it's gotta come out. You can't keep it inside. So anything from the Beatles to the Stones, from Led Zeppelin to Aerosmith and AC/DC and so on and on.

Petra Zeitz: Do you go to see other shows a lot?

Brian Wheat: No, not anymore. When I was a kid I used to go to a lot of shows—the Scorpions, UFO and AC/DC. The only shows I've seen lately were AC/DC and I've seen about six Paul McCartney shows. He's still my favorite. I can't really go to shows in Sacramento anymore. There's always people haunting for autographs and I couldn't enjoy the show anymore. Also when you're doing as much touring as we have done, when you're not on tour you don't wanna go to a rock show anymore. Maybe it's being a bit jaded. I'd much rather stay at home and be with my wife and my dog than go out to see a rock show. Unless it's Paul McCartney, you know.

Petra Zeitz: Have you ever worked with guest musicians and who would you like to work with in that case?

Brian Wheat: Never worked with guest musicians and won't work with guest musicians. A Tesla record is a Tesla record and not Tesla with a little help from our friends. I wouldn't want to be in any other band but Tesla. I wouldn't want to play with anyone else but Jeff, Frank, Tommy & Troy. I wouldn't want somebody else to come and sing on my record. A silly dream is to play with Paul McCartney on one of his songs or something, as a personal thing for me. He's the guy who wrote "Yesterday," man! But when it comes time to do a Tesla album, it's only the five of us and no one else is allowed—not even Paul McCartney.

POP & ROCK MUSIC

A B C

ABC was founded in 1980 by singer Martin Fry in the British industrial town of Sheffield. ABC produced a line of strong and trendy love songs. In 1982, they became an international success with their bestselling album "The Lexicon of Love." In addition, the group's hi-gloss image made them pin-up favorites. They achieved Top 30 single and album success in the United States.

After several line-up changes in the mid-eighties, the band disappeared from the charts. Martin Fry and guitarist Mark White became the only remaining original members. ABC managed to re-emerge with "Be Near Me" from their "How to Be a Zillionaire" album in 1985. "When Smokey Sings" came out two years later and again was a huge hit on both sides of the Atlantic. Martin Fry had just recovered from Hodgkin's Disease. He reunited with Mark White and went on to record several more ABC albums.

In 1991, the band was signed to Parlophone Records and their newest offering "Abracadabra" was released in August. The mixture of pop, dance and soul proved to be extremely commercial.

The following conversation with Martin Fry took place in October 1991.

Petra Zeitz: Did you call your new album "Abracadabra" because you're into magic yourself?

Martin Fry: No, a magician says "Abracadabra." It's a big corny magical word and it's understood internationally. That's why I decided to call our album "Abracadabra." How could I resist a title that had an A, a B, and a C in it. Nobody quite knows what this word means though. It's like "Voilá, here comes the magic."

Petra Zeitz: "Abracadabra"

ABC

is also your first release on Parlophone Records. Is that the only difference between this one and your previous albums?

Martin Fry: We have been making records for quite a long time now. It feels like a very short time, but I mean, we formed in 1980. It's weird because I never really thought I would be making records for more than ten minutes. It took me by surprise when somebody said that I had been around for ten years. It was a bit frightening. I feel, like I'm turning into a dinosaur. But yes, our last studio album was called "Up" and it was very instantaneous, very much inspired by House Music. Some of our records are neurotic—I think, that's why you make records. This time we wanted it to be really polished and very melodramatic. "Abracadabra" is kind of elegant and relaxed as well at the same time. But it's not a complete zigzag departure from a lot of the other music we have made in the past. It's just a more cosmopolitan record, I suppose.

Petra Zeitz: Why did you change labels and sign with EMI [Parlophone]?

Martin Fry: Just an occupational hazard of still wanting to make music, you know. It was time to move on for bigger and better things really. We were on Polygram before and in 1991 our contract expired. It was good for me and the group. We consider that time as our apprenticeship and now we're just starting.

Petra Zeitz: Do you feel ac-cepted as an established act by Parlophone or are you being treated as a completely new band?

Martin Fry: It's like transferring to another soccer team, I suppose. We realized for the first time in our lives that we had a reputation or a past. It's strange having a past, because I tend to live very much in the present. That's what I'm like as a person. I like the past and I remember it well, but the music I like is contemporary and I like modern things. I have made more than five records and more than five people have bought it. In pop music, that is sort of an achievement, you know.

Petra Zeitz: How do you feel when you listen to your new material on the radio?

Martin Fry: My heart starts beating fast. I generally feel that our songs always sound like half the volume of anybody else's music. It's because I'm worried—it's my baby. I recognize it even before it comes on. I'm sure a lot of people have that. It makes you realize how international music is, in a way, or what a privilege it is to make a piece of music. We arrive in a city and hear a song we've made in the taxi. It's amazing.

Petra Zeitz: Do you remember the first song you ever wrote?

Martin Fry: Yes, it was a song called "Boomerang." I wrote it way back in 1981, I suppose. It was about being thrown out and returning. I wanted it to be like James Brown meets Frank Sinatra, but it never made it onto our first album.

It was a bit of a fraud masterpiece. We made a video as well. At the time video cameras were brand new and this guy I knew had one, so we made this video for "Boomerang," "Do As I Say" and another track called "Surrender." I have still got that video at home and it's fantastic. We thought it was so sophisticated to make a video and we played them to the record companies as well. God knows what they thought, but they must have liked us because Polygram got us to sign with them.

Petra Zeitz: Do you still enjoy making videos?

Martin Fry: You never quite learn how to do it right. It's not like driving a car where you get a couple of lessons and then you can drive a car. With videos something always goes wrong. That's the beautiful thing about it. People always have 101 ideas and everybody is trying to make the greatest moment of film history. That's when things start to get terribly wrong. So videos are still a major challenge. ABC has done about 12 videos. We started off wanting to make "Citizen Kane" and each time we made a video the idea got gradually simpler. Actually we started at around the same time as MTV, so I can just remember life before videos. We made a video for "Love Conquers All" with a director called Mark Romanac in Los Angeles. He was living there, so we went out to Los Angeles but we wanted to make the most European looking video we've ever made. That was an achievement. It looks like pages of *Interview* magazine. With "Say It," the next single, we worked with a guy called Markus Nispel who does a lot of videos of C C Music Factory. He works in a really graphic way. The video was shot in New York with a cast of thousands, just people that were hanging around.

Petra Zeitz: Do you think a bad video can spoil what was a good song?

Martin Fry: Yes, if you see a video which makes your jaw drop, something that was really badly executed or really bland, you just turn off, don't you? I don't think a great video could sell a bad song either.

Petra Zeitz: Even if it's being played to death on MTV?

Martin Fry: Like Paula Abdul, you mean? I guess you get brainwashed. There's this Bryan Adams record, "Everything I Do," which has been at number one in Britain for over 16 weeks. So by week 15 I started to think I should go out and buy three copies because I felt left out. The rest of the population must own one, you know what I mean? People just get brainwashed into buying records.

Petra Zeitz: Have you ever considered taking on a part in a feature film?

Martin Fry: We tried to make a little film once with Julian Temple, the guy who had directed *The Great Rock'n'Roll Swindle* and much later did *Absolute Beginners*. Our film was called *Mantrap* and it was about ABC traveling through Europe. We realized we actually had to talk in this film because it had a bit of dialogue. Instead of doing an on-the-road documentary, we tried to make a James Bond type of film. It put me off acting for life! It must be really hard being an actor. I have no great aspirations left.

Petra Zeitz: Many rock singers have gone into acting though. Do you dislike the mixture of making music and acting in films?

Martin Fry: No, but a lot of rock singers have got massive egos, so they have to go somewhere else outside of music to let it out. I think the best singer turned actor was Johnny Rotten [John Lydon]. He did a film called *Killer Cob* and he was great in it. Unfortunately he never made another film after that one. I suppose David Bowie and Sting have done it. So has Bob Dylan, but with him I thought: "Don't give up your day job, mate!"

Petra Zeitz: When ABC started out in the early eighties you had more musicians in the band. Since Mark White and yourself are the only remaining members, are you looking for musicians to join the band?

Martin Fry: We have never been a group like U2, you know. We have a different way of doing things. Mark and I write all the songs. We have always met with a lot of different musicians. We see making a record and writing the songs as the most important things. It's like being a film director of your own movie. You can cast people, you can use different cameras. The songs are the filmscript. So we get different musicians to work with us in the studio.

Petra Zeitz: How do you and Mark work together?

Martin Fry: I write all of the lyrics. Sometimes a song sparks from a phrase or a saying. Sometimes it starts from a bass line, from a couple of chords. Sometimes Mark writes a complete backing track. Then the music will change to accommodate the mood of the vocal. It's just a case of recording a song on a little Walkman cassette player and if it sounds good we take it into the studio.

Petra Zeitz: How long does it take you to record an ABC album?

Martin Fry: It varies, maybe three or four months. "Abracadabra" took a long time, though. We started recording it when the World Cup took place—that was a distraction and there was a very despondent mood throughout England because they didn't get to the finals. For about four months everybody was sitting in pubs, just staring into the beer. So after that, we could continue making our record again.

Petra Zeitz: You have not been on tour for a long time. Do you have no desire to play in front of an audience?

Martin Fry: I would like to tour on "Abracadabra." I have not played live for ages. Every time there was an audience ready to go and see ABC, we had either moved on to do the next record or we were successful in the States and had gone there to promote our work. But we didn't really feel the desire to tour. Live music is weird— sometimes it's really entertaining, sometimes it's terrible. I like seeing Madonna and Prince, big shows like that. You can learn a lot from playing live. You get to see who your audience is. It's like we're working in a vacuum sometimes in the studio.

Petra Zeitz: Have you noticed if there are fans who have been following your career since you started?

Martin Fry: Yes, there are some in each city. We're not like Michael Jackson but it's rewarding when people show their loyalty. They sometimes show you a photograph they took of you standing together with fans. We don't make records every week, so it's nice to have these fans. They have a very protective attitude toward the group.

Petra Zeitz: You live in London now. Did you leave your hometown Sheffield because it didn't have a music scene?

Martin Fry: Sheffield is a small city, an industrial steel city, but it does have a music scene. In the north of England people are very down to earth and quite friendly. We formed in Sheffield, the Human League is from there, Def Leppard and Joe Cocker are from Sheffield. I saw Joe Cocker last week. He's lived in Los Angeles for 25 years, but he is still a typical Sheffield, Yorkshire, character. He's a legend in Sheffield. It's a very insular city. People just entertain themselves and they're not bothered about going to London.

Petra Zeitz: Do you enjoy living in London?

Martin Fry: Yes, I like living there for the time being. London is a beautiful mess. It's built on villages, so you can drive around for ten years and suddenly you find a new part of London. In a way, London is frustrating and it's filthy and ready to collapse—not quite as much as New York is—but, it's got no more than another 30 years. London is still an inspiring place, though.

Petra Zeitz: You had a greatest hits album out last year. Were you responsible for selecting the songs, or was that done by the record company?

Martin Fry: The record was called "Absolutely ABC" and we edited it ourselves. It was strange listening to all the songs from a ten-year period. For a long time I thought we have been zigzaging and going in different directions, but when I listen to a lot of the music it all runs together. That was a nice sensation. It made me realize that you shouldn't fight what you are.

Petra Zeitz: Would you say that your music sounds very British?

Martin Fry: I guess it does in a way. It's hard for me to say because black music has been a big influence on everything we've done. We tried to make records in America and we failed. I don't think any of our records sound very American. There is something really English about what we're doing. You can't put your finger on what it is, but I think it happens because most English people are neurotic and obsessed with little details.

Petra Zeitz: How are you being viewed in America?

Martin Fry: We are successful in America, but people there tend to think we are eccentrics.

That's why they like to buy ABC records, because we're very English or very European. They like that particular quality.

Petra Zeitz: Which direction are you going to take next?

Martin Fry: I think pop music is becoming really theatrical again. I can't put my finger on it. I think the real art is to make something very melodic, something that touches people. For two years I only listened to House music or hardcore techno music. But now I like Seal and even Simon & Garfunkel songs that are really melodic. I never really know what's around the corner—I just pretend that I do in interviews.

CROWDED HOUSE

Crowded House was founded in 1985 by Neil Finn who was a former member of New Zealand's most popular rock band Split Enz. The Crowded House trio was completed by Nick Seymour on bass and Paul Hester on drums. Together they went on to become one of the most successful acts in their native Australia.

In the summer of 1986 Crowded House's debut album was released worldwide. It gained platinum and provided the band with the two US Top Ten hits "Don't Dream It's Over" and "Something So Strong."

In 1991, Crowded House released their best album to date called "Woodface," featuring for the first time Tim Finn as a fourth member. Tim, like his brother Neil, had been a member of Split Enz in the early days. Later on in 1991 Crowded House toured the United States once again, leaving behind enthusiastic audiences and raving critics.

In November 1991, Crowded House's management announced that by mutual agreement of all concerned parties, Crowded House and Tim Finn had decided to once again go their separate ways. While the band was still committed to promoting "Woodface," Tim was eager to begin work on this next solo record.

The following conversation with founder members Neil Finn and Nick Seymour took place in Bonn, Germany, in October 1991. At this stage Tim Finn was still a member of Crowded House.

Petra Zeitz: You played in Hamburg last night. How did the show go?

Neil Finn: It was great. We went on at one o'clock in the morning, so we had a lot of hours to fill in between the

Crowded House

soundcheck and the show. But it was a really good crowd. We had a full house last night and they were really up for it.

Petra Zeitz: How come Tim Finn got to join Crowded House. Where has he been all this time?

Neil Finn: Tim was a plumber and a fireman before. [*Laughs.*] Well, after Split Enz broke up he did a couple of solo albums and did a bit of promotion for those. He hung out in some of the ritzier spots of the world with his beautiful actress girl-friend. That sounds pretty good, but he was basically mis-erable most of the time. He wants to be glamorous, but he can't quite accept it.

Nick Seymour: True, I don't think that during all the time I have known him there was ever a time when he was not com-plaining about something. It's still going on. This morning we woke up in the bus and the only thing I could hear was Tim com-plaining about how little sleep he had gotten the whole night.

Neil Finn: He said that 50 times! I was very broken too but you have to go with it. At least we had time to rest. We're bitchin' about Tim now. We're deep into the tour, you see, and people's little foibles come to the surface and tend to be amplified and exaggerated.

Petra Zeitz: Do you get on each other's nerves when a tour gets too long?

Nick Seymour: You have to have a lot of tolerance. It's the nature of being a musician. It comes with the job. It's one of the things that stopped a lot of the musicians that I knew when I was around 18. I'm 32 now and a lot of those guys are no longer in the business. They won't be musicians anymore because of the lifestyle, not because of the music. They still have the hunger and the desire to make music and are still as passionate as ever, but they just can't tolerate being at such close quarters with other creative people. It's quite a compromising lifestyle, but you do get the release when you perform. You can't trade anything with how good a show can be when all the musicians are feeling the same way.

Petra Zeitz: Is Crowded House more a live act than a band whose records one buys?

Nick Seymour: I would think so. That's a very large part of appreciating the wholeness of Crowded House. Just listening to our records is not really getting the whole picture of what we are all about by any stretch of the imagination. Would it be 50 percent, do you think?

Neil Finn: Now at the moment it's everything because that's what we're doing. Live music is where our potential shows through at the greatest level. Some people that like us live have problems with our records, because they seem too crafted to them, a little too neat and orderly. We criticize ourselves for the same things. It's very difficult to get live energy onto a record, but what we're aiming at is evident on stage. We can be the best band in the world on any given night and we have been.

Nick Seymour: What you strive for, too, is to be able to one day make an album that actually represents the spirit and the joy of playing live together. It's a mystery, but we work towards that point and we will get there someday.

Petra Zeitz: You mentioned before that you think it's strange that people who do not speak English listen to your music. Do you feel your audience actually pays attention to what you say in your songs when you're performing them?

Neil Finn: I think so, yes. Certain lyrics seem to bring a response, particularly in English-speaking countries where people are able to catch every phrase. I feel that there is a connection.

Petra Zeitz: Your songs sometimes have really intelligent lyrics. How much importance do you put on the meaning of the words?

Neil Finn: The words are important to me for sure, they're almost 50 percent of the song. Well, not quite because I think a song is lost without a good melody, but particularly in recent times I have been very concerned with what I am singing. I have to get behind it to deliver it with some feeling. There is enough rubbish out there in the lyric department without me contributing more to it. Some songs are better than others. Some of my lyrics I feel dissatisfied with, and others I feel are very well rounded. It doesn't so much matter to me if they make sense, but that they contain interesting imagery and that they set your mind going.

Petra Zeitz: What prompted you to write the song "Chocolate Cake" ["Woodface" album] which has a really biting humor.

Neil Finn: It came from a conversation that Tim and I had about all these weird and wonderful things we had seen. It's a worldwide thing that wasn't especially aimed at America, although people came to think that. There is a line in the song that mentions America, but it's just a whole cast of characters. Tim told me a story about this woman he had seen in a New York restaurant, eating a huge meal and then turning to her husband saying: "I don't know, honey, another piece of chocolate cake or the cheque?" It sounded like a good line because it seemed to sum up that concept of consuming and wanting more sugar all the time. There were also all sorts of headlines in the *National Enquirer* that popped up, and characters that seemed to be particularly over the top.

Petra Zeitz: There was also the Tammy Faye Bakker reference.

Neil Finn: She's the wife of a television preacher called Jim Bakker who was arrested for fraud. He also had a sexual liaison with his secretary. Tammy is an overly made-up woman, like a hysterical kind of cartoon character. She came on TV with her mascara running all the time, pleading her husband's innocence. But the way she looks, she embodies the loss of reality. She just looks bizarre. So she cropped up in the song, too.

Petra Zeitz: Where do you feel most inspired to write your songs?

Neil Finn: At home. I've always thought that I would love to get to the point where I'm writing on the road, but it always seems very difficult. You're too much in a transitory state of mind all the time. You can get general ideas but it's very difficult to finish them up on the road.

Petra Zeitz: Nick, you did the artwork for all Crowded House albums. Are you an artist as well as a musician?

Nick Seymour: I would like to think I am. I'm most happy when I'm doing that.

Neil Finn: Compared to the average musician, he's an artist.

Nick Seymour: I've done all the album covers so far. I'm trained as a printmaker, so I did silkscreening and stuff like that at art school. I've been leaning towards the graphic side of fine arts, as supposed to actually being a painter of canvas. I've got a lot of work at home and I've had a couple of small shows. Some of these exhibitions have been on the premise that I'm a celebrity because I'm in a band. One day I would like to have an exhibition of work that was on my own merit. You never know, a young painter is 40 years old and that's a *young* painter. It takes you most of your life being able to get your language down, so that you don't even have to think of making pictures anymore. You just make a couple of marks and people tell you you're a genius.

Petra Zeitz: Why do you prefer to record in America?

Nick Seymour: It's easier service-wise. There are rows of experts around who can come in at a moment's notice and do anything you want. The mechanics of recording are much easier.

Petra Zeitz: Is it true that you left Australia to live in the States?

Nick Seymour: We don't actually live in America, although everybody thinks we do. We have recorded there a fair bit, but we have never lived there properly. We went to America to start the first Crowded House record. We live in Melbourne, Australia. At the moment we haven't chosen to live anywhere else, but there are disadvantages to where we live. When we're out of sight we're out of mind to some extent. We don't feel as connected to the way things are happening sometimes.

Petra Zeitz: But Australia has a well functioning music scene as well, doesn't it?

Neil Finn: Of course it does, but when you're there you just lose touch a little bit. It's very easy to become apathetic when you're in Australia because the lifestyle is very good. You can get a bit too relaxed.

Nick Seymour: Mind you, there's a lot of Australian observation of the northern hemisphere, of things that go on in the northern hemisphere. All the literature, the movies and the magazines from the northern hemisphere seem to make it to Australia. So, because of their isolation factor, Australians seem to observe rather than participate. It's a very interesting place to live because of that.

Petra Zeitz: Well, it's also very beautiful . . .

Nick Seymour: Aside from that, it is! Some parts are very beautiful and some parts are extremely boring. The suburbs of the cities are pretty dull. In some places you can drive a good 500 miles and the landscape doesn't change. It has got a certain endlessness to it, a feeling of neverending space. Some people feel very uneasy with that. There is a certain unease running through the Australians' psyche. They are displaced Europeans who were used to small and crowded places. They got into this big, wide land and they feel a little bit uneasy.

Petra Zeitz: But your generation was born in Australia. Do you feel uneasy, too?

Neil Finn: There's a strange melancholy that sets in sometimes on certain days.

Nick Seymour: It's funny. I was born and grew up in Australia and I actually miss the desire to go into the bush and hang out. Europe is so overpopulated that it doesn't have as much wilderness, but I don't mind not having it. In Australia you can really get away from other people and just be surrounded by wildlife and the sounds of birds. There are also stretches of primeval nothingness, just great sandy deserts. But when it rains in the desert, the next day things will have grown overnight. It's pretty amazing. Australia does have a really bright, fresh light source. Australia is the oldest continent in the world, and yet the light, the rock surface and the bush looks fresh all the time compared to American deserts which always have a dustiness. The weather elements and the pollution have jaded the landscape.

Petra Zeitz: Since you mentioned pollution: People are worried about the hole in the ozone layer. How did that change the Australian lifestyle?

Neil Finn: Well, it is a factor. In the last few years the ultraviolet levels have doubled during the time the hole in the ozone layer has been over the place we live in. It only happens close to Christmas, in November, I think. But it's only a three to four week period. People in Australia have to be mindful of the sun all the time. In the northern hemisphere there's a lot more stuff in the atmosphere, whether it's man-made or whether it's a natural thing.

So it's always very intense out in the sun and people with pale skin like us have to be really careful anyway. It's not particularly worse because of the ozone layer, but people are more conscientious about putting sunsreen and hats on.

Nick Seymour: I think that because you take the brightness of the sun for granted you don't purposely go out to get a suntan, like the way Americans or Europeans do. I have friends in London who are just blown away by the fact that the sun shines; they are lying out there trying to change their skin tone. Australians probably used to be a lot more like that than they are nowadays, in the sense that this continent does have the highest rate of skin cancer in the world. But the bottom line is Neil and I are musicians and musicians don't get suntans. We just stay in little rooms with air conditioning and no windows.

Neil Finn: Exactly! [*Laughs.*]

DNA

"Taste This" was the debut album by re-mix specialists Neal Slateford and Nicholas Batt. As DNA they had become established figures in the world of dance music by releasing a re-mix of Suzanne Vega's "Tom's Diner." Five million copies sold resulted in commissioned work for several other artists, including Dave Stewart and Candy Dulfer. In 1992, DNA released "Taste This," a collection of 11 dance floor tracks in several different styles. They had another successful single with the up-beat number "Can You Handle It?," originally a hit for Sharon Redd in 1981.

Neal and Nicholas first met in a club in their hometown Bath, in western England. Nick worked as a soundmixer for live bands and Neal was a local DJ. They decided to form a re-mix and production team. "Tom's Diner" and "La Serenissima" were the first two tracks they produced.

DNA are more known for their production work than for their own material. The following interview—one of the first they ever granted—took place in February 1992, while the duo was promoting "Taste This."

Petra Zeitz: How did you get together as a production and re-mix team?

Nick Batt: We both worked at the same nightclub. I worked there four or five nights a week and Neal was a DJ on Friday nights. I didn't actually work on Friday nights for a long time. So we finally met. Being a DJ, Neal was interested in getting into doing some remixing, trying out a few ideas. I had a computer and a sampler at home. I had the equipment to do that.

Neal Slateford: That's it really. I said: "Do you fancy trying out some ideas" and he said yes. And then immediately the first thing we ever did was a

DNA

worldwide hit single. It was quite a surprise.

Petra Zeitz: Why did you choose Suzanne Vega's song "Tom's Diner" to be your first project?

Nick Batt: Because it was there! It was a cappella and we thought we could do something with it.

Neal Slateford: I had the original record because I do like Suzanne Vega anyway. I was just playing it in the car and it's got this really strong rhythm in it, but there was no music. So, I thought, we could put a beat under it and it just worked very well. It's one of those things, one of those lucky records that comes along once every couple of years.

Petra Zeitz: How did Suzanne Vega react to what you had done to her song?

Nick Batt: She laughed apparently when she heard it for the first time. Then she allowed us to put it out. I don't think she expected it to be her biggest ever record, which it was.

You have to ask her what she thinks about that. We worked with her again on the album. We co-wrote a track with her called "Saltwater."

Neal Slateford: We met her a couple of times and we do get on. We have some fun together. She's come to our hometown and we have been to hers. We went over for tea and we get on fine. We can just phone her up and offer to let her listen to our tapes.

Petra Zeitz: Is your album a collection of previously produced tracks or were all the songs recorded specifically for "Taste This"?

Nick Batt: No, a couple of older tracks are on there because the record company felt they would sell the album. The rest of them were written specifically for the album—in a hurry. It's our first record and it all happened rather spontaneously because we're not songwriters normally.

Petra Zeitz: How do you compose your songs?

Neal Slateford: We don't write like normal people. Lyrics are always last because we're crap at writing them. We approach it the same way we would approach a re-mix: we just shove down loads of ideas, go back to it a couple of hours later, pick up the ones that sound good, throw the rest away and get a singer involved. We don't sit there with a guitar and work out chords.

Nick Batt: We tend to start with a mood or a groove, or a feeling and then build up from there, arrange it into a song-form type of shape. We come up with the melodies ourselves or we work closely with a singer. We may well develop a method in the future, but at the moment it's very haphazard. One of the tracks came very quickly. I just sat there and played a verse, a chorus and a bridge and thought: "Uhm, there's a verse, a chorus and a bridge—fine." I didn't have the melody or the lyrics, but I had an idea. That's about the most traditional we got, I think.

Petra Zeitz: Are lyrics important in dance music?

Nick Batt: Not fantastically. If we are working with a singer who's coming up with some lyrics, we would make sure that they're not offensive. Or we write them ourselves in which case it's total gibberish. Obviously, in other forms of music the lyrics are the main feature, but they're not very important in dance music.

Neal Slateford: If a rapper came in wanting to do a rap about the Ku Klux Klan, we'd probably say no but within reason we let them do what they like.

Petra Zeitz: Do you play any instruments?

Nick Batt: I play a bit of keyboards and a bit of guitar. And I'm trying to learn the drums.

Petra Zeitz: How is a re-mix actually done when you have a finished record by another artist and want to re-mix it?

Nick Batt: You get the master tapes. (We didn't need it for "Tom's Diner" because that was a cappella.) Normally the record companies send us a tape and ask us if we are interested in doing a re-mix of it. We say yes or no. When we say yes, they send us a copy of the master tape, a 24-track or whatever it's on.

Neal Slateford: We then whack it all up on the desk. We obviously keep the vocals and if there's anything else that we like musically we keep that, too. Usually we end up throwing 90 percent of it out and starting again just re-writing. We usually start off with the beats, try different breaks and loops, you know, just to get a feel for it. Then we do a bass line, and shove other stuff in.

Nick Batt: The thing with the computer is that you can just keep filling it up. You can play the length of an entire song on a bass line, switch it off, do another whole one and then find the bits that worked the best. You can join them all up. The computer is very flexible.

Petra Zeitz: Have you turned down any offers for re-mixes yet?

Nick Batt: Loads! We may need the work, but we don't need it that badly. When "Tom's Diner" first came out, we were getting forty or fifty tapes a week. It was ridiculous. We turned down Engelbert Humperdinck, I think. We won't do it just for the sake of it.

Neal Slateford: When people ask us to do these silly things, we think: "Why would they want a dance mix on that? And why do they think that we would even think about doing it?" I mean, what's the matter with those people? If we don't like the track, we turn it down. There have been one or two instances where we have just done it because they offered us such a big amount of money. It would have been stupid to turn it down, but in the main, we try to do stuff that we like. We've turned down Erasure and we turned down James Brown because it wasn't very good. We turn down a lot of stuff, I mean, more than we actually do.

Petra Zeitz: Are there any singers you particularly would like to work with?

Neal Slateford: Well, Chaka Khan, Bette Midler—I would like to do a dance record with Bette Midler—the Bee Gees. Those are the singers, but I would also like to work with some of the American hiphop producers, Public Enemy and that kind of stuff. That is a diverse selection for you, isn't it?

Petra Zeitz: Do you get to work with the original artists when your're doing a re-mix of their song?

Neal Slateford: No, not usually. You just get the tape. Sometimes they might ring up and say: "I love this guitar solo, please leave it alone," but usually they just send you the tape and let you get on with it.

Petra Zeitz: What kind of music do you listen to for pleasure?

Neal Slateford: We don't like music.

Nick Batt: We both have got a very broad musical taste. I like all sorts of music.

Neal Slateford: I'm more into the dance music than he is. I do like a lot of hiphop, but I had a Suzanne Vega album. So there you go.

Petra Zeitz: What would you predict is going to be the next big thing in dance music?

Neal Slateford: If I knew that I would own a record company. I wouldn't be just mixing. The real big thing in dance music in England at the moment is disco. There's a real disco revival. People are having big disco nights in London. I think it's got something to do with the backlash against the techno thing, which is very sparse. For as many people who love that sort of music there's also people who don't. I think they're fighting back in England.

Petra Zeitz: What is the American dance music scene like compared to what is going on in England at the moment?

Neal Slateford: In America they are a lot more broad-minded in the way they compile their dance charts. In England the dance charts are based on what's being played in a small amount of black music clubs so you get a lot of soul or hiphop. In America you can have all that stuff, but they'll also put something like Jesus Jones or EMF in the same charts. That's quite good.

Petra Zeitz: Do the two of you plan to stay in the background or do you want to present yourself as pop stars now?

Nick Batt: No, that's not what we do. We're quite happy the way we are. This is our first coming-out if you like. We prefer to stay roughly where we are. Being a pop star can be very distracting from making music. This interview is our concession to EMI's worry that we haven't got an image.

Petra Zeitz: Are you being pushed to have an image?

Nick Batt: Yes, we are pushed to have an image. They can be important for album sales, so we're told.

Petra Zeitz: Can your music be reproduced on stage?

Nick Batt: I'm sure it could be, but it wouldn't be very easy. There are six different singers on the album and that's our repertoire of songs, so it wouldn't be possible to do a show without a great deal of expense and coordination. It's very unlikely. I would like the idea of it, but it's not really feasible at the moment.

JULIAN LENNON

John Charles Julian Lennon was born at Shefton General Hospital, Liverpool, on April 8, 1963. For both his parents, John and Cynthia Lennon, those were heady days indeed. Only three weeks before Julian's birth, The Beatles had hit the number one position on the British charts. An astonishing trail of record-breaking events that was to catapult John Lennon and The Beatles into international fame had begun.

For Julian, his infancy and childhood was spent in transit. Since Liverpool could not contain the Beatles, Julian and his parents moved to London when he was a year old. Later on in 1964, John Lennon bought a house in Weybridge, Surrey.

Julian was only five years old when John and Cynthia were divorced. The following spring John married Yoko Ono, and Julian moved back to Cheshire to live with his mother. He went to school in Hoylake where he met another pupil who shared his enthusiasm for old rock'n'roll. Together Julian and Justin Clayton formed a schoolboy group.

Julian kept in touch with his father and actually made a guest appearance on John Lennon's "Walls and Bridges" album in 1974.

By the time Julian was 17, he and Justin had jammed around with other musicians. Then the news shook the world on December 8, 1980, that John Lennon had been murdered outside his New York home. It struck a deep and bitter blow inside Julian. Within two days, he was on a plane to New York where he spent several weeks with Yoko and his half-brother Sean. Not surprisingly, Julian sought refuge in music.

During 1981 and 1982 he gathered around him a commune of musicians. Now living

Julian Lennon

in a London flat, Julian contemplated the route his music should take. In 1984 his debut album "Valotte" was released and was an immediate worldwide success. It was even nominated for a prestigious Grammy Award. Julian followed his sudden success by going on tour with his new band, including his old friend Justin Clayton with whom he had co-written much of his material.

Despite the initial success, a second album, "The Secret Value of Daydreaming," failed to meet commercial expectations and Julian's 1989 offering, "Mr. Jordan," flopped badly. He continued to go on tour, establishing an international fan base, but public interest seemed to be more in his name than in his music. Tired of discussing his father with the press, Julian moved to Los Angeles and tried to make a name for himself.

In 1991 he burst back onto the music scene with a mature and interesting album, "Help Yourself." The single "Saltwater" gave him his first UK top ten hit in seven years.

The following interview with Julian Lennon took place in March 1992. Much to Julian's relief I did not discuss his father nor other family issues. This is a conversation with a successful and honest young man talking about his music.

Petra Zeitz: In one of your new songs you say "In your life you must help yourself 'cause there's no one else." Did you write this from your own experiences?

Julian Lennon: Very much so. I felt in the past that I had relied on too many people and their opinions. I generally found that I was regretting a lot of things because of that. So in order to achieve what I wanted to achieve in life, whether it be on a personal level or a career level, I had to take charge and help myself.

Petra Zeitz: Do you learn a lot about yourself by writing songs?

Julian Lennon: Yes, especially with this album "Help Yourself." It was very much a self-help therapy, where you relieve a lot of your pressures in life, a lot of tension or problems, and you put it into your music and lyrics. Later on, once you've finished that, you look back at what you've done and realize that, in reflection, you have made some good changes in life. So yes, it's very good that way.

Petra Zeitz: Are you ever

worried about revealing too much of yourself in a song?

Julian Lennon: Sometimes, but I think most people can relate to what I say, to a lot of stuff that I write, and if that in some way can help them through their own lives and their own problems, then it's fine to do that. I think we all feel the same way sometimes.

Petra Zeitz: Sometimes yes, but I don't always want other people to know what I feel.

Julian Lennon: Well yes, but obviously it doesn't get too detailed. It's just an expression and it's not the fine print at the bottom.

Petra Zeitz: You've lived in New York for some time and now you're based in Los Angeles. Do you feel at home in the Unites States, or are you there for working reasons?

Julian Lennon: On this earth I feel so much like a gypsy that everywhere that I have lived so far I didn't really feel at home. I have such a keen interest and intrigue in the rest of the world that I constantly travel. I constantly visit and stay in other places. So I don't really have a foundation as such. Although I have a house and live in LA, and I go and stay there when I'm not working and even when I'm

working, it doesn't feel very concrete to me. It doesn't feel that stable. I'm already thinking of moving on.

Petra Zeitz: Do you have to go to exotic places to be able to write songs? I know your first album was written in France and the third one was written in Switzerland.

Julian Lennon: No, my songs can be written anywhere. "Help Yourself" was written in a grey room, half the size of this, overlooking a car park in Los Angeles. So it doesn't matter where you are.

Petra Zeitz: Could you see yourself moving back to England then?

Julian Lennon: No, because I've lived there for 20 years of my life already and the world is a big place. I know what Britain is. Now I know what America is and it's time to move on. There are too many other experiences in life for me just to sit around in one place. Life is for living, exploring and challenging. I would probably go crazy if I had to stay in one place.

Petra Zeitz: Where are you planning to go?

Julian Lennon: My next thought at the moment is Australia. I've had very, very pleasant experiences in Australia.

It's a wonderful country. The weather is wonderful. The people are lovely over there. It's a certain lack of aggression and pressure in Australia which I've never felt anywhere else in this world. Australians tend to work hard and play hard. They enjoy life to the extreme. I think the rest of the world tends to get a little too caught up in their problems, instead of just looking at them, resolving them and then moving on. And again I just had a very good time. I think it's a lovely country. I'm always on the move. I get to see other countries, but as a base, as somewhere to live, Australia is definitely a possibility for the future.

Petra Zeitz: Would you want to get involved in the music scene over there too?

Julian Lennon: Yes, sure! Australia's a lot more laid back in the music scene as well because there are only 16 million people on the whole continent. In England, there's 16 million in London itself! So workwise things are a lot less pressured, a lot more laid back. It gives you more of a chance to be heard.

Petra Zeitz: Musicians around you have been with you right from the start. Are you a very close unit now?

Julian Lennon: Well, there's only one guy, Justin Clayton, who I've known as a good friend for 17 years now and who I've been writing with for that time too. There isn't a band as such. It's pointless having a band when I'm a solo artist. I work with Justin all the time, but writing only happens on and off. So to keep a whole band paid and looked after is well out of my reach. Also, other people in bands want to move on and do other stuff. You don't want to sit around waiting for me all the time, it's boring.

Petra Zeitz: Are you planning any further tours?

Julian Lennon: Yes, at some stage, no plans yet though. I've been on the promotional road for eight months now and I haven't even started in America. What I'm trying to do is build a good foundation everywhere so that people know I'm still around and that I'm not a flash in the pan and I will be here for many, many years to come. I still have a lot of that to do, to re-establish myself, to build a foundation again with the public. After I feel satisfied in doing that, then I might be playing live.

Petra Zeitz: Each one of your four albums sounds very different from the others. Do you want to keep changing your sound or have you found your ideal style on "Help Yourself"?

Julian Lennon: With every new record you do, you find another element of what comes out of you. But I find it very, very boring to just write the same style of music over and over again. I like to be creative and as diverse as possible. I have so many influences in life and musically I have a very collective taste which ranges from classical to jazz. I couldn't imagine sitting down and writing the same song for the rest of my life, which a lot of people do.

Petra Zeitz: On the "Mr. Jordan" album your singing voice was very different. Is all that intentional?

Julian Lennon: Sure, it has to be! What I said about writing the same song also goes for singing in the same style.

Petra Zeitz: You have used three different producers on the four albums you did. Did they have an influence on your style?

Julian Lennon: Especially with the last one. Bob Ezrin had a lot of influence on that. Working with different producers is more of a learning and growing process. Not everybody can find their own niche, but I've

learned a lot from Phil Ramone, from Pat Leonard, from Bob Ezrin—all the producers—and it's enough to know exactly what I want now. More than likely I will produce the next album myself.

Petra Zeitz: Have you sat in the producer's chair before?

Julian Lennon: All the albums I've done I co-produced, even though it didn't say so on the covers. Obviously because my involvement is 100 percent, a lot of my creative ideas go into it. The first chance to produce on my own I had with "Help Yourself" when I took two potential singles and went back in the studio to re-mix them and replay some things. Unfortunately I don't know whether everybody is going to get to hear that, but definitely for the first re-launch release in America the song "Help Yourself" is a completely different version which I did myself. I'm very happy about it and I'm already itching to go back in the studio to do some more stuff. The re-mixes that I have done, which are for "Help Yourself" and "Get a Life," are a lot more aggressive than the work on the album. I've enjoyed that more than what's on the album because it has a different edge.

That's why I'm looking forward to producing the next one.

Petra Zeitz: Doesn't remixing songs give you the feeling of never finishing the songs?

Julian Lennon: No, it's intuition. You instinctively know when the song doesn't need anything else. But it's good to have a chance to do remixes just to have alternative versions. You normally leave doing the remix to somebody else, but I've decided to try it myself. To play around with the songs I have written is like a second chance which is a lot of fun.

Petra Zeitz: Do you feel comfortable in the studio?

Julian Lennon: Yes. It gets very tiring at times, not knowing whether you've made the right decision or not, coming back and forth and trying different things. To put down good music that has sincerity, honesty and depth in it takes time. It takes time to nurture all those things, to let them grow naturally.

Petra Zeitz: You play all kinds of musical instruments. What are you best at?

Julian Lennon: I mainly write on piano and guitar.

That's what I'm best at.

Petra Zeitz: I found an old interview where you said you didn't want to voice your political opinions. On "Help Yourself" there are some political songs like "Imaginary Lines" and "Keep the People Working." Has your attitude changed in that sense?

Julian Lennon: Well, before I was afraid, purely because of the inevitable comparisons and criticism from the past. But now, I've reached a point in my life where I really don't care what other people think about what I do. First and foremost it's got to be what makes me happy, and if that means speaking about political issues or talking about environmental issues or any other issues, then I'm going to do it. The response so far has been very good. It has only been my first effort. It's been a good response and leads me to believe that this is probably what I'll do a lot more of in the future.

Petra Zeitz: Was there a particular incident that prompted you to write "Imaginary Lines"?

Julian Lennon: There was this writer that I have been working with, a guy called Anthony Moore, who is a lyricist. We both took a trip from Los Angeles down to Mexico for the weekend to get away and just to sit down and think about some ideas. On the way, crossing the

American–Mexican border, we were horrified to see how many thousands of people basically stood there 24 hours a day, dreaming and looking at America, and wishing that they could be there. Obviously California was originally Mexican land, before it was taken away from them. California is very rich and fruitful and Mexico isn't, so that's very unfair. "Imaginary Lines" was initially written about that, but refers not only to physical borders, but also to mental borders that we have to confront all the time. This is not a free world by any means.

Petra Zeitz: Do you support any environmental groups?

Julian Lennon: I'm getting involved in them. I did some work for Greenpeace while I was out in Australia, and a couple of other things. Slowly but surely. I don't like preaching what to do, but I think it's very important to keep up the awareness of problems we're facing. I feel a lot of people, including myself, tend to get complacent about problems. Unless they are resolved, they are just gonna get worse, and we're not going to have anything left.

Petra Zeitz: Do you get time to write new songs when you're out to promote an album?

Julian Lennon: No, I've been on the road for seven months, I'm doing 12 to 16 interviews a day. It's kind of impossible to even try eating lunch, never mind writing other songs.

Petra Zeitz: Does all this promotion work bother you?

Julian Lennon: No, again if you believe in what you do and in your project, then you do whatever it takes.

Petra Zeitz: You've done four albums in the space of eight years. Is it difficult for you to get back into the business each time?

Julian Lennon: It's always a bit of a challenge, but again, I want stuff to be sincere and honest and meaningful, all that stuff and it takes time. When you finish an album, which could take six months to a year to do and then you're on a promotional tour for God knows how many months. Then maybe you have a couple of weeks off or you start rehearsing for a tour. Then you go on tour for six months to a year, you take a month or two off if you can, then you start considering sitting down to write for the next album. So if you just don't particularly care that much about what the song says, then you can write music and throw it out quickly. I can do that, but I don't want to.

Petra Zeitz: How did you come to sing a duet with Paul Buchanan ["The Other Side of Town" on the album "Help Yourself"] of the Blue Nile?

Julian Lennon: I heard the Blue Nile's "Hats" album two years ago and I flipped! I said, "This is the best thing I've ever heard!" Paul was on a plane to Los Angeles and we were able to meet. There are a lot of experiences in life that run parallel for he and I as far as relationships and things like that go. There's a lot of pain and it was very easy for us to sit down and talk about that stuff. "The Other Side of Town," the song we wrote together, is probably my favorite song of all the work I've done so far. Paul and I remain great friends. He is doing another album with the Blue Nile and I will probably do some work with him on that.

Petra Zeitz: A lot of your songs are written in collaboration with friends and other writers. Is it easier for you to work with a partner?

Julian Lennon: Not always. Sometimes it happens out of a desire to work with other people, sometimes it was out of a need, especially with Anthony Moore, because "Help Yourself" was the first time that I wanted to write about different issues in life. Anthony Moore had great experience as a writer and as a lyricist. I just wanted to see what somebody else's perception of what I saw was. It was very much a learning process. I wanted to work with Paul Buchanan out of a desire because I think he's great. It's nice working with other people. Again, being a solo artist, I can sit in my room for days and years writing my own stuff. But to meet other people that are very interesting, that I have a curiosity about, that I can sit down and have a lot to talk about with, and to finally write songs from that is very exciting.

Petra Zeitz: Your albums contain many ballads, but on stage you're more of a rock'n'roller. Do you have a preference?

Julian Lennon: The thing with albums is that you can only put so much emotion on them. When you play live it's a different situation. You have a lot more chance to show what the song is all about. Obviously with an audience right in front of you, you get instant reaction from them. Generally when I sit at home and write on the piano,

I write a lot of ballads, but when you're standing on stage and you have five people behind you playing great music, you don't want to sit there and sing a quiet ballad. It's not that I have turned my back on harder-edged music, and for the next album I would like to consider doing a lot more raw material, not necessarily harder punching, but a lot more raw and in your face. I love my last album to death, but it's very produced. It's very smooth all the way around. I would like to bring a little bit of a raw element back into it.

Petra Zeitz: You recorded a few songs for soundtracks in the past. Do you want to expand that element of your songwriting?

Julian Lennon: I've done one or two things, but there's nothing I can feel really proud of. I write a lot of classically oriented music from time to time. I feel that some of the music I do is very visual, you can close your eyes and picture many things. So it is a definite consideration for the future, if and when I can find the time, to do a soundtrack. Again once I feel I have established myself enough and have a good foundation, I can take two months off and write a film score or write other things.

MARILLION

This British rock band came into being as Silmarillion in 1979, its name being inspired by J.R.R. Tolkien's book of the same title.

The band emerged from Aylesbury where their Scottish lead singer Fish had gone to build a career for himself in the rock business. The band quickly shortened their name to Marillion and their local following started to grow due to their extraordinary live shows. Marillion's first album, called "Script for a Jester's Tear," was a chart success in the UK and provided the band with a couple of hit singles. It was their fourth album "Misplaced Childhood" that moved them into the top league of British rock acts. It contained the single "Kayleigh," which became a worldwide success and has now earned the "classic rock" status.

Marillion became a major international concert attraction with Fish's charismatic theatrical appearances earning them a good reputation. After the release of "Kayleigh" Marillion's penetration of the United States market remained limited, but they continued to have chartbreaking albums in the UK and in most other territories.

After long-standing musical and personal differences, Fish left the band and went back to Scotland to pursue a solo career from there. He was replaced by singer Steve Hogarth, who lacked Fish's theatrical appearance, but actually had a much better voice than his predecessor. Hogarth premiered with Marillion on the 1989 album "Season's End." The band then toured the United States, Canada, Brazil, and Europe and released a documentary film on video entitled "From Stoke Row to Ipanema." In 1991 Christopher Neil produced their album

Marillion

"Holidays in Eden" which further established Steve Hogarth as Marillion's new front man.

The following conversation with Pete Trewavas (bass/vocals) took place backstage in Düsseldorf, Germany, during Marillion's 1991 world tour.

Petra Zeitz: What did the band do between "Season's End" and the latest album "Holidays in Eden"?

Pete Trewavas: We toured with "Season's End" for quite a long time. We finished in Spring 1990, and then we spent six months writing "Holidays in Eden." Basically we started from scratch writing an album as a five piece again. With "Season's End," Steve (Hogarth) brought along songs that he had, and we brought along a lot of music that we had already written as a four piece after Fish left. So when we wrote "Season's End" it was quite an easy process, but with "Holidays in Eden" we had to learn how to write as a five piece group together. Steve is a keyboard player as well as Mark (Kelly), so they were very aware of not treading on each other's toes. Steve consciously didn't want to come along with a song and say, "I want you to play this and I want you to play that" because that's a way we have never worked together. So we took a while to find our feet and that's probably why it took so long to write the album. But we stuck to our guns because we didn't want to record anything before we thought we had enough songs that had a good enough quality. That took, as I said, six months. Then we spent two months recording the album and finished it in March 1991. Since then we have been promoting singles and doing TV shows, that kind of thing. We started touring in September, toured around England and this is our third gig in Europe.

Petra Zeitz: How did you de-

cide on Christopher Neil to produce "Holidays in Eden," instead of producing it yourself?

Pete Trewavas: We hadn't worked with him before, but he approached us or we approached him—I can't remember now—to do the "Season's End" album. But at the time we felt that having a new singer was enough of a change. We felt that if we changed producers as well, the style of the music could change a little bit too much. So we decided to produce "Season's End" ourselves. But we used an engineer called Nick Davis who's worked with Chris Neil a lot in the past. Finally, when we came to do this album, we found we had some quite commercial songs and we thought of Chris Neil as a producer again. His son is actually a big fan of Marillion, so Chris knows the material. He also wanted to do more rock stuff than he has in the past. He's done an awful lot of pop music, but he's been producing for about 20 years, so he's done everything from reggae to Sheena Easton to Mike and the Mechanics.

Petra Zeitz: Weren't you worried that he would put too much of a pop feeling into your music?

Pete Trewavas: Yes and no.

Obviously whenever we suggested that to anybody they said: "Oh dear, you're gonna be selling out," but we started off and worked with Chris for a few days. And he was really into the more album side of the songs as well as the commercial side. He brought a lot of good things to the album. He helped us with the first track, "Splintering Heart." That song was very much on one level until Chris came along and showed us the way to go. His arranging abilities are much better than ours in a lot of ways. He knows how to bring a song out, whereas we tend to bury it under complicated musicianship which can sometimes hinder a song. It just depends what you're into.

Petra Zeitz: Where did the title "Holidays in Eden" come from?

Pete Trewavas: That came from a lyric that was written for us by a chap called John Helmer who wrote half of the lyrics on the "Season's End" album. When we came to do the "Holidays in Eden" album, that was one of the first lyrics he gave us and probably the best lyric he presented to us in the whole session. It's supposed to be a relatively true story about this terribly nice young lady who goes away on holiday to South Africa or South America, somewhere like that, and gets completely into the culture. She goes a bit wild and crazy and comes to a stage where she doesn't really want to come home. But when she does get home, she's changed so much that she can't relate to her old life and her friends can't relate to her. She just wishes she's back on holiday. That lyric certainly appealed to us, hence the title track. We can relate to it because we spend a lot of time traveling around the world. It can be hard to get back to normal life—whatever normal life is. I'm not sure about that these days. I guess everybody's idea of normality is quite different.

Petra Zeitz: When Marillion started out you had a cult following. Do you know if the same people that supported you then still come to see you now?

Pete Trewavas: We do see some of the same old faces. We're very lucky because we had a cult following for a long time. I think because we play a lot live we built up this reputation of being a live band which has done us a lot of good. These days, we're getting a lot of new people interested in the group. Unless you see a group live, you don't really understand what the group is about. There are an awful lot of preconceived ideas. We're featured in some of the heavy metal magazines and people think we're a heavy metal band. Other people think we're boring old hippies, they've heard that we sound like Genesis which we don't. There are so many different ideas that people have in their minds about what we are that I think it's good for people to give us a chance live. Through playing a lot live, that was really the way the band broke, and because of that we have managed to keep our following. What's great about that, from our point of view, is that it means that we haven't got the record company breathing down our necks saying, "Come on boys, we need the next single!" They know we're an album band and we sell on the strength of our live reputation far more than on our last single success.

Petra Zeitz: When did you drop the name Silmarillion?

Pete Trewavas: That must have been dropped in about 1981, I think, or even 1980. Silmarillion is the title of a book by J.R.R. Tolkien. We're back to the old hippie stuff again! I think the story had something to do with a brilliant jewel, but I don't really know to be honest. I haven't read the book because I heard it is kind of boring, but the name appealed to the people in the band at the time. When I joined which was in 1982, the band was just called Marillion. The name seems to have worked.

Petra Zeitz: Could you see a time where people don't expect you to include "Kayleigh" in your stage show?

Pete Trewavas: I don't know actually. People like the song and I don't mind playing it. It's part of our history and it's something that we're very proud of. We are very proud that we had this success a few years ago, but also, having said that, we're very proud of what's happening now. Our following is getting bigger again. Obviously when Fish left the band, things seemed a bit dice for a while. We were very confident about what we were doing, but we had to convince the audiences that Marillion wasn't just carrying on because we had mortgages to pay. The band actually meant something to us. People often ask how long we think we can sustain our career with Marillion, and I really think the band can really go on until we think we have run out of things to say—musically and lyrically. But we have an awful lot going for us at the moment. Since Steve joined it's like a new band.

Petra Zeitz: Is it difficult for Steve Hogarth to sing the older material that people remember being performed by Fish before?

Pete Trewavas: No. I mean it can be; I know what you're saying. We never asked Steve to re-enact what Fish was doing on stage. We had the approach that Steve should be comfortable singing what he wants to sing. I think a singer can only sing something well if he really believes what he is singing about. So Steve chose his favorite songs out of our favorite songs, I suppose. We had a list of songs that we knew worked well live and Steve chose the ones that he wanted to sing. Other songs from earlier albums were so unique to Fish because he had his own style of singing. He wasn't a natural singer, by any means, but he did have an unusual way of putting songs across. He used to frighten people sometimes. For Steve trying to sing these kind of songs would be like acting on stage. But stuff like "Kayleigh" does have a pretty universal message and I think people can relate to it as much as Steve does.

Petra Zeitz: Do you keep up with what Fish is doing now?

Pete Trewavas: No, no. I'm quite interested in a way because a friend of mine plays guitar for Fish. I wish him well for the future. I think there's enough room for both kinds of music. Good luck to him, but I wouldn't rush out to listen to every song he's singing. We're more busy thinking about our future than his.

Petra Zeitz: When you now listen to the albums you have recorded with Fish, are you still pleased with them or would you like to change things?

Pete Trewavas: It's like any piece of work that you do really, you can always pick fault in it after you've done it. The idea is, I suppose, to try to get better at your craft. That's something you can hear through the ages of Marillion. As soon as I have finished an album I find things I want to change. We never quite managed to capture the feeling of our live shows on a studio album. I guess part of that is that when you're recording in a studio everything you're playing is under a microscope. Every little noise gets blown out of proportion and you get half a dozen people thinking about that note you just played. It can be a bit unnerving. We're trying to get better every time we do it. It's really strange because there are two definite sides to this industry, you know. The one side is the going out and performing to an audience and then the other side is trying to be a perfect musician in the studio. They are almost completely different ideas.

Petra Zeitz: Are you trying to take your music further on stage?

Pete Trewavas: Yes. I think that's an inevitable process of playing live. It's nice to be able to recreate the record, but part of being a good live band is to do a little bit more. If I played the same thing night after night on the same song, I'd get bored soon. The thing about Marillion is that we can actually play together. We get off on certain songs, but we don't play songs that you can't hear the song in. I remember seeing some bands like, for example Level 42, who do that. They get off on a completely different thing and you forget which song they were supposed to be playing. Sting does that as well. We don't go that far, but we play about with the songs that we've written. It's nice to do that.

Petra Zeitz: Are you going to release another live album?

Pete Trewavas: Yes. We have recorded some dates on this tour in England. I think the idea is to record some of the dates on the next tour we do with another album, and then put out a live album of what will be then the last two tours. We're not really sure, but definitely we will release another live album.

ROXETTE

Dreams can come true and for the Swedish pop duo Roxette they did. The way which the band's phenomenal success outside Sweden occurred makes a remarkable story. A United States student on an exchange visit to Sweden was very taken with Roxette's music which he kept hearing on the radio. He took a CD of the "Look Sharp" album back home to Minneapolis and asked his local radio station to play something from the disc. They aired the first track ("The Look") and, as a result of overwhelming listener response, syndicated the song to other radio stations. The process continued with some stations even playing fifth generation cassette copies. *Billboard* magazine registered "The Look" in their airplay charts as a new entry at No. 50 before Roxette had even concluded a US record deal. They signed to EMI and within two months

"The Look" was at No. 1. Two further No. 1 singles quickly followed.

Per Gessle and Marie Fredriksson formed Roxette in 1986, although their friendship extends back over 14 years. Both had established themselves individually as two of Sweden's most popular performers.

Per was front man to the band "Gyllene Tider," who were very successful in Scandinavia until they split in 1984. He continued his career as both solo artist and songwriter. Marie was Sweden's top female singer with her three solo albums selling in excess of 100,000 copies each.

Roxette's debut album "Pearl of Passion" went platinum and, during the summer of 1987, they undertook their first tour of Sweden, breaking attendance records wherever they appeared.

In October 1988 Roxette re-

Roxette

leased their second album, "Look Sharp," which went straight to No. 1 in the Swedish charts where it remained for three months. It also was to bring them into the eyes of a worldwide audience.

In January 1991 a third album, "Joyride," was released. The title was inspired by a quote from a Paul McCartney interview: "Writing songs with John Lennon was one long joyride."

"Joyride" became even more popular than its predecessor. It topped the US charts for several weeks, won platinum awards in all parts of the world, and made Roxette a household name. The two singers and their backing band spent a whole year on the road playing to enthusiastic crowds worldwide.

The following conversation with Per Gessle and Marie Fredriksson took place backstage in Düsseldorf, Germany, in October 1991. The duo was in a hurry because their concert was to begin only about 60 minutes later.

Petra Zeitz: Who is in your band for this world tour?

Marie Fredriksson: We have been playing with most of them since 1986 and our keyboard player, for instance, is our producer as well. His name is Clarence Öfwerman. Our bass player is also our engineer. So we know them very well and we feel like a big family. All of them are Swedish.

Petra Zeitz: You've been well known in Sweden for quite a long time now. How do your audiences over there differ from the ones you are encountering on this world tour?

Marie Fredriksson: We were playing in Rotterdam last night and the crowd went totally wild. It was fantastic! I think the audiences at home are very good as well, but they are a little bit more shy. Basically, it's the same everywhere, though.

Petra Zeitz: Do you prefer live playing to working in the studio?

Per Gessle: I have been touring a lot ever since I started out in the late seventies. I think it's interesting to tour, especially because you can meet your fans. They are the people who buy the records. On the other hand, being in the studio is nice too. I like both. I know Marie likes to tour a lot.

Petra Zeitz: With many of your fans being very young, do you feel like role models?

Per Gessle: No. I think you have to be yourself. I also think that our fans are not particularly young. The average age of the concert goers is 20 to 22. A lot of journalists were surprised by that because people seem to think we only attract 9 to 12 year olds. This is not the case. We get a lot of people from every age. We have the Phil Collins audience as well as the New Kids on the Block audience. This is why we sell so many records I guess.

Petra Zeitz: Can you understand the motivation of your fans to wait around hotels or stand in front of the venues for hours? Is that something you expected to happen?

Per Gessle: No, not really. I think it was the same thing when I was a kid myself. I stayed outside a door in Gothenburg for seven hours to see David Bowie in 1973. That was probably the same thing.

Petra Zeitz: You are often compared with ABBA. Does that bother you?

Marie Fredriksson: We are always being asked about ABBA. We're very proud of ABBA; they did a lot of good songs but it was such a long time ago. I don't think we consider ourselves as a similar band.

We're only being compared with ABBA because they were a successful Swedish band and so are we.

Petra Zeitz: If you do not like to be compared with ABBA, are there any other bands you would like to be compared with?

Per Gessle: We were raised on late sixties and early seventies music and that's where our roots come from. People always want to put you into formats, you know. We do what we do and we've based everything around our inspiration from the sixties and seventies. In our music you can find a lot of T-Rex, a lot of the Beatles, and a lot of early Joni Mitchell stuff. The reason why we started Roxette in the first place, coming from two very successful solo careers, was that we wanted to make records that we would buy ourselves. We're both big fans of what we do, otherwise I don't think we would have this type of success.

Petra Zeitz: Were you surprised at the success you've achieved?

Marie Fredriksson: Yes. When we started—it feels like a long time ago now—we thought maybe we could reach Europe. We never thought we could make it in America and Australia as well. Now it's the whole world and that is a fantastic feeling.

Petra Zeitz: Are there a lot of other good Swedish bands around that maybe we haven't heard of yet?

Per Gessle: To make it happen in the music industry is very difficult when you come from a small country. Today, there are quite a few bands who got signed by international labels, like the Electric Boys, Army of Lovers, and the Creeps. The music business itself is getting more and more global.

Petra Zeitz: I heard you're recording some of your shows. Are you going to release a live album soon?

Per Gessle: No, there won't be a live album yet. We are recording a lot of shows, but we keep the option of a live album for the future. We want to go ahead with our next studio project after the tour. It feels like it's still a bit too early in our career because we have only had two albums out internationally. When Phil Collins releases a live album it makes sense because he's been in the business for two hundred years.

Petra Zeitz: How does it feel

to be honored with a postal stamp in Sweden?

Marie Fredriksson: That's a great honor! It's hard to believe because when I think of stamps they always have the king and the queen printed on them. So it feels very weird for us, being a pop group, to be on a stamp.

Petra Zeitz: Do your lyrics have any special message?

Per Gessle: When I write songs, I try to think in two ways: on one hand, I try to write very personal lyrics that are important to me. On the other hand, I try to write fun lyrics like "Joyride" or "The Look." They are in the "Magical Mystery Tour" tradition which is weird but fun. I'm reading all these letters we get and I found out that songs like "Listen to Your Heart" or "It Must Have Been Love" come across very well. Everyone can identify with a person in the songs. But, to an-swer your question, we don't have a message as such.

Petra Zeitz: With all this success, do you still get a chance to do normal things like go to the movies or go shopping?

Marie Fredriksson: When we are traveling like this, on a tour, there is not so much time. But we do it when we have time. It's not a problem that people rec-ognize us and ask for auto-graphs. People are very friendly and they have a lot of respect.

Petra Zeitz: You don't have much private life left, but of course both of you have part-ners waiting for you in Sweden. How can you cope with this?

Marie Fredriksson: You learn to live with it. Of course you miss your private life sometimes, and you miss your friends and your family, but you never know how long this success will last. So we have to take care of it and have as much fun as we can.

CURTIS STIGERS

Curtis Stigers was born in Boise, Idaho, in the late sixties. His interest in music began at a rather young age and he started to play the clarinet in a classical style. The boy soon discovered that his instrument was not very useful for the music he wanted to play. Curtis was into jazz, rock 'n' roll and the blues. Towards the end of high school, he switched to saxophone. Every Tuesday night he attended jam sessions by jazz pianist Gene Harris. It was there that he learned to play the saxophone well. Later on, Curtis joined a punk band called "The B-Sides" as their drummer and played with a local blues band, supporting the likes of John Lee Hooker and Albert Collins.

Once Curtis discovered that he could write songs, his ambition became to front a band. He left Idaho and went to New York. Clive Davis, the man who had given Whitney Houston her break, agreed to take him on. Curtis began writing songs for his debut album and recorded them. Produced by Glen Ballard and Danny Kortchmar, the album "Curtis Stigers" was released on Arista Records in late 1991.

Both the album and the single "I Wonder Why" proved to be immensely popular, resulting in Stigers' first Top Ten success. With critics and audiences on his side, Curtis Stigers is on his way to becoming an established figure in the world of contemporary rock and pop music.

The following conversation with Curtis Stigers took place in March 1992.

Petra Zeitz: Has the saxophone always been your main instrument?

Curtis Stigers: No, my first instrument was a clarinet when I was eight or nine years old. I was old enough to join the school band. I wanted to play

Curtis Stigers

drums or trumpet or something, but unfortunately—or fortunately, depending on how you look at it—my cousin Diane had just graduated from high school. She had been a clarinet player and I inherited her clarinet because we couldn't afford anything else. I was disappointed at first, but I ended up playing it for eight years. I played mostly classical symphonies and stuff like that. About a year later, I started playing drums. I played drums for a long time too. That's what I played in rock and punk bands in high school. I switched over to saxophone sometime during high school. I eventually stepped up from the rock bands and the drums and started playing sax. It's sort of complicated, but I played clarinet and drums a lot—long before I played sax. From clarinet to sax was an easy change because the two instruments are very similar.

Petra Zeitz: Was the saxophone an instrument you particularly admired?

Curtis Stigers: It was an instrument that I admired, but it was also an instrument I could use to play rock 'n' roll, jazz and the blues. With the clarinet I couldn't do all that. I just played with a marching band and played symphonies. With the sax I could play in clubs and experiment in all the different types of music that I liked to play.

Petra Zeitz: What type of music did you intend to play when you first became a musician?

Curtis Stigers: It was hard for me to decide on just one type of music. I loved rock 'n' roll, I loved Led Zeppelin and hard rock, but I also was really into Steely Dan and I liked jazz. I never really decided on what I wanted to play, so I did them all. I had to stop playing sports. I had to stop doing everything because I had so much studying to do as a musician. To this day I couldn't tell you what's my favorite. I love to play jazz and I still do it. Not necessarily on my first album, but when I was signed to this record deal, I was actually playing in a jazz trio. My music is a mixture of everything because I'm a big fan. I have a record collection that goes from the Violent Femmes to Stevie Ray Vaughan to Sarah Vaughan.

Petra Zeitz: When you played with a blues band in your hometown you got to support some very famous blues players.

Curtis Stigers: There was a great bar in Boise called the

Bouquet. I was a sax player in the Monday night house band. We opened for Robert Cray, Albert Collins, and some very cool bands. There was this circuit of musicians that came through Boise. There was a big blues scene in Portland and in Seattle so those people would make it to Boise every now and then. I got to see a lot of really cool music when I came out of high school. Robert Cray was amazing, you know. That was before he made hit records, when he was just a blues guy. I couldn't believe that he wasn't better known because he was such a great singer and guitar player. And then, about two years later he exploded.

Petra Zeitz: Do you come from a musical family?

Curtis Stigers: My grandmother played piano and sang. My grandfather played cowboy songs on the guitar, but none of them were professional. My mother is a good singer and a big Rolling Stones fan. She's really into rock 'n' roll and the blues. I heard a lot of music at home, but I was really the first to say: "Alright, that's what I wanna do and, I think, I can make money out of it, too."

Petra Zeitz: Is this now the first time you're earning a living from making music?

Curtis Stigers: No, strangely enough I started making money playing in bars during high school. I was only in college for one year and right out of college I started making a great living. When I was 18 years old I was living in Boise, Idaho, paying my rent and living quite well playing music. There were only a few times in my life when I had to take on other jobs. When I moved to New York, the competition was so great and it was such a struggle that I had to stuff envelopes and xerox. I became a photographer's assistant and a courier to supplement my income. I made a pretty decent living before I moved to New York, but I had to go out and move there to get a record deal. There was no way that I was going to do it in a little tiny town.

Petra Zeitz: Did you go to New York on your own?

Curtis Stigers: I knew a couple of people there. I knew a married couple and I stayed with them for a few months. I didn't know any musicians at all and I went to jam sessions a lot to meet musicians. I went pretty cold turkey. Boise, Idaho, is a small town in the Northwest. It's actually west of the Rocky Mountains, just north of Utah.

It's gorgeous. It's a beautiful well-kept secret. There are wilderness areas where you can't even ride a bike. My own private Idaho! Every now and then it has a thriving music scene. There are six or seven clubs you play at. Being in that kind of conservative environment makes you want to be liberal.

Petra Zeitz: What did you have to do to finally get the record contract?

Curtis Stigers: I had all these well-laid plans. I had a band with drums, keyboards, bass, and guitar. We were playing at all the right clubs: at the China Club and at the Bitter End, which are places where record companies go and hang out. Nothing really happened from those, but I was also playing in this jazz trio, like I said. We played more than jazz. We eventually started playing soul music and somebody came into this restaurant accidentally. This was a restaurant that really no record people came into, but all of a sudden there were six record labels interested in me because one person had come in. I was really lucky. It just happened, I think, because I did what I was doing best, which was to draft from a lot of different types of music and play the things that I love to play instead of trying to cater to one type of music.

Petra Zeitz: Did you have the artistic freedom to record whatever style you wanted to play?

Curtis Stigers: Mostly yes, strangely enough. Usually you hear about people being railroaded into doing this type of music or that type of music. It wasn't that way with me at all. I made a record of mostly my songs. I picked the producers, and I got to choose the musicians. Again, I was very lucky. I know that there are a lot of people who had to compromise but I made exactly the record that I wanted to make.

Petra Zeitz: Were you surprised to have a Top Ten success?

Curtis Stigers: I was very surprised. I was surprised to get to make a record at all and to be writing with the people I got to write with. Just to have a hit record is so hard in this day and age. There's so much competition, so many record labels and new artists. I'm lucky and I hope it doesn't stop.

Petra Zeitz: Would you say that you've found your style on this record, or are you planning to do something completely different next time around?

Curtis Stigers: I may some day make a jazz record. I'm influenced by so many different things, who knows what I will be doing in ten years. I can barely see past tomorrow. I know the day after tomorrow I'm going to play another gig and I'm going to have a great time. The record will evolve as I choose to dive into the different types of music that I play.

Petra Zeitz: Were the songs written specifically for this record, or did you already play them in clubs before?

Curtis Stigers: Some of the songs were already there before I had the record deal. A lot of the songs I wrote for the record. I wrote 25 or 30 songs, 9 of which are on the album. So there's a lot left over, some of which will hopefully go on the next record. I have to sit down and write for months and I have to take time off to become a songwriter. It's a job in itself. I don't write in hotel rooms or in bars. When I got the record deal, I was given six months to write. It's another job I have that I love as much as I love playing or recording.

Petra Zeitz: On which instrument do you write?

Curtis Stigers: I usually collaborate with co-writers. I don't play keyboard or guitar very well. I can play, but not well enough to make me happy. Usually my collaborators are piano players or guitar players. I write lyrics and I specialize in melodies. As far as the chords are concerned I need the collaborators to help me realize what the chords are. I could write songs by myself, but it would take me months, whereas I can sit down with Glen Ballard and write two songs in two days. It's a much quicker process. Not only do you have a piano player there, but you have someone who has a whole other person's worth of ideas inside of them to add to the picture. It makes the music much stronger.

Petra Zeitz: Are your lyrics personal?

Curtis Stigers: Yes. I think it's very hard for me to imagine writing songs about things I made up. There are certainly parts in my songs that aren't autobiographical, but a lot of the songs are. I start with an emotion I know quite well and then maybe I become a novelist a little bit. But for the most part the songs are honest and very close to home.

Petra Zeitz: Do you learn something about yourself when you're writing songs?

Curtis Stigers: Oh yes. I hope that I've worked through a lot of problems and a lot of mistakes I've made. I learned by writing them down six months later. I've learned about jealousy. I've learned about insecurities, about letting your imagination run wild when you should be a little more rational. Love makes you crazy. Being in love—or being out of love for that matter—is the greatest irrational factor in people. Love can make the chemicals in your head go waggly-waggly. I've written these feelings down and then attributed them to a character in my song who is obviously me to a certain extent, but it's somebody else too. I sort of handed off my insecurities and my jealousy to this poor guy in my songs and he's got to deal with them now.

Petra Zeitz: Are there any possible guest musicians you would like to have on your future records?

Curtis Stigers: There's a million of them. I would love to work with Sam Moore of Sam & Dave. There's so many I don't know where to begin—Joni Mitchell, Donald Fagen, Bonnie Raitt. I got to play sax with Bonnie on New Year's Eve. When I got to sing with Donald Fagen recently I was like a 12-year-old kid. Another person who I think is a great singer is Annie Lennox. I would love to write a duet with her. I have so many idols. It's hard to list them right now.

Petra Zeitz: When did you realize you wanted to be a solo artist instead of being a member of a band?

Curtis Stigers: When I was in Idaho I had bands. I fronted them, but they were really bands and we all made decisions. When I moved to New York I couldn't have a band because I couldn't afford it. I didn't have anywhere to rehearse. You know the term garage band comes from people actually having garages at their houses, but I didn't have a garage in New York City. I couldn't rely on other musicians because I had to pay them to show up. I became a solo artist because there was no other way. It was a necessity. I was forced to have a vision. I was forced to become a songwriter. I was forced to grow up by moving to New York. It was good for me. I'm glad to work that way. I like having the collaboration of people coming in and adding their own touches to things, but I think music is a lot more focused and a lot stronger if you have it realized before a band comes in and has its way with it.

Petra Zeitz: Where did you get the band you're touring with now?

Curtis Stigers: Some of them are old friends and some of them are very good new friends. When I finished the record I had the task ahead of me of putting together a band to support the record. It turned out to be a great band. The rhythm section is fantastic. They have both played with Suzanne Vega for several years. The guitar player played with Asia and made his own record. It's an all-star band, but at the same time they're my best friends and they are great people. That is something that's hard to find. I mean, how many times have the Rolling Stones broken up because they hate each other? They love each other at the same time. My band hasn't had any personal problems at all yet and I'm knocking on wood and hoping that they won't. Everyone is so much fun and we love the music so much that it's great to play together.

THEY MIGHT BE GIANTS

John Linnell and John Flansburgh have known each other since grammar school. They became friends in high school in Sudbury, Massachusetts, where they worked on the school paper and recorded some songs together. After high school they moved to different states. Linnell played in the Rhode Island band the Mundanes. Flansburgh played in a couple of hobby bands during his time at college in Ohio. Both of them moved to Brooklyn in 1981. They started working on their first home recordings and played in clubs in the Lower East Side district, calling themselves They Might Be Giants.

By the mid-eighties they started to get noticed on the downtown scene for their live performances. Many people in and outside the New York area discovered They Might Be Giants through their dial-a-song service. They offered songs recorded especially for this phone line and the only charge was that of a regular call to Brooklyn.

The band's 1985 demo tape was reviewed in *People* magazine and they were approached by a small record label regarding an album release. A quick succession of events vaulted the band into the national spotlight. Their self-titled debut was widely praised and sold over 100,000 copies in its first year of release. The Giants also became MTV regulars.

After the release of their second album "Lincoln," the band signed with Elektra records. In 1990, They Might Be Giants released their first major label single "Birdhouse in Your Soul" which became a Top Ten hit in the UK. Two enor-

They Might Be Giants

mously successful albums, "Flood" (1990) and "Apollo 18" (1992), followed.

They Might be Giants still rehearse in John Flansburgh's apartment in Brooklyn. The following interview with him took place in February 1992, after NASA had declared They Might Be Giants to be the official rock band for the 1992 International Year of Space.

Petra Zeitz: Since you finished recording "Apollo 18" you seem to be traveling the world to promote it. Is that the case?

John Flansburgh: Yes, we're traveling an insane amount.

We're in a different city every day and I feel 100 years old.

Petra Zeitz: You made the successful "Flood" album in 1990. How does "Apollo 18" compare to it?

John Flansburgh: It's a wilder sounding record than "Flood." We're very happy with the way it came out. It's the first record that we produced entirely ourselves, so we're very proud of it on a personal level. It's a very different record in a number of ways. John bought a couple of saxophones when we started making the record, so there's a lot of horns on it. We just have a better understanding of how to get around in the studio.

Petra Zeitz: Didn't you want to hire a producer this time?

John Flansburgh: We hate working with other people. On most of the songs you just hear the two of us, but some friends of ours also play on the record. Usually we only have people coming in if it's an instrument we really have no ability to play. We have violins on a couple of songs and John tried playing the violin and it was really torture for me. So we hire a professional violinist when we need violins. By and large we're not afraid to do everything ourselves. I play mandolin on some songs. I'm not a very good mandolin player, but the spirit is there. We're not trying to be Steely Dan, you know, we don't want to be perfect.

Petra Zeitz: How can you recreate your studio music in a live show when you can't play that many different instruments all at once?

John Flansburgh: A lot of melodies that are played by different instruments on the album, we play on an accordion or on the guitar. In a concert, John plays the accordion and I play the guitar. We also have a drum machine and a sequence space. It's very minimal compared to the record, but it's more rock'n'roll. The live show is a very different musical experience than our records.

Petra Zeitz: Do you tour extensively every time a record comes out?

John Flansburgh: Yes, we spent all of 1990 on the road doing 170 shows. We also played in Japan, Australia, England and in Germany. It's funny, but we didn't get to places like Spain or France. I'm always interested in playing in the more exotic places. Being on tour in England is fun because we have a lot of fans there, but the fact that the culture is so similar to the Unites States makes it less exciting. At home, we usually play in theaters, but it really depends on the size of the city.

Petra Zeitz: Do you enjoy playing festivals too?

John Flansburgh: When we first started doing it, it was very scary. You'd look out and there was just a sea of people. It was very hard to get used to. Then you realize that it's a very casual, happy experience. A festival is not quite as intense as playing in a club or playing in a theatre, so we started to relax about it. We used to be overwhelmed by the fact that it was the biggest crowd we ever played for. It actually is just the opposite because you're very far away from people and they can't hear you that well.

Petra Zeitz: How long have the two of you played together as They Might Be Giants?

John Flansburgh: This is our ninth year of performing together. We met each other in grammar school and became friends in high school. John is a year older than me, and in school you can't be friends with somebody who is a year younger. It's against the rules. So it wasn't until we were a little bit older that we actually became friends. We worked on the high school newspaper together.

Petra Zeitz: Were the two of you into the same music at that time?

John Flansburgh: In a way we're lucky, because we have grown up with the same music. We were teenagers in the same town and we discovered a lot of the things together. I think we have very different tastes in music, but we have a lot of similar experiences. John is very into melody and harmony; he's a very musical person. I certainly enjoy melody and harmony, but

I also like to hear people screaming.

Petra Zeitz: Are you the one who wrote titles like "My Evil Twin" and "Dig My Grave"?

John Flansburgh: John and I wrote "My Evil Twin" together. "Dig My Grave" I wrote after I saw a lot of thrash metal bands play. Some of my friends are into thrash metal and they took me to the shows. It was the first time in a few years that I actually got a chance to see a lot of bands perform. So I think a little bit of that seeped in. The title of the song is actually taken from a bunch of folk songs that all have the title "Dig My Grave." I have this record that collects four of five versions of a song called "Dig My Grave" and they're really mild folk songs. I thought it was great and so I wrote another song called "Dig My Grave."

Petra Zeitz: How did you come to be chosen by NASA as the official band for the international year of space?

John Flansburgh: It was an amazing accident. We were talking to people at NASA about getting photographs for our album cover. So they knew who we were and they knew that we were going to be having a record with a space theme or a space title. So they told us about this program and thought this might be something that we were interested in. We were very flattered that they thought we would be good spokesmen. I don't know if we are. I don't even know what we're supposed to do. They've already told us that we don't get to go up in a rocket, but we have had unlimited access to their photo files, which was very nice. The international space year is actually independent of NASA, but it's a program to promote international space exploration and try to create an international space agency. They want to specifically stop the space exploration as being an excuse for military research. It's a really powerful, positive thing. We were happy to be part of it.

Petra Zeitz: Do you feel patriotic?

John Flansburgh: No, we're not patriotic. It was nice to be involved in something that actually could create something better out of the government. The international space year was set up to get back to a more positive idea of what it means to explore space. It's one of the few things about technology that I think gives people a better spiritual feeling.

Petra Zeitz: Are you fans of science fiction adventures and shows like *Star Trek*?

John Flansburgh: We're not the kind of people who read science fiction at all. We're more interested in the amazing real aspects of science. We don't like the fantasy elements. It's the actual difficult beauty of the world and space that we're interested in.

Petra Zeitz: You changed your record label a couple of years ago. Why did you want to sign with a major company?

John Flansburgh: We wanted to release our records on one record company worldwide. It was really practical because if we had stayed on an independent label that had that capability it would have been fine. But it was just getting to be a real headache and one thing about independent record labels in the US is that they tend to not stay in business for more than five years. At the time it seemed like a big accident was about to happen and we wanted to make sure we weren't the victims of this accident.

Petra Zeitz: Isn't it difficult to be a top artist on an independent label and suddenly become one of many on a major label?

John Flansburgh: In some ways it's exactly the same. In

other ways it's quite different. When you're on a big label the rules that have been set by the superstars are obeyed for you. We don't have to debate a lot of issues. For instance, we don't like to do autograph appearances because it makes us feel strange and we can just say to a major label, "We're not going to do it" without them taking it personally. Whereas when you're working with a smaller label they have a very practical understanding of what it means to do something or not to do something. They get really mad if you're not willing to do it. In some ways, you're actually more free when you're on a major label. But there are also struggles: We had to take a stand to produce this record ourselves. We really wanted to arrange our songs and we thought it wasn't up for debate. The difference between major and independent labels is nothing compared to the difference between working with people or working by yourselves.

Petra Zeitz: You're living and working in New York. Isn't the music scene rather elite there?

John Flansburgh: I have a lot of musician friends in New York who come from a very different musical background. What has made us friends has nothing to do with music. It's interesting to me that somebody would say that the scene is elite, because I go to parties and I don't feel that I don't belong there. When we started playing in the East Village it was a very jaded, cynical version of the Fillmore in San Francisco during the hippie days. They had three bands on a night and they made a point of the three acts having nothing to do with one another. That made it more like a community in a way because you all were performing. Ultimately it happens at the same time. It was challenging to us and I certainly don't think musicians in New York stay in their ivory towers.

Petra Zeitz: How would you describe your music if you had to categorize it?

John Flansburgh: Usually when people ask me to describe it, I describe what instruments we play and that our songs are two minutes long and that they have verses and choruses. I think we're like the Beatles only with messed up lyrics. There's no easy category for what we do. We're pretty much by ourselves and it would be weird if another band came along that was like us.

Petra Zeitz: If you have to

choose an opening act, would you have somebody who is a bit like you or rather a band that's completely different?

John Flansburgh: We always like to work with people who don't have drums. We usually had solo performers opening for us; a lot of times they had things in common with us. They were singer/songwriters with a sensibility that was so much like us, but that's not necessary. I think it would be nice to have a girl group open for us. Sometimes I feel like the whole rock business is so male-oriented that it's really boring. There are just not enough women in rock. There are not that many of them and when they get famous, it always happens really fast.

Petra Zeitz: Is it difficult these days to actually survive in the music business?

John Flansburgh: You know, we're not ambitious. I live in the same apartment I lived in before we even started the band. My rent is very low. We're happy with being able just to make the kind of music we want to make. We're really on our own and I don't feel like we're in competition with anybody else. We're just doing our thing.

Petra Zeitz: Has your band name anything to do with the baseball team the Giants?

John Flansburgh: It's funny, because on the New York sports pages, whenever the Giants lose they always say "They Might Be Giants." It's actually the title of a movie made in 1971. The movie is not very good, but we thought it would be an interesting name for a band. Since we named it that, everybody in the sports world is very into using it. But we're not the kind of people who are interested in sports.

CELTIC CONNECTION: BANDS AND MUSICIANS FROM IRELAND AND SCOTLAND

BIG COUNTRY

Big Country, a guitar-based rock 'n' roll band, was formed in Scotland in 1982. Ex-Skids guitarist Stuart Adamson and his friend Bruce Watson got together with the rhythm section which Pete Townshend had used to record his album "All the Best Cowboys Have Chinese Eyes." It consisted of Tony Butler on bass and Mark Brzezicki on drums. They had been working together as session musicians for a while, using the name "Rhythm for Hire."

Steve Lillywhite produced Big Country's debut album which raced up the UK charts in May 1983. With hit singles like "Fields of Fire," "Look Away," and "The Sneer," Big Country soon became a household name. Their worldwide following consisted of pop, rock'n'roll and heavy metal fans. In 1985 they took part in the legendary Live Aid show and in October 1988 they were the first Western band ever to perform at a Russian stadium in Moscow.

Big Country's 1991 offer "No Place Like Home" was the first album without Mark Brzezicki. He left temporarily to resume his session career. After working with Midge Ure and Pete Townshend, he rejoined Big Country in 1993.

The following Big Country interview with founding member Stuart Adamson took place between the finishing of the "No Place Like Home" album and the group's embarking on a world tour in 1991.

Petra Zeitz: Tonight you will be performing for a television special. Does the show feel different to you because of the TV cameras?

Stuart Adamson: No, you're never really aware of that. When you do things in front of a live audience you tend to be involved with the audience and don't think about the television

Big Country

cameras. You go and play your gig. It is important, though, that the atmosphere of the gig comes across well on television.

Petra Zeitz: Is Big Country more of a live act than a studio band?

Stuart Adamson: We have always been very much a live band and very traditional in the sense that music is a fairly distinctive, direct thing between people. Live music has certainly always been the biggest motivator for us. The studio is important, too. I love writing songs and all that side to it, but the reason why I wanted to be a musician in the first place was for the live performances. I have grown up doing it and it still feels very special to me.

Petra Zeitz: You have just released your new album "No Place Like Home." Did you have a chance to realize all your ideals on this project?

Stuart Adamson: Usually what happens with an album is that it takes me two or three weeks to sit back from it, but I never left this one since we finished it. I'm really delighted with it—everything we've done—I'm pleased with the songs, I'm pleased with my writing and with the production. It's definitely the best album I am capable of making at this moment in time.

Petra Zeitz: Has your style changed since Mark Brzezicki left the band?

Stuart Adamson: I think it has, but it happened naturally. We have always been a rock'n'roll band, in the traditional guitar/bass/drums format. Our new album is even more rock and less folk-oriented than the previous ones. There are certain elements in our music which I always identify with Big Country, and there are also new things happening. That is a natural process in any band.

Petra Zeitz: You were quoted as saying, "I want to write songs that people are touched by." What, in your opinion, makes a good lyric?

Stuart Adamson: I try to do something new each time I write a piece. There have been millions of love songs that have all been in exactly the same style. I like to write songs that tell a story or recreate a mood, you know, evoke a mood. I do it like the folk musicians. Some of my lyrics are personal and some come from completely outside sources. It always depends on what kind of song I'm writing.

Petra Zeitz: Since you mentioned folk music, did you ever use any traditional Scottish instruments for your recordings?

Stuart Adamson: No, not really. We never used proper bagpipes or anything like that. That's a common misconception. Our only traditional Scottish instrument is called the electric guitar!

Petra Zeitz: When you first started Big Country, rock'n'roll was quite unpopular and new wave music was sweeping Britain. What made you want to form a rock band in those days?

Stuart Adamson: Music is not necessarily good because it's being played on guitars, but I think it helps. I have played guitar since I was 11 years old. I joined a band called the Skids which became quite successful. Even before forming Big Country I had a very clear idea about what I wanted to do, which was to find musicians that were not just great players but people who shared the same attitude towards the music that I had. I have now come to realize that the attitude is more important than how well you can play. So all I was doing was that. I think my music was also a reaction against what was going on at the time, but mainly, being a guitar player, it was natural for me to form a guitar-based band. As a musician I always have to trust my own instincts. I write songs that I enjoy, and songs that I love, and songs that mean something to me. And I hope that other people will catch up on those feelings. At the time it didn't really feel that we were flying in the face of any fashion but I certainly felt that we were very individual and we were proud of that—always have been and always will be.

Petra Zeitz: Has being a mainstream rock band become any easier now?

Stuart Adamson: Yes, it's much easier these days. Since we first started, many guitar-based bands have emerged. It also gave live music a kick. Far more bands go out and tour now than they did in the early eighties.

Petra Zeitz: Are you a career-oriented musician?

Stuart Adamson: No, not at all. I'm involved in Big Country because I want to make music that I feel inspires other people as much as I'm inspired by it. It takes time to produce such music, but I don't mind the gaps between albums.

Petra Zeitz: Which bands were you influenced by in your early days?

Stuart Adamson: I was influenced by a lot of different things. My mother was a big fan of all types of music. She used to work in a record shop. I heard everything from folk music to the Rolling Stones, the Kinks and country & western stuff. The first band I ever saw live was Led Zeppelin. I was only 12 years old and watching them was just amazing!

Petra Zeitz: How did you come to choose the other members of the band?

Stuart Adamson: Bruce Watson, the other guitar player, lived in the same town as I did. He was in a band with my brother-in-law and I really liked to watch them play. I liked

Bruce's attitude towards what he did. Tony and Mark had been in a band called On the Air and they supported the last tour of the Skids. They were very tight together so I asked them if they wanted to join.

Petra Zeitz: Did being Scottish at first interfere with you becoming successful? As far as I know the British music industry is still based around London.

Stuart Adamson: At the time I was with the Skids, being from Scotland did prove to be a problem because everybody had to go to London to make it. But as the new wave movement got its strength, more A&R men would come outside London to find artists. A lot of the independent labels were set up in places like Glasgow and Manchester. That encouraged people to go up and look for bands in other areas. Since I first started, there have been quite a few Scottish bands who have been successful and that has opened the way for more musicians.

Petra Zeitz: Is there still a "homecoming atmosphere" when Big Country plays in Scotland?

Stuart Adamson: Oh yes, it's something I have always appreciated. It's nice to be admired by your own country.

Petra Zeitz: You performed in Moscow and East Berlin in 1988. Would you like to play in Russia or Eastern Europe again?

Stuart Adamson: I'm absolutely desperate to go back. I would like to meet the people again. I'd like to speak to the same people I spoke to last time and find out how their lives have changed and how they feel about things. Everything happened so quickly, I mean, it's hard to keep up with things. It's a very inspiring time to be a European but I think it's going to be very difficult as well. We would be foolish to pretend that suddenly everything is going to be nice for everyone. It just doesn't happen like that. But I think people in the East have certainly far more chances to be themselves now and to find their own potential. It's really fascinating.

Petra Zeitz: Have all of these political changes affected your life in Britain?

Stuart Adamson: To be quite honest, particularly in the British government, people are very wary of the wave of nationalism sweeping Europe. If that happens at home we may end up with a divided Britain again. But I hope we can build something positive out of all these feelings.

THE CHIEFTAINS

Paddy Moloney's traditional Irish folk band the Chieftains has been regarded as a cultural ambassador for over 20 years. Ever since the Chieftains' first album was released in 1964 they have spearheaded the revival of traditional Irish music. Their line-up today consists of Paddy Moloney on uillean pipes and tin whistle; Michael Tubridy on tin whistle, concertina and flute; Sean Potts on tin whistle, Martin Fay on fiddle, Pedar Mercier on bodhran and bones as well as Derek Bell on harp, oboe and tiopan.

Their inclusion in this volume is justified by the long and impressive list of rock stars they have been asked to work with. Most famous undoubtedly for his collaboration with Van Morrison, Paddy Moloney, himself a real character, has also worked with Paul McCartney, Mick Jagger, Sinead O'Connor, Mike

Oldfield and the Pogues, to name but a few.

The Chieftains toured the States frequently and were once invited to the White House where they were received by Ted Kennedy in 1983.

The following conversation with Paddy Moloney took place during rehearsals for a St. Patrick's Day television special which was filmed at the Royal Opera House in Belfast in August 1991. One of the Chieftains' musical guests that night was Roger Daltrey who afterwards confessed: "There are only two bands I really enjoy playing with—The Who and The Chieftains!"

Petra Zeitz: Can you explain some of the origins of Irish folk music?

Paddy Moloney: The Chieftains have been together for 30 years now, but the music goes back hundreds of years. It has never been written down, but

Chieftains

has been passed on. My grandfather was a flute player and everybody else in the band had relations who played Irish music.

Petra Zeitz: There are some amazing facts about the Chieftains. For example, you hold the record for having played to 1.3 million people.

Paddy Moloney: Yes, and the pope came on after us! Actually we opened a mass gathering for the pope in Ireland and we played for about 20 minutes before he touched down in his helicopter.

Petra Zeitz: The Chieftains had their own music festival in London in July 1991. Did you collaborate with other musicians to reach a wider audience?

Paddy Moloney: The whole festival was very successful from the point of view that for the last 30 years we have been guesting on other people's albums. This time we invited them! We had five different shows with many surprise guests and a lot of things happened all the time. The last concert was with the Pogues and turned out to be total madness. They are usually wild, but that night they tried to appear composed because they were with the Chieftains. We did two hours together and it was amazing. We also played with a philharmonic orchestra. Another guest I have to mention was Midge Ure. And one of the big surprises of the London festival was Mary Hopkins. She sang in Welsh and her voice was just incredible. I think that was the beginning of a new relationship between Mary and us.

Petra Zeitz: Mary Hopkins made her last successful record in the late sixties when she was signed to the Beatles' Apple label. Is she trying to make a comeback now?

Paddy Moloney: She's been off the scene for a long time, but she really enjoyed that night with us. You never know, but it could be very interesting. We may do an album with her one day.

Petra Zeitz: Last night and tonight you're performing with Roger Daltrey of the Who. Aren't two different worlds merging into each other?

Paddy Moloney: Music is music, no matter which area you come from. Roger was just incredible. I mean, he's the guy that used to throw television sets out of the window! Last night you couldn't believe this guy. We did more songs than we actually planned to do. He sung them like a true Irishman would. We call it *Sean-nos*. It's the Gaelic word for old-style singing, and here's this *Cockney* kid who sings in a true Sean-nos style.

Petra Zeitz: You have been collaborating with rock stars for a rather long time now. What is it that gets you involved over and over again?

Paddy Moloney: I have to be honest and say that traditional Irish music is what the Chieftains are best at. The other projects are good fun. One of the things we are trying to get across is that on stage all music comes together. It's a combination of personalities and it works. Roger Daltrey was saying yesterday that two years ago he was playing in Detroit to 80,000 people in a huge stadium and tonight he gets on stage at the Belfast opera house and loves it as much. As I said before, music is music. It doesn't matter if it's Irish music or Spanish music or even Chinese music. I don't get much time to listen to anything at home but when I do I usually listen to classical music like Mozart.

Petra Zeitz: There is a growing awareness now for what is called "world music"— traditional music coming from mainly Third World countries. Do you follow this development?

Paddy Moloney: Yes. That is one of the things I am most interested in. I would like to develop it even more. For example the structure of Indian music is sometimes very similar to traditional Irish music. I have met the Indian sitar virtuoso Ravi Shankar on several occasions, and maybe we can work together one day. I consider projects like these a great honor for the Chieftains.

Petra Zeitz: You have been involved in many soundtrack recordings. Is that an area you are particularly interested in?

Paddy Moloney: It is. I get to know the director, get to know about the film project and get a copy of the script. Sometimes the screenplay is not all that helpful, but if you get a synopsis, a storyline, you can get a feel for the film. I see the music like a vision or like a painting, long before I get to watch the rushes.

Petra Zeitz: What kind of audience reaction do the Chieftains receive when they play in places like China or in the States?

Paddy Moloney: Before we went to China we were warned that audiences there would behave rather quietly. But they weren't. At the end of each concert we had a jam session with Chinese musicians playing their own instruments, and it was terrific. We do these jam sessions in every place we go and it warms up the audiences to us. We are very successful in America. I mean, we never stop! We have been on tour for the last 20 years.

Petra Zeitz: Thank you for your time. I know you have to attend rehearsals now.

Paddy Moloney: Actually, I could go on forever. I hope that what I was trying to say has made more sense than I think it has!

FISH

The Fish story began on April 25, 1958, when Derek William Dick was born in Dalkeith near Edinburgh. His only singing experience until the age of 21 was a spell with the school choir from which he was ejected for not attending rehearsals.

Fish studied forestry, ultimately at Bowhill Estate in the Scottish borders where he joined his first band Blewitt. In May 1980 Fish decided music was a more appealing career than forestry. He eventually left Scotland. In the English town of Aylesbury he joined a band called Marillion. His first live appearance with them in March 1981 inspired him to study stagecraft and to experiment with costumes and make-up.

Over the next seven years Marillion proved to be one of the biggest international successes of the eighties, with each album and tour winning them legions of new fans. In 1988 dis-

agreements between Fish and other members of the band became very serious. The singer was as unhappy with the band's music as they were with his lyrics. Consequently, Fish decided to quit in September 1988.

He realized he wanted to return to his roots and went back to Scotland where he bought a farm near Haddington. He began to convert an outhouse into a recording studio and started to work on his first ever solo album to be called "Vigil in a Wilderness of Mirrors."

July 1990 saw Fish finishing his first solo tour, and a few months later he was given his first acting role as persecuted Scottish religious immigrant, Daniel Nielson, in an episode of the U.S. television series "Zorro."

A bitter court battle between Fish and his former record label (EMI) put him on ice for almost a

Fish

year, but in March 1991 he signed a new worldwide contract and started work on a new album. "Internal Exile" was the first recording made at "Funny Farm Recording Studios," a residential, 56 channel (32 digital, 24 analogue) complex that has since become available as a commercial studio. In early 1993, Fish released an album of cover versions which was not very successful.

The following conversation with Fish took place upon the completion of the "Internal Exile" album in October 1991.

Petra Zeitz: One of your main concerns these days must be the construction of your new studio complex. What made you want to run your own studio?

Fish: I knew I had to find a place at my farm where I could write, audition members of the band and rehearse for a tour. I also needed a recording facility to give me more freedom. So we—well, I didn't spend a lot of money on it—the bank and some other people spent 1.3 million dollars on it, and the place suddenly went from being a little demo studio to being an international residential recording studio.

Petra Zeitz: Did you record all of your latest album there?

Fish: Yes, I did. The studio was finished in July 1991, and we almost immediately started recording the album there. We were the guinea pigs, I mean, all the little gremlins were there waiting for us—and they came out in legions! The recordings were running very late, but from a financial level I needed to get the album out before Christmas.

Petra Zeitz: Why was that?

Fish: Well, the last album was in January 1990 and 18 months is a long time to wait for an album. This record should have been out last March, but because of the problems I had with EMI, I wasn't allowed to release any material. Everything was so late but we had to get the album out so that we could get Polydor to give us more money to prepare the tour. I wanted people to know that I was still alive and had not just disappeared in the Highlands of Scotland with a bottle of whiskey.

Petra Zeitz: Still you found time to have a MTV special filmed at your recording studios.

Fish: We had quite a few journalists sitting in the back of the studio doing interviews. MTV came up to do an interview and I couldn't get the time to actually sit down for two hours. So we did a deal that I went in and did the vocal on the B-side of the first single, and they got to film it. The vocal that MTV filmed was the actual vocal that was used on the record. Time was just so against me.

Petra Zeitz: Although the public has not heard from you for a while, you have not been lazy for the last two years?

Fish: Far from it. We had major problems that would turn grown men into jelly! The last two years were extremely pressurized and so intense. For both my management and the guys who work for me, anything that comes along now is easy compared to what we've been through in the past. Because of the EMI thing I couldn't work, I couldn't even tour because promoters wouldn't put up the money for the tour. If I had tried to deal with the EMI case living in London, I would have gone clinically insane. It was that heavy, I mean, being 33 years old and suddenly finding you're not allowed to work. My entire life was just lying there on a pile of paperwork. It was really scary. Even though the phones were ringing all the time in Scotland, I was a certain distance from London. When it

was really bad I could go for a walk on the beach or go into the hills.

Petra Zeitz: You left Scotland when you were in your early twenties. What made you want to return there?

Fish: I really missed it. I never realized how much I actually missed it until I went back in 1988 with Marillion, and we took over this castle. The idea was we were either all going to kill each other, or we were going to come out as a new band. Nothing happened. We just went up there, and I realized the whole thing was heading to the wall. I did not relate to these people anymore, nor the music they were making. By doing that—leaving the castle, going to pubs, meeting people and seeing old friends—I realized that I was Scottish. I wasn't British! Even though I had been living in the south of England for eight years, I never had a home there—all I had done was buy a permanent hotel room. I felt I never had roots there and I missed the sense of community and the sense of belonging to somewhere. When I lived in England, one of the neighbors on my right hand side had lived next to me for two years and I spoke to him five times. I think I was in his house once and he was never in mine. I had asked him to come to parties but he did not want to socialize with me.

Petra Zeitz: What happened after you left Marillion in 1988?

Fish: First of all, my wages went down. It was like: "Thanks very much, goodbye Fish. You want to be solo? Take this!" And I ended up with nothing. I even auditioned for jingles for M&M, and I got $300 for that. I was desperate! I also auditioned for a part in the musical "Metropolis" in London. It was then that I decided to move up to Scotland. I said to my wife: Look, we've got a choice here—we can either move to the southwest of England or to Scotland because we can't afford to live in the house we have. We sold the house and my mum & dad found this place in Haddington [Scotland]. It was a farm house with a lot of buildings around it. One of the buildings was dry and had a really nice roof on it, and it was the ideal size to put a studio in.

Petra Zeitz: Why is there such a big difference between living in England and living in Scotland when both places belong to Great Britain?

Fish: The Scottish thing is that I'm in a place now where nobody cares what I am. Nobody suddenly says, "Oh Fish, you're the rock star." You know, it's more if you're an asshole, you're an asshole, and if you're a good guy, you're a good guy. People take you at face value and I really like that. I like being able to talk to my local policeman and go drinking with the milkman in the pub, play squash with one of the farmers, things like that. They are really down-to-earth people, no pretense, no insincerity, a lot of depth. And you see, my family is there. I have a nine-month-old daughter now and being there has been great for my head. I really love my country. And the thing with the studio is also that I am able to put something back into my country. I am politically basically a socialist. I sometimes feel very guilty about the amount of money that we use up, but I'm not a Ferrari kid or a Porsche boy. With the studio, I'm providing a facility to the East Coast of Scotland and I'm going to be able to help young Scottish bands. I'm going to be able to give them the option to record in Scotland, rather than having to go down to London which is a hell hole.

Petra Zeitz: Are you pleased

with the development of the music scene in Scotland?

Fish: There have always been hundreds of Scottish bands. I really admire Runrig for what they have done. They've done it from Scotland and that's what I'm doing now. And like I said, it's being part of a community rather than just being the rock star that lives down the road. You are actually a member of the community, you're involved in little charity gigs and—the same as Runrig do—you take the music to people, rather than let people travel six hours to come and see you.

Petra Zeitz: You have recently embarked on an acting career as well.

Fish: I had always wanted to get into acting and I got a chance to do "Zorro," which is an American production where nobody dies, nobody gets killed, there's no sex, no swearing, all the baddies get pies in their faces—it's crap! But it was my first ever chance to act. When you do videos the whole thing revolves around you, you are the center of attention, but when I went onto the "Zorro" set and I was just another extra, although it later said: "Special guest star Fish." This year I got a chance to do some serious

drama in a three-part thriller written by David King. It was done for the BBC. I play the part of Ferguson who is a hitman. I'm the one who gets to do all the clean-up work, but I always mess up. I strangle people and the rope breaks, things like that. Acting is a profession I respect and I'm willing to put a lot of work into it.

Petra Zeitz: Do you still play Marillion material when you're on tour?

Fish: My object is not to be a cabaret artist. I'm not into performances for nostalgic reasons. To be honest, it would be the same if I was in Marillion now, the new albums would start to dominate the proceedings. I have actually picked some Marillion numbers but I refuse to play them for nostalgic reasons because I believe we can do them better now. We're more of a rock'n'roll band now than Marillion ever was. There's a lot more soul, feel, passion and energy in my music than there used to be.

Petra Zeitz: What was your contribution to the Marillion material?

Fish: A lot of people misunderstood what my contribution actually was. They said, "He just writes the words." I put a lot of feeling and a lot of soul into what they were doing, and I think it's evident when you listen to the new Marillion albums and compare them to my stuff. You can hear that there's a difference between the feeling and the energy level.

Petra Zeitz: Have you ever watched Marillion perform with their new singer, Steve Hogarth?

Fish: I actually saw them two weeks ago. It was a very strange experience, a bit like watching your ex-girlfriend making love to somebody else. It was really weird. But I mean, when I saw it, all it did was qualify my reasons for leaving the band. I could not identify with the material they were playing, I could never sing what they do now. It's very clever musically, but it's not my cup of tea. I prefer a more dynamic, attacking form of music. I'm more of a performance artist than a singer. I met Steve Hogarth after the gig and he is a really nice guy. We were both nervous meeting each other, it was quite funny. I still consider the guys my friends. I think they were very bitter and very annoyed about the fact that I left the band. They never expected me to leave, but I did. I think it has done both of us a lot of good. They mean as much to me now as the Scorpions do, or Aerosmith or Little Feat or whatever. I'm interested in what they do, but it doesn't matter anymore.

HOTHOUSE FLOWERS

Liam O'Maonlai and Fiachna O'Braonain met at Gaelic speaking school where music classes were spent playing and learning traditional Irish instruments like the tin whistle and the bodhran (a goat skinned tambourine). Liam went on to become all–Ireland champion with the bodhran, while Fiachna won several traditional instrument competitions.

They later took to the streets of Dublin where they played what could be described as "Gaelic Blues." They played for pocket money and fun, calling themselves "The Incomparable Benzini Brothers."

Liam and Fiachna later added drummer Jerry Fehily, bassist Peter O'Toole, a former lumberjack and maker of fine musical instruments, as well as Leo Barnes on saxophone. They called the new line-up Hothouse Flowers.

Bono (singer for U2) stamped his seal of approval upon the band by releasing a Hothouse Flowers single on U2's own label, "Mother Records." Within 18 months they became the biggest band in Ireland, regularly pulling crowds of 2,000 or more wherever they played.

When their debut album, "People," was released by a major label in June 1988, it shot to No. 1 in the Irish charts. The rest of that year was spent consolidating their lives following their tour of Europe, Japan and the United States.

Hothouse Flowers recorded their second album in New Orleans, Rockfield and Dublin. Entitled "Home," it was released in June 1990 and proved to be an international success.

The following conversation with Fiachna O'Braonain and Peter O'Toole took place in London while Hothouse Flowers

Hothouse Flowers

were touring the U.K. in support of "Home."

Petra Zeitz: Do you prefer to play small clubs rather than huge concert venues?

Fiachna O'Braonain: I like to be able to play both types. In a large place, the distance between the band and the audience sometimes becomes too big and you begin to feel isolated on stage. But I wouldn't want to just play clubs anymore.

Petra Zeitz: Hothouse Flowers headlined the annual Glastonbury Festival in England which gave the band a kind of hippy image. Is that something you reject?

Fiachna O'Braonain: No, we don't reject it, but it's a bit frivolous. People always look for labels to put on us and "hippy" is just the latest one of them. Before that it was "Celtic soul." We had all kinds of things said about us, but in a way it's understandable because people want to make categories for everything. We do it ourselves, too. When we listen to music we try to categorize it.

Peter O'Toole: Music is only about a fifth of what's going on in Glastonbury. There are so many other things of interest. There's people who travel around and they all meet up in Glastonbury which is apparently a very spiritual place. Unfortunately I don't know anything about it, but when you go up there you see people making tents. They spend about two weeks there rather than just stay for the 3-day festival. These people come early and leave late. They all used to move on to Stonehenge, but that's now been banned. Musically, I think Glastonbury is great. This year they have Ry Cooder, the Happy Mondays and Sinead O'Connor to name but a few.

Petra Zeitz: What kind of music do you listen to for pleasure?

Fiachna O'Braonain: I generally like the music that's made with real instruments, but, then again, there are people like Prince who use machines to make music and they are absolutely amazing. Recently I listened to The Band, the Neville Brothers and I also like Neil Young's album "Freedom."

Petra Zeitz: You seem to be part of the "Dublin Band Explosion" that has happened recently. Is the Dublin music scene very special?

Fiachna O'Braonain: Music in Ireland generally tends to be less affected by fashion than it is in other places. That is the main difference. The effect that it has on the music is that the music tends to be more from the heart. A lot of music seems to be designed to make money. By and large the music scene in Ireland is healthier. But there are so many bands around and we just don't have enough venues for them.

Petra Zeitz: Are you going to keep your base in Dublin?

Fiachna O'Braonain: In Ireland, anyway. I mean, Dublin at the moment is home, but it needn't necessarily be there forever.

Petra Zeitz: Is it important for you to be in Ireland to feel inspired?

Fiachna O'Braonain: We can write music anywhere; it is just important for the five of us to be together. We generally jam or write songs during soundchecks. We just have the tape rolling in the desk and get up and play. Sometimes we come up with something and keep working on it. Other times one of us will have an idea and we will meet in our rehearsal room and play it. Other times we have the lyrics first and look for something musical to go with them. Generally speaking, eighty percent of our material is written during jamming. Liam is mostly responsible for the lyrics, but we all look at them and maybe write a couple of lines. On the album "Home" we do a traditional Irish folk song. It's a Sean-nos song that Liam has known for years and we decided we wanted to include a piece in the Irish language. When Liam and I go on holiday to the West Coast of Ireland where they speak Irish all the time people say: "Why don't you sing in Irish? If you're able to speak it, you must sing it!"

Petra Zeitz: Don't you find it quite unusual to use traditional Irish instruments in rock music?

Fiachna O'Braonain: It's hard to say whether the music we're making with traditional instruments is rock music. We don't have the rock'n'roll attitude which is a bit of a turn-off anyway. In Dublin that is quite a joke, but especially American bands tend to behave in a certain way just because it's part of their image.

Petra Zeitz: You toured America on several occasions and have been well received by the critics. How did Americans in general react to your music?

Fiachna O'Braonain: They loved us! We got a great response from the American audience. People travelled from here, there and everywhere to see us.

Petra Zeitz: You were actually called "the Irish Beatles" or the "new U2" in the States. How do you feel about that?

Fiachna O'Braonain: That's funny! I like the "Irish Beatles" one. [*Laughs.*] I'm Paul then.

Petra Zeitz: Do you feel people in America can relate to your "Irishness"?

Fiachna O'Braonain: I suppose they have a very limited knowledge about what's going on in Ireland. In America you get people coming up to say: "Hey, my grandfather was Irish, or my father was Irish" and they always love to make that connection. Nine times out of ten their grandfather probably was Irish, but you hear it all the time. I sometimes felt like turning around and saying: "Mine was too, funny enough!"

Petra Zeitz: Why was your album "Home" recorded in five different studios?

Fiachna O'Braonain: It just happened that way. We wanted to record our new songs when they were fresh and we still enjoyed them. Sometimes if you leave it for too long you lose the feeling for a song. So, for example, we went to New Orleans in the middle of an American tour and recorded a few tracks there.

Petra Zeitz: There was quite a long gap between your first album "People" and this one. How has the band developed during that time?

Fiachna O'Braonain: We have learned an awful lot about recording. Listening to our gigs, we felt that "People" was slightly too much of a studio album. So we wanted to record more with a live atmosphere. We had to work with a couple of different people in order to achieve that because a lot of producers find that way of recording quite difficult. But we thought, 20 years ago bands didn't find it difficult to go into the studio and just play!

Petra Zeitz: Would you like to release a live recording from one of your shows?

Fiachna O'Braonain: Yes, that would be great. Last night this person came to the gig with a video bootleg of a show we did in Japan. We saw a rush of it on the bus and the quality of it was very good. We made a live video of a concert we did in Dublin and we will do a live album one day. It's a bit scary when you're up on stage and you know the gig is being recorded. You never know if you're playing for the audience or for the tape, but of course, you always end up playing for the audience.

Petra Zeitz: One of the producers you used this time was Daniel Lanois who has also worked with U2. Did he prove to be a good choice?

Peter O'Toole: We all felt Daniel Lanois was great, just his way of working and his kind of technique. He told us how to work in a small environment like a small house or even a room. He said you don't need a studio to record an album. That appealed to us because we find some studios are intimidating; they are equipped with all sorts of great machinery, but they don't have any instruments in there. For a musical studio that doesn't make sense. There's a great place in London called Townhouse 3 where they have a quite good recording room, but down the back they have a room with hundreds of instruments, percussions and everything. That, for a musician, is more important than having all these little effects and stuff.

Petra Zeitz: Do you prefer playing live to working in a studio?

Peter O'Toole: Ultimately live, but I think we really enjoy recording, too. It's interesting to go in and hear yourself back on tape and overcome that difference. The difference between the energy you have when you're playing live and the energy you have when you're playing in a studio is incomparable, because there's no people there. We get really turned on by people.

RUNRIG

Runrig are one of Scotland's best kept secrets. At home they have long established themselves as national heroes, very Scottish and proud of it. The band centers around singer Donnie Munro, who has been appointed rector of Edinburgh University, and the two brothers Rory and Calum MacDonald who provide all the original material. They released three albums on their own Ridge label before being signed by Chrysalis. Through their charismatic live appearances in Great Britain, Europe, and Canada, they won a considerable following. Their annual show at Loch Lomond in Scotland attracted 50,000 people in 1991.

Some of Runrig's songs are sung in Gaelic. The lyrics are powerful images of Scottish landscapes but also criticize the destruction of nature.

The 8th album, "The Big Wheel," was their fastest selling product so far. From it came their hit single "Hearthammer."

The following conversation with Donnie Munro took place in August 1991 just after "The Big Wheel" had entered the UK charts at No. 4.

Petra Zeitz: Were the songs on your first album, "Play Gaelic" all sung in Gaelic?

Donnie Munro: It was all Gaelic songs. That album was recorded when we were all students. We had grown up in the west of Scotland where there was Gaelic language and Gaelic culture. As kids we had that as our first influence, but then, like with all young kids growing up, the appeal of international rock and pop music was too great to resist. You tend to forget about the things that are in your own immediate life and you are attracted to this much more glamorous and exciting world. By the time we got to university, we started looking again

Runrig

at the things that meant a lot to us in our background. So we decided to record some new songs in what was our first language. This album was a deliberate thing to say that we think Gaelic culture is valuable.

Petra Zeitz: So your mother tongue was Gaelic before you even learned English?

Donnie Munro: Yes. It was our first language in the home. But by the time we went to school, at the age of five, we had to speak English all the time and we basically forgot about our own language. We were not encouraged to speak Gaelic at all and the generations before us, like my parents' generation, they were actually punished for speaking the language because it was considered to be of no use. That was a big mistake because any language and any culture is very important. It's what makes everybody different and hopefully more interesting.

Petra Zeitz: Is there a Gaelic culture revival happening now?

Donnie Munro: There is, yes. People take time to learn. I think the political history of Scotland was one of the reasons why they didn't want the language to be too strong. If you have a language and a cultural identity with a difference, it allows more potential for political rebellion against authority. So the authorities were quite happy to see the Gaelic culture descent, but that has changed now. They are even putting a lot of money into Gaelic television. I hope it will make a difference.

Petra Zeitz: In your lyrics you often express political awareness. Do you think music is a good tool to achieve political changes?

Donnie Munro: There are instances where music has been instrumental in changing the heart or the minds of people to question certain circumstances. If you look at the American protest music of the sixties and through the Vietnam period, that obviously had an impact on a whole generation of people to make them question the value of taking part in the war. There certainly is a place for music to have that role, but I see mostly that music is reflecting situations rather than shaping or controlling them. Musicians and writers, like most other artists, absorb the influences and react to situations they find themselves in. Although our songs have political or social comment, we would never consider

going forward into a situation of campaigning on any issue. People are attracted to music first and foremost because of entertainment and wanting to feel good. It can be very offputting to go to a concert and have somebody standing up there for an hour and a half, trying to politicize you in any kind of way. I wouldn't like this to be done at all. Some artists do it, but not us.

Petra Zeitz: Concerts are the biggest part of your job, aren't they?

Donnie Munro: The entire success of this band has been based on live music. Our album "The Big Wheel" went into the UK charts at Number Four. Normally when you get an album going into the top of the UK charts it goes in because a band has either had a hit single which has been played to death on the radio or has been hyped in some way or form. As a band, we have never had anything like that. We have never been hyped by anybody or anything. We have never been the darlings of the music press and we have never been considered the next hip thing to be involved with. So in many ways the only reason why this album is at Number Four is because enough people have seen the band in a live situation and enjoyed it enough to go out and buy an album. We are very happy that this is the case because anything that happens above that now is a bonus.

Petra Zeitz: Do you basically recreate your records on stage or do you try to take the music further in a live situation?

Donnie Munro: Any band's dilemma is often that they do fantastic recordings and when you go to see them live you end up being disappointed. Runrig did this big outdoor show in Scotland three weeks ago. We played for 50,000 people on the banks of Loch Lomond on a tremendously beautiful day. After the show we met a journalist who has seen us many times before. He buys and likes our records and he often reviews them. So he told us we were a really strange band because mostly when he goes to see bands in concert, he puts their records on afterwards and usually the record is much better than the band he has just seen. With us, he said, it is exactly the opposite. Maybe there is a lesson to be learned that we need to do our albums more in the form we do our live music.

Petra Zeitz: How long do you work on an album in the studio?

Donnie Munro: This album took us three months from start to finish. That's not a long time by the standards of many people. There are different ways of working. You can go into the studio with a very vague idea and spend a lot of time experimenting and trying out things. I like to go into the studio and be quite immediate to feel a fresh attitude to the songs. If you labor a long time in the studio your head drops and you want the work to end. That comes out on the records, you know, you can feel it. So we try to avoid that.

Petra Zeitz: Have you played in North America yet and what was the reaction there like?

Donnie Munro: Many people have said to us that Canada should be a great place for the band because a lot of the Canadian population is made up of Scottish families. So we went to Canada and we had a great time. We played an outdoor festival at Winnipeg for 20,000 people. That was our first concert in Canada, so it was nice for it to be on that scale. The thing that we noticed though is that Canada seems to suffer a great deal from being the next door neighbor of the States. All of the Canadian bands that we met there were begging us to give them the names of agents in Europe because they felt that they couldn't break out of Canada. It's a huge country in terms of its size, but when you compare its actual population to the size of the area, it's quite small. The music industry and the opportunities for Canadian musicians are quite limited. But we will go back to Canada and also tour the United States. To make an impact in the States is a great challenge for us.

Petra Zeitz: The lyrics of your songs are always rather poetic. One could read them like a poem without having to listen to the music.

Donnie Munro: I know that if Calum was sitting here he would be very embarrassed for me to say this, but I think Calum's writing stands up on its own without melodies. He would hate to be thought of as a poet, though. I think this is because of the stereotypical idea that poetry isn't everyone's cup of tea. Some people think it's an art form for academics, and songwriters usually have an easier access to communication. I think that's why Calum would be happier thinking of himself as a songwriter rather than a poet.

Petra Zeitz: Have you ever felt any resentment from the English music business because you have made it out of Scotland?

Donnie Munro: The big thing about London is that there was a time when everybody who wanted to be successful had to live there to get noticed. We have done the opposite. We didn't go to London and we hardly ever played there. We set up our own label and didn't ask for record deals. But we became noticed because we started selling large quantities of albums. The London record companies noticed our records appearing in the independent charts and so they contacted us. Everything was done by our rules and not by the rules of the music industry. I'm glad we did it that way because we learned a lot by running our own record label and by having to set it up with our own money. We had to take the risk of whether a project would be successful or not. We learned the whole process of recording, manufacturing, designing and marketing. So now that we are with a major record company, we know exactly what we want them to do.

Petra Zeitz: Does your own label still exist?

Donnie Munro: Yes, it does. We always left the potential to sign other artists. We still have our own back catalog. Maybe at some point in the future we will either record new artists or use the label to put out solo projects by the band members.

Petra Zeitz: Would you like to do a solo album yourself and if so, would your solo music be much different than Runrig's?

Donnie Munro: I would like to record a solo album, but I would need to work very hard, I think. I have written plenty of songs but they still need a lot of work. It would be nice to get other musicians in to work along with some of the band members. My music would be different because Calum and Rory write the songs for Runrig. Calum, Rory and I have always been very close, we grew up together, and we have very similar backgrounds. When they started writing these songs, the band really grew and became serious about performing. Their confidence as songwriters grew as the success of the band developed. But all the other band members, in their own right as musicians, write their own songs. Peter Wishart, the keyboard player, writes a lot of music for television. We all have material for possible future solo projects, but at the moment the band takes up everybody's time.

ANDREW STRONG

Still a fresh face in the music business, Andrew Strong was born in Ireland in Wicklow County in 1973. His father was Rob Strong, a singer with the Plattermen. At the age of eight, Andrew had his first chance to perform on a stage and he loved it so much that by 11 he was singing regularly in public.

Five years later he was discovered by the successful movie director Alan Parker and given a leading role in *The Commitments*, now a rock 'n' roll movie classic. As in real life, Andrew played a singer with a rock band. After completing the film and recording the soundtrack album, Andrew Strong, by now 18 years old, was signed as a solo artist by a major American record label. Having witnessed Strong's first concert appearance, the British newspaper *Mail on Sunday* proclaimed: "In terms of stage presence Andrew Strong is at least 37! It's a rare thing to find confidence without arrogance, but he's got it. This rasping-voiced prodigy will enjoy himself for some time yet."

The soundtrack album, "The Commitments," with Strong on lead vocal became such a big chart success all over the world that a follow-up "The Commitments II" was also released. In the summer of 1992 Andrew Strong was due to record his first true solo album.

The following conversation with Andrew Strong took place just before Andrew and his band played at the international "Filmball" in Munich.

Petra Zeitz: How did you get the part of Deco in *The Commitments* as you were only 16 years of age at the time?

Andrew Strong: At first I was hired to come on and sing as a session singer during auditions. Alan Parker heard me sing "Mustang Sally" and about four days later I got a phone call

Andrew Strong

from John Hubbard, the casting director, saying: "Congratulations, you got the part of Deco." I hadn't even applied for it!

Petra Zeitz: Was it difficult for you to suddenly be thrown into acting when you were basically a musician?

Andrew Strong: No, I found the acting very easy. The only thing I felt a bit conscientious about was Alan Parker. When you mess up he gets really angry, but that's just the type of person he is. It's like in school when you have a soft teacher and a hard teacher. With the hard teacher you make sure you do your homework every night and suddenly you're good. The filming itself was a lot of strain, but we pulled through it all together as a bunch.

Petra Zeitz: What was working with Alan Parker like?

Andrew Strong: It was great! I have been offered a couple of other movie things, but I wouldn't do them unless the director can complement Alan Parker. As soon as I do my solo album I will go on a world tour and then I would like to do another movie. Next time it's not going to be a musical film, but I would like to play a gangster or something like that.

Petra Zeitz: Were you sur-prised that a low-budget movie like *The Commitments* did so well everywhere?

Andrew Strong: Yes, I was surprised. I didn't realize it was going to be so successful in places like America, but then, when I went to Los Angeles it was at Number four in the box office charts and I thought, "Wow!" Apparently it was big all over Europe, too.

Petra Zeitz: Is the atmosphere of the movie true to reality? Is that what Dublin and the music scene there is all about?

Andrew Strong: In a way it is. It shows the ups and downs of a band, it shows good gigs and bad gigs. It's like, you tell me how many guitar players have Fleetwood Mac had? It's like that.

Petra Zeitz: Did you put a lot of yourself into the part of Deco, the lead singer of The Commitments?

Andrew Strong: I just put my body into it—that's all. Deco is the type of person who talks before he thinks. He's got an attitude problem and nobody likes him. He doesn't listen to anybody; he has no respect for people. Myself, I do have respect for people and I listen to what people have to say and stuff like that. At the beginning, I didn't want to play the bad guy, but on the way it was good, because— this is what people tell me— when you see Deco singing you intend to forgive him.

Petra Zeitz: Did you read Roddy Doyle's novel *The Commitments* before the film was made?

Andrew Strong: No, I haven't read the book to this day.

Petra Zeitz: I didn't like the end of the movie, where on the verge of success, the band breaks up.

Andrew Strong: Everybody's ego clashed at the end and there's no point being in a band if you're not happy. If any one of my musicians wasn't happy, I wouldn't have him in the band. I have to have people around me who are happy all the time. If you're depressed, don't come near me!

Petra Zeitz: The Commitments was so-called "Dublin soul" music. Who are your favorite bands?

Andrew Strong: I love soul music, but just because I'm in a soul band doesn't necessarily mean that I just like soul. I love all different types of music. I love rock 'n' roll and funk. I love the Average White Band, AC/DC, Aerosmith. I'm into every type of music.

Petra Zeitz: Are you into Irish music as well?

Andrew Strong: Yes, I love traditional music because I have to respect the people who play it. A lot of people can put down the traditional Irish music, but to me it's probably one of the hardest things to play. I don't put it in my own music, but I love it as a pastime.

Petra Zeitz: Did you ever strive for any career other than music?

Andrew Strong: I wanted to be an architect but that was when I was very young.

Petra Zeitz: Did you have a band before you got the part in *The Commitments*?

Andrew Strong: I've been in bands since I was 11, but just before appearing in the film I went to boarding school getting myself an education. I used to watch my father's gigs and be the roadie for him. The band I have now has been together for six months. They're all friends of mine from Dublin. Most of them actually played on the Commitments' albums. They are like the real Commitments because in the film you see mainly actors. My music is quite different to the Commitments' stuff, though. I play more funk rock but I'm probably going to have to sing "Mustang Sally" and "Try a Little Tenderness" for the rest of my life.

Petra Zeitz: You're going to record your next album in San Francisco. What made you choose this location?

Andrew Strong: My producer likes it but I've also stayed in Berkeley before and I thought it was pretty cool. It's the real hippie kind of thing there just because I have a ponytail people come up to me and say: "Peace, man, peace!"

MIDGE URE

Born in Glasgow in 1953, Midge Ure found his first success with a band called Slik whose single "Forever and Ever" proved to be a No. 1 hit in the U.K.

Midge Ure became a prime mover in the new romantics scene of the early eighties. After a short spell with the Rich Kids, he formed Visage with Steve Strange on vocals. Their synthesizer-based sound on "Fade to Grey" and "Mind of a Toy" soon established them on an international level. Midge Ure left Visage to join Ultravox in 1980. Their hit single "Vienna" was regarded as a milestone in innovative new wave music and earned them several prestigious awards.

In 1984 Ure found worldwide fame with Bob Geldof with whom he co-wrote Band Aid's "Do They Know It's Christmastime." It became the fastest selling single in history.

Since his departure from Ultravox, Midge Ure has released several solo albums and organized various all-star bands for charity events. He also became a renowned director of music videos.

In late 1991 Midge Ure toured Europe with his own band, supporting the album "Pure." The following conversation took place on the eve of his show in Cologne, Germany.

Petra Zeitz: Are you an observing follower of the music scene these days?

Midge Ure: For about three years we have gone through this dance-oriented stuff, but now people are getting fed up with hearing the same tempo with very little music involved. The strange thing is that if you look back at musical history any big musical phase that came, be it dance music, new wave, new romantics or whatever you want to call all these things, when the

Midge Ure

period was finished, the next big thing that came along was the exact opposite of what had just been. After heavy metal came disco music, after punk came gentle, electronic music, and so on.

Petra Zeitz: You were very much involved in the new romantics movement in the early eighties. Have you always been interested in innovative music?

Midge Ure: I hate all the terms the media came up with. New romantics, to me, was a look, rather than a sound. I remember pictures of A Flock of Seagulls and Duran Duran at the time, and I always saw Ultravox as something different.

Ultravox had been around for four years before this whole thing happened. I got interested in synthesizers via Germany. They had innovative bands like La Düsseldorf, Can and Kraftwerk. That was what I was listening to at the time; it was a direct influence to me. I was making pop music before and then I heard this and it excited me. I took some elements of it, merged it all together and out came Visage and, to a certain extent, Ultravox. Then, of course, everyone copied what we were doing and they called it new romanticism!

Petra Zeitz: Why didn't you want to be the singer on the Visage project?

Midge Ure: I wanted to be a producer. I was tired of being in bands at that time. I wanted to go into a studio and realize my ideals, which I had never been allowed to do up until that point. I put some really good musicians together, wrote some interesting pop music and Visage was the first outcome. I was very pleased at having been given a chance to do that, but then I succumbed and joined another band—I joined Ultravox.

Petra Zeitz: Have you now assembled a regular band again?

Midge Ure: I don't have a fixed band all the time. Most of the guys I'm playing with these days have appeared on the "Pure" album, but never all at the same time. I worked with them individually, so when it came to putting a band together it was quite obvious who I was going to ask to do it. I have two drummers, one of them is Mark Brzezicki who used to be in Big Country, two keyboard players, a bass player and myself. So there's five of them and they all play amazingly well.

Petra Zeitz: How does "Pure" compare with your other material. You are with a new label and you have generally gone through some changes.

Midge Ure: I think "Pure" has a musical connection with my last album "Answers to Nothing" but it bears no resemblance at all to my first album, which was called "The Gift." Although that one was the most successful solo album so far, it now seems to be a bit of an oddity. It was a real mixture of ideas, and I think I started to get the ideas right on the last album, and now "Pure" finally is what Midge Ure sounds like as a solo artist. It has taken up a while to get into an area I'm happy with.

Petra Zeitz: On "Pure" you

have used some old, traditional instruments like Uillean pipes, yet ten years ago you were primarily known for electronic, synthesized music.

Midge Ure: I think you just change your ideas. Ultravox always said that we would use whatever instruments we could get our hands on to achieve the desired effect. A lot of what we were going through at the time was electronics, but we still mixed electronics with violins, or we used electronic and acoustic drums together, which had never been done before. We used a variety of instruments. Six or seven years ago, my ideas began to change to the extent that, on the last Ultravox album, I worked with the Chieftains for the first time. They recorded a song called "All Fall Down" with Ultravox and I thought it was a great combination. We also did a thing called "All in One Day," where George Martin orchestrated a whole track and we did it with a complete orchestra. So, at that time, I started to think there were other areas of music which are just as interesting as using a synthesizer.

Petra Zeitz: Do you support the idea of illustrating a pop song with a video?

Midge Ure: Videos have now become a necessity. When the "Vienna" album came out ten years ago, Ultravox asked the record company if we could do a video. We had to really push them into letting us do it. Now it's written in your contract that for each album you have to do at least two videos. It's a bit of a pity in a way because I like to listen to music and imagine what the writer and the singer are saying, imagine the scenario, imagine my own movie in my own head, the way I used to do when I was a kid. I used to put my headphones on and go into this other world, imagine all the characters and everything that way going on in the song. Videos eliminate that. Once you've seen the video, it has killed your imagination and you constantly refer back to the video when you hear the song on the radio.

Petra Zeitz: Do your own videos correspond with your imagination or are they the ideas of the appropriate director?

Midge Ure: I'm always the director; that's the difference with me. I'm the one in charge for the videos. Most people get an outside director involved, tell him or her their ideas and then he or she goes out and makes whatever video they think. I don't want that. I script and direct them myself. I also did most of the Ultravox videos, and some for Fun Boy Three and for Bananarama. It's just something I find interesting.

Petra Zeitz: Don't you find it difficult directing other artists' videos then?

Midge Ure: I went through a period of doing some bits for other people, and then I went off making videos totally because I got tired of it. Everyone was basically making the same video, you know, someone would make something interesting and then a hundred other people would come in and make the same video, using the same story and the same idea. So I just got tired of it for awhile. I started getting back into it again a couple of years ago.

Petra Zeitz: In the mid- and late eighties you were often responsible for putting all-star bands together for charity concerts. Has that run its course now?

Midge Ure: I'm still getting asked to do it. Amnesty International has been haunting me for the last week because they are organizing a big concert for their 30th anniversary. Although I'm obviously very sympathetic to AI, I just can't bring

myself to put together an allstar band again. There must be someone else who can do that! They pressure me like hell for me to get in charge and do the business. It can be fun sometimes, but right now I physically don't have the time to do it. I don't think it has run its course, though. There will always be rock-oriented charity events. But I'm not convinced that a concert or a record is the answer to anything. I know they can generate a lot of money as well as a lot of public interest, but I've seen a few big, globally satellited concerts recently where I was wondering if these guys on stage knew why they were there. I wondered if they actually understood what they were there for. They just came on and sang their new single, plugged their new album and their tour, and didn't even mention the reason why they were there. I've become a bit cynical about it. I don't think the feeling was right on a lot of those charity gigs recently.

Petra Zeitz: I think for Live Aid the feeling was absolutely right but later events got a bit out of hand.

Midge Ure: I agree! I think the industry got its claws in it and realized it's a massive publicity machine. Everyone saw what happened to U2 and everyone saw the Queen albums going back into the charts after Live Aid. It was simply because those bands were brilliant and they certainly didn't do it for publicity, but the record companies thought: "Wow! Let's get our bands on the next show that happens, whatever it happens to be!"

Petra Zeitz: Did you enjoy performing with the all-star bands?

Midge Ure: Oh, it was wonderful! For the Prince's Trust concerts in England the band consisted of Eric Clapton, Mark Knopfler, Phil Collins and Elton John, and then our guest singers were Tina Turner, Rod Stewart as well as Paul McCartney. It was fantastic! All those guys are only as successful as they are for one reason: It's because they are actually very talented people. And they have no egos, they all work with each other, they are all as well known as each other so they just go on stage and it's good fun for them, too.

Petra Zeitz: Would you like to produce other artists?

Midge Ure: I get asked to do that a lot. The problem with taking on productions is that you also take on egos. If there are five people in a band there is always one that hates what you do. If I make myself do it, I have got to have the temperament to deal with that, but with the egos and internal problems that bands have right now I just don't want to. When I stop doing my own music I may do some production work.

BLUES
GUITARISTS

ALBERT COLLINS

Albert Collins was born in Texas in 1932. He took guitar lessons from his cousin, Lightnin' Hopkins, who taught him to tune his guitar in a minor key. Hopkins himself had switched from organ to guitar upon hearing John Lee Hooker's "Boogie Chillun."

By the age of 15, Collins was playing the clubs with Clarence "Gatemouth" Brown. He formed his own band only two years later. In the fifties Collins achieved certain chart success and later became a household name during the electric blues craze of the sixties. In 1969 he headlined at the Fillmore East in New York. In the seventies Albert played gigs in Washington State where he first met upcoming blues man Robert Cray.

Through the eighties he released a series of seven albums which included the Grammy-nominated classics "Ice Pickin'" and "Cold Snap." In 1985 he recorded "Showdown" alongside Cray and Johnny Copeland, bagging a Grammy for that year's best blues album. Albert Collins played on Gary Moore's million-selling "Still Got the Blues" album and played with Eric Clapton in London.

In 1991 Collins released his much acclaimed "Iceman" album and went on tour with his current band "The Ice Breakers."

Composer John Zorn described him as "the greatest blues man alive."

The following conversation with Albert Collins took place at his London hotel during the "Iceman" tour in early 1991.

Petra Zeitz: When did you start playing the blues?

Albert Collins: I was 16. My father played guitar, but not professionally. My cousin taught me how to play. I also have an uncle that played guitar. Now, he is a minister in Dallas, Texas.

Albert Collins

So it got around the family a little bit.

Petra Zeitz: How do you feel about the blues revival of the nineties? Did it have any effect on you?

Albert Collins: Well, I've been living in Las Vegas for the last five years. I didn't think there was a blues society in Las Vegas, but there is! I've played Las Vegas twice, down in the valley. I think the blues scene is pretty good right now and I hope it will stay that way. I've seen it changing for about five years, but if it stays where it is now it's going to be all right.

Petra Zeitz: What kind of changes did you witness?

Albert Collins: It took Stevie Ray Vaughan and Robert Cray to create an interest for the blues out there. I wouldn't say Robert is directly playing the blues, but the kids are listening to him.

Petra Zeitz: Have you ever lived in Chicago?

Albert Collins: No, but I cut all of my records out of Chicago. My record company was there and most of my musicians come from Chicago. I lived in LA at the peak time and I now live in Las Vegas. Chicago is the blues capital. Memphis used to be the blues place, but it migrated to Chicago. Originally the blues came from down South, like Mississippi, Alabama, South Carolina, and Texas.

Petra Zeitz: You have now started doing part of your recordings in London. Isn't it strange to record "Chicago Blues" music in England, instead of in the States where its roots are?

Albert Collins: No, it's nice now. The first time I played London was in 1979. I performed in a club called Dingwalls which is now closed. There were a lot of racial problems at that time and I didn't go back to England for years. And then all of a sudden London popped up again. I now enjoy playing there.

Petra Zeitz: You recently teamed up with a lot of other blues players. Did you enjoy the concerts you played with Eric Clapton in London recently?

Albert Collins: I really did. It was the first time I got a chance to meet Eric. See, when I played Live Aid in 1985 I knew he was going to be on later and I tried to wait around for him but I had to fly out to play another job. I walked right past him and the guy who was taking me to the airport said, "You want to meet

Eric Clapton, you just passed him right there!" I turned around and saw him, but I didn't get a chance to meet him. But the Royal Albert Hall concerts in London [with Clapton, Robert Cray, Jimmy Vaughan, Buddy Guy & Albert Collins, in March 1991] were really nice. Robert and I had played together about four years ago, but it was amazing for me to be able to play with Buddy, Jimmy Vaughan and of course Eric. I like that kind of stuff, it makes me keep up on what I'm doing. To be with other guitar players is very inspiring to me.

Petra Zeitz: Do you sometimes feel inferior to any of them?

Albert Collins: No I don't, but I don't know how the other guitar players feel about it.

Petra Zeitz: How did you get to work with Gary Moore on his "Still Got the Blues" album?

Albert Collins: What happened was that I cut a tune called "Too Tired." Gary thought it was my tune and he asked me to come and work on his album and we did that "Too Tired" together, but the tune was really a Johnny Guitar Watson tune. So anyway, Gary and I got to be friends. I met up with him and I'm glad I got to play with him. We also did a video together.

Petra Zeitz: Weren't there a few incidents during the filming of that?

Albert Collins: Not really. It was done in a little town in Michigan called Port Deposit, a little seaport town. It was nice, we got up and started, then there came a storm so we had to quit and go back the next day. I enjoyed it. The people in that town were very nice and enthusiastic.

Petra Zeitz: You're also on the "Mr. Lucky" album by John Lee Hooker.

Albert Collins: We did "Backstabbers" together. The whole album will be really nice.

Petra Zeitz: Is there anybody left you would like to work with?

Albert Collins: I want to work with Eric again next year. He has invited me to do another series of shows with him and I'm looking forward to that.

Petra Zeitz: Is a white man able to play the blues the same way a black man can?

Albert Collins: Color makes no difference, dear. Music is music, but they always try to keep this to black and white, but it just won't work. It's very ignorant because prejudice is no good. I tell all these young kids if you put me and a white guy in a corner, roll a tape and let us play the same note, nobody in the streets could tell if we were black or white. I never thought that music would be syndicated to the black and white thing; that's the only thing in music that I don't like.

Petra Zeitz: Are you going to keep on being on the road as long as you physically can?

Albert Collins: You know what? I feel good. I feel like your age! The touring doesn't bother me because I've never been on drugs in my life, dear. I tell everybody, all the youngsters, that in order to function properly you mustn't be on drugs. I used to drink hard liquor but quit doing that in 1983 and I don't smoke cigarettes now.

Petra Zeitz: Do you still encounter a lot of drug-taking around you?

Albert Collins: The music business is still full of drugs. I tell my musicians, who probably have a little problem, you know, the old habit, I just tell them: "You do your thing, but you don't do it around me!" I have no drugs in my possession so I have no problem.

Petra Zeitz: Has the audience reaction to the blues been

the same abroad as it is back home?

Albert Collins: It used to be different but now the blues is more accepted around the globe. Actually audiences in Europe give you more inspiration than they do in America. American people are spoiled through listening to all types of music. They have the blues, rock 'n' roll, country & western, and middle-of-the-road. People abroad just love American entertainment. It makes me feel good playing in Europe because they appreciate our music.

Petra Zeitz: Do you listen to any other types of music in addition to the blues?

Albert Collins: Sometimes I listen to fusion-jazz, I listen to rap, which has been around for years before the kids picked up on it. I keep my ears open. I used to listen to a lot of country music, too. I also like Buddy Holly. I was on the same label as Buddy Holly and I got a chance to meet him before he died.

Petra Zeitz: Is there anybody out there who, in your opinion, has the potential to make it big in the blues world?

Albert Collins: I haven't paid much attention yet, but I know a young man coming up now is Robin Forward. He's a very fine guitarist. I hope that Jimmy—his name will be Jimmy Ray Vaughan from the next album—will carry on with what his brother, the late great Stevie Ray Vaughan, did.

Petra Zeitz: You knew Stevie Ray quite well, didn't you?

Albert Collins: Oh yes. I played a concert with Stevie three days before he got killed.

You know I always have a flashback because I think if I was there on that particular night and the fog was in, I wouldn't have let him go on the helicopter. I would have made him ride with me. We would have arrived together but he wouldn't have been on that helicopter.* He would have paid attention to what I said.

**Stevie Ray Vaughan died in a helicopter crash on his way back to Chicago after playing a concert with Eric Clapton in 1990.*

BUDDY GUY

As a leading figure on the Chicago and United States blues scene for over three decades, Buddy Guy has long enjoyed a cult status amongst the world's elite guitar players. Jimi Hendrix once cancelled a gig so that he could see Buddy play. Jeff Beck and the late Stevie Ray Vaughan admired him, and Eric Clapton said in a recent interview with *Musician* magazine: "Buddy Guy is by far and without doubt the best guitar player alive . . . If you see him in person, the way he plays is beyond anyone. Total freedom of spirit."

George "Buddy" Guy was born in Lettsworth, Louisiana, on July 30, 1936. At 17, he was gigging in the blues bars of Baton Rouge, and by 1957 he relocated to Chicago. His impact was immediate: Muddy Waters force-fed him salami sandwiches in the back of a Cadillac after realizing that the young guitar-ist hadn't eaten for three days. His no-holds barred performances not only enabled him to beat out the likes of Otis Rush and Magic Sam in "Battles of the Blues" but also made him a hero with the blues-boomers of the sixties. He later opened the highly successful Legends club in Chicago.

As a sideman to the likes of Muddy Waters and Howlin' Wolf, as half of a duo co-featuring his fellow Waters alumnus singer/harpist Junior Wells, and as an artist in his own right, Buddy Guy is a true legend of the blues. His most definite statement on record is his 1991 release "Damn Right I've Got the Blues" on the British Silvertone label. It was recorded in London, England, and produced by John Porter. The album included contributions on guitar from three of Buddy's long time friends and admirers, Eric Clapton, Jeff

Beck and Mark Knopfler. In addition the Memphis Horns appeared on several tracks, and Little Feat's Richie Hayward was on drums.

In the nineties Buddy Guy continues to tour and play blues clubs all over the world. The following conversation took place shortly after the release of "Damn Right I've Got the Blues" in mid–1991.

Petra Zeitz: You've been playing the guitar since you were 17 years old. What made you pick up the instrument?

Buddy Guy: I don't know. I talked to my grandparents before they passed away and even they couldn't go back and find anybody that was musically inclined in my whole family. I used to try to make guitars even before I knew what a guitar looked like. I didn't even have a magazine that had a guitar in it. I used to take wire, rubber bands, strings, anything I could stretch tight enough to get a sound out of it, and try to bang away at it. I just loved it! A question I get asked now is, why I did not become a straight rock guitarist. But I listened to Muddy Waters, Howlin' Wolf, T-Bone Walker and I just fell in love with that music. After all of my old friends passed away I

found myself almost the last one who liked their music and could kind of imitate them because their shoes will never be filled. And I wanted to make sure that I could keep that music alive. The last thing Muddy Waters told me while he was alive was "Don't let the blues die." I'm still working on it, but I'm no comparison to the way those guys could play it and sing it. I just do the best I can and hope somebody will say: "Well, at least he did play with them while they were alive."

Petra Zeitz: Is it true that one has to have a traumatic experience to be able to play the blues?

Buddy Guy: I don't think that's true. To play it you just have to love it. To be a good athlete you don't have to have such a bad experience because that won't mean you'll ever be good at it. I love the blues and if you love something hard enough it's gotta work. It's like two people in love. If you love one another, nothing can get between that. That's the way I am with the blues. I've been in love with it from childhood until now. I've been with it for too long to quit it. I think I'll be with it until I leave this world.

Petra Zeitz: You come from

Louisiana but relocated to Chicago in 1957. Did this move have any effect on your music?

Buddy Guy: Not really. I mean you experience more and you learn more in Chicago and suddenly you're playing something you weren't playing when you lived in Louisiana, but that's just experience the way I look at it. Later on came different amplification, different guitars and they made different sounds. It did sound like the person himself was different, but I don't think that was true. During the sixties we had the Chicago Sound, the Motown Sound, the Memphis Sound and all those different sounds, but we didn't come up with these names—some journalists decided that. Out of Chicago we had a lot of harmonicas and guitars, out of Detroit they had a lot of groups and horns, same thing in Memphis, but I guess the beat was different. I had one of the old record players which would play 78s and you could slow the speed down to 45. You can hear blues even out of Stevie Wonder! I learned a lot this way.

Petra Zeitz: Has the blues scene changed much from those days to now?

Buddy Guy: Not much, be-

cause there's really not a lot of us left to play it. When the late Muddy and the Wolf and all those people were alive and playing the blues, they were so good at it that everything they sung to me seemed like it was something different, but if you sit down and listen to it, I think music is music. You could try and learn how to play like Muddy Waters or B. B. King, but sooner or later there's something you are gonna have that God gave you and it makes you different. Regardless of how hard you try to be exactly like a particular person you admire, your idol or whatever you want to call it, you will always be different. And that's what happened to me when I copied those people. I didn't invent anything, I didn't invent the blues.

Petra Zeitz: Do you feel nostalgic about the time you were playing with Muddy Waters and T-Bone Walker?

Buddy Guy: When I first started in Chicago, I couldn't draw two people! Nobody knew who I was. I met Muddy and he said: "OK, Howlin' Wolf and I will stop by while you're playing and a few people will come." I was getting all excited and I was making $5 a night, but when I got off stage that night the club owner told me: "You owe me $20. Muddy Waters and the guys drank up $20!" Next time I saw Muddy I said: "I can't pay my rent. You drank up $20!" but he said: "That's the price you have to pay to have Muddy Waters and Howlin' Wolf come by to listen to you!"

Petra Zeitz: There are a lot of young players out there now copying Buddy Guy.

Buddy Guy: Well I guess that's the way it happens. There are a few kids who are going to be good. I think, unless the blues is heard and seen as much as the rest of the music, the young kids might lose interest in playing it because they want to be on MTV. Young people have to be influenced by it, and they have to be able to make a decent living out of it. We have to have some young people who catch on and play the blues just like Junior Wells and myself do.

Petra Zeitz: Do you think the blues can survive in the age of MTV and short-lived pop trends?

Buddy Guy: I was watching TV before you came in and I thought, I would love to see Muddy Waters come across there, but I haven't seen that. Actually the year Michael Jackson won all the awards was the same year that Muddy died. I was watching him and then they'd have a big picture of Muddy on the national television. I said it would have been great for him to look up and see that while he was alive. My mother told me just before she passed, "Son, if you have any flowers to give to me, give them to me now, so that I can smell them. I won't smell them when I'm dead!" If the blues will get the exposure I would like to see it in my lifetime. I think we'll have a lot more of it. I want it to be on TV, on the radio, I want more media on the blues than we have been getting. Lately Stevie Ray Vaughan, Bonnie Raitt and John Lee Hooker have raised some eyebrows and you hear more about it now than I ever heard in my life. I just hope it doesn't go away again. It's been around a long time, longer than any of the other music you play. From what people have told me, the blues and spirituals are the oldest music forms we've got.

Petra Zeitz: "Damn Right I've Got the Blues" is your first record for over a decade. Does this album represent where Buddy Guy is at today?

Buddy Guy: I certainly hope so. I was just telling some people this morning that I haven't listened to it. They are picking up a Walkman now and I've got the tape. I didn't want to listen to it yet because I'm kind of jagged to myself. I always hear things I could have done better and I get mad at myself. So I told my family to wait until they hear it on the radio. Someone can then tell me how good or how bad it really sounds. As of now I've been hearing more good's, I haven't heard one bad yet, so I begin to feel maybe I should listen to it in the next three or four days.

Petra Zeitz: Are you saying you haven't heard a single track since you finished recording?

Buddy Guy: I didn't want to. I had to listen to "Mustang Sally" because we had to do it live. I had some rough dubs they sent me before they put the record out and I kind of briefed that and said: "That's enough. I don't want to hear no more." There is always something that's not right and I don't want to hear it.

Petra Zeitz: You chose a very fitting title for your album. I heard there's a story behind it. Would you like to tell it?

Buddy Guy: I was sitting in my club one night. Everybody was jamming and it was pretty full of people. When it was time for me to go up and play, some fans of mine were asking me if I was going to play the blues and I made the statement: "You're damn right, I've got the blues!" It just stuck with me and I decided to write a few lyrics around it.

Petra Zeitz: You recorded the whole album in a London studio.

Buddy Guy: I've been anxious to do that for some time. It's been 12 years since I had an album and what happened was that when I got the opportunity to do it, several labels approached me at the same time as Silvertone did. Something told me in the back of my mind that I wanted to come to London because my mind would flash back to Hendrix who was here, doing it. Eric [Clapton] is here, doing it. Beck is here, doing it. And these guys make good records and they are the greatest people in the world to work with when it comes to recording. It seems to me they have started and landed more than the people in America did, even though they learned a lot from the jazz days which no longer exist. But they seem to do a good job at it and if everybody is happy with this record, sooner or later I'll be the happiest man alive. I'm happy about having an album, but I'll be more happy if it is a good one.

Petra Zeitz: Was the fact that you did not make a record for over a decade a conscious decision on your part?

Buddy Guy: No I just don't think any record company wanted to have much to do with the blues. The blues has never made a lot of money for either the artist or the record companies until lately when the late Stevie Ray Vaughan, Bonnie Raitt, and then John Lee Hooker had good albums out. Suddenly record companies would say: "Wow, we better give this guy a shot at it again." During the Chicago days, at the height of the blues boom, Chess Records kept recording it whether it was making a lot of money or not. We never found out what they were doing, but I know they would put out blues records by all the great players. Chicago itself was a blues town and Chess Records even did a lot of jazz stuff. But when they went out of business, I don't know any other label that went straight after blues artists. I heard B. B. King mentioned lately that blues is more exposed now than it ever has been in his lifetime, and he is a bit older

than I am. I have to agree with him. I believe the blues is more exposed now.

Petra Zeitz: Has John Lee Hooker's successful "The Healer" album influenced your decision to sign with the Silvertone label in London?

Buddy Guy: No, it wasn't that. The first time I went over to London was in February 1965. I went alone and came to play with a group of kids called The Yardbirds and Rod Stewart was opening for me. I also came on the American Blues Festival organized by this German guy, Horst Lippmann, and I was playing with Big Mama and John Lee Hooker. I was having so much fun—I was the back-up band. The British people treated me so well, so I felt at home in a way of speaking. And then after that I became good friends with Eric [Clapton], the Rolling Stones and all of the guys who were doing well. I thought: "Gee, I should have left the States when I was 20 and just moved to England to record."

Petra Zeitz: Your new album was recorded very quickly, more like the original blues albums in the forties and fifties were done. Was that your intention?

Buddy Guy: I don't know if it was done as quickly as that. I went to London and tried to be Buddy Guy for a change, because I never was Buddy Guy when I went into a studio in the States. They would never let me play the way I play in person. When I was in the studio before, people were giving me so much advice: "It's a little bit too loud, or you're playing too much, or you're not playing enough." When I go to the audience I don't have anybody to say that and it seemed like to me I would get something over to the audience and I started to ask myself: "How come I can't do this in the studio?" I got the freedom to do it on this album with Silvertone and I'm very happy about that.

Petra Zeitz: Guest musicians on your album include Mark Knopfler, Eric Clapton and Jeff Beck—quite an impressive line-up. Can you tell me about working with these people?

Buddy Guy: Over a period of 12 years I would see Eric, I would see Beck, I would see the rest of the people that were on there and they would say: "Man, if you ever record I would love to go into the studio with you." And I said: "OK, if we get the opportunity you'll come!" Actually, the contract with Silvertone gives me the opportunity to do a live album as well. I think it might be a little rougher than this one, but when I play live the people bring something out of me. I get encouraged when I hear people around me. The BBC called me in 1987 because they wanted me to do a special show with Eric Clapton and they said: "The reason we called you is that Eric very seldom smiles and we asked his manager what it takes to make him smile and he said, 'Go and get Buddy Guy!'" Whenever we get a chance to play together we have a lot of fun. I smile a lot, too, because he's great.

Petra Zeitz: Would you say that your live concerts are more like jam sessions?

Buddy Guy: Yes, but the playing is still there. It just seems to me that the public brings an extra out of me because when they are there I always try extra hard. I think I owe the people exactly what they came out to see. And I don't think I should hold anything from them because I've got enough to give them 120 percent which is not that much.

Petra Zeitz: Do you prefer to

play in small clubs like the one you own in Chicago?

Buddy Guy: My club is not small. The first one I had in Chicago was small but the one I've got now holds about 400. That's pretty large compared to an ordinary blues club. The blues clubs in the fifties where I met Muddy were holding about 100-120 people. Naturally when the sixties came up we started playing outdoor things and bigger halls because we started mixing more with the rock groups. A lot more people will show up now to see the blues because the rock guitar players, the soul singers, and whatever, have a tendency to drop in on you. By me owning the club in Chicago, people always expect somebody to show up. They hang out at "Buddy's" because they never know who they are going to see.

Petra Zeitz: Do you choose the artists who play in your club?

Buddy Guy: No, if it was left up to me everybody would play there. Right now, every Monday the club belongs to the musicians. Whoever comes in and signs up to play can play. It's only limited to how many acts we can fit in from the time we open to the time we close. If I

get a chance and I don't get in anybody's way, I get up there and jam with them, too. For some strange reason I never get tired of music, I just love it to death.

Petra Zeitz: What types of music does a legendary blues guitarist listen to for pleasure? Do you enjoy any other form of music besides the blues?

Buddy Guy: You can come in and catch me. I'll pull Eric, and B. B. King, but if you come to my house you'll also find George Benson, some jazz, Count Bassie, Benny Goodman and so forth. B. B. King once told me that he didn't listen to too many guitar players because if you listen to horn players' solos and piano players' solos, you have a tendency to find something that maybe no other guitar player has. I listen to everything!

Petra Zeitz: You've teamed up with Junior Wells a lot during the eighties, and you even went on several tours with him. Do the two of you still work together?

Buddy Guy: We still play together. But when you play in small clubs and have two people there on stage, they limit the time you're supposed to play. It was getting to the point that I was able to play two songs and Junior played two or three, then we had to take a break. The audience did not know that—they were saying: "We go and see them and they don't play. Buddy plays two songs and Junior three and that's all they give us!" In the meantime the owner of the club wanted us to cut the show. So I told Junior one day that we were cheating the few fans we had and we had to stop it. We haven't always played together. He had his band in 1965 and I never was a member of Junior's band. We decided to play together right after we toured with the Rolling Stones in 1970. He had a band problem and I asked him to join my group. We tried it and it led up to the fact that neither one of us had time to play enough for the people who were still supporting us after we didn't make records for so many years.

Petra Zeitz: You published your autobiography *Don't Start Me Talkin'* recently. Did you intend to finally put the record straight about your history and that of the blues?

Buddy Guy: I was approached by a publishing company because they had heard

me mention writing a book once in an interview. People were writing books about us and half of the stuff wasn't true. I have talked to journalists and have seen some articles on myself which weren't true. So I wanted to write a book myself because I can tell the truth. I wasn't going to lie about what I have done and what I haven't done. A lot of journalists lie to sell a book, but I wanted people to know the truth about a blues musician. I've been through a rough time in Chicago, I've had guns put in my face, I've gotten no money for playing all night from 9 P.M. to 6 A.M. but the club owner had no money to give me. All these things were flashing back when I decided to write this book, some of the things I went through, some of the help I've gotten from people like Eric, the late Stevie Ray Vaughan, Jeff Beck, and the British people who didn't have to do this. They did it because of their love for the music.

Petra Zeitz: Do you have a highlight in your career you would like to share with us?

Buddy Guy: Yes, I have several. Actually, a big one in my career was for Eric to invite me to his Royal Albert Hall shows.* I understand that was something special because that place wasn't built for the blues. Another one was when B. B. King called me and I saw him and decided to walk by. I didn't want him to say anything because I was playing his tunes that night. But he stopped me and said: "Don't you go by me. I want you to come on the same show with me and play!" That and the Muddy Waters days are some of the highlights of my life. I have to think about that every day.

*In 1990 and 1991 Eric Clapton invited friends to perform with him in a series of concerts at the Royal Albert Hall in London, England. Both times Buddy Guy was amongst the selected guests. Albert Collins was invited in 1991.

CHRIS WHITLEY

Still a rather fresh face on the scene, Chris Whitley belongs to a new generation of folk blues musicians who grew up listening to old recordings by Robert Johnson, Muddy Waters and Elmore James.

Born in Texas in 1960, Chris Whitley has never spent more than a period of six or seven years at the same place. His parents moved to Oklahoma, but were divorced when he was only 11 years old. His mother took him to Mexico where they lived for a year before moving on to Vermont. It was there that Chris Whitley first picked up a guitar and started playing the Johnny Winter song "Dallas" which is still one of his all-time favorites.

At the age of 17 Chris left school and went to New York City. He started playing in clubs and bars and even in prisons. Twice he went to live and work in Belgium where he met his wife. His first daughter Trixie was born abroad. By 1988 new blues clubs had opened up on Bleeker Street in New York and Chris finally seemed to have found his niche. He met the highly successful producer Daniel Lanois who invited him to his own studio in New Orleans. The sessions resulted in Whitley's much acclaimed debut album "Living with the Law."

Chris is the only active folk blues player using an open-tuned national steel guitar. His song "Kick the Stones" was included in the movie soundtrack of *Thelma & Louise* in 1991. He also supported Tom Petty & the Heartbreakers on a nationwide tour, being selected for this job by Petty himself.

The following conversation with Chris Whitley took place in February 1992.

Petra Zeitz: You have played in clubs for years and now you're recording and touring.

Chris Whitley

Has your live experience paid off?

Chris Whitley: The concerts have been good so far. I think that people are surprised with the differences in the shows.

What I'm trying to do on stage is quite different from the record. It's a bit more rock, a bit more aggressive. I just like that. My first record is the kind of thing I wouldn't want to do live because it is too passive and quiet. I can't see me doing that in a live situation.

Petra Zeitz: Does that mean your next record will be more aggressive and suited to your stage performances?

Chris Whitley: I think so. I hope it'll be a little crazier. I don't want to fix my ideas on it too much.

Petra Zeitz: You were called a blues guitarist by the media. Are you very influenced by blues music?

Chris Whitley: Not very. I am influenced by it a lot somewhere, but I don't know very much blues stuff. I only know three or four people and it's all very old blues, none of it is new. I find most modern blues really boring, I don't like it at all. There are elements in it that I appreciate, but I just find it quite boring. My music is a mixture of a lot of stuff. For instance, I play slide guitar, but the way it is usually used, I don't like most electric slide guitars for its sound. I'm looking for something else, you know. I put limits on myself. I play the sort of music that I think I understand a bit, just by what I feel through it. It's what I do the best and what I seem to do the most honestly, but why that is, I don't really know. As a songwriter and writing with a certain blues tint, I try to get the most expression out of those limitations.

Petra Zeitz: Is honesty what you're looking for in music?

Chris Whitley: I'm looking for where I can be the most selfish, doing what I want to do the most. I don't think of my music in the same terms as most pop music is conceived. But I don't know, maybe I do.

Petra Zeitz: Who are your main influences?

Chris Whitley: I liked a lot of people. I think I'm encouraged rather than influenced by the people that I've liked the most. They are different people for different reasons. Some songwriters I respect a lot, some people I like as guitar players or singers. The guitar players I like are old Johnny Winter, Muddy Waters, Jimi Hendrix and Jimmy Page. These are all people I grew up with as a kid. My parents were listening to Led Zeppelin, Hendrix and stuff. As writers I like Joni Mitchell, Bob Dylan, David Byrne and Iggy Pop. As singers I really love Al Green and Stevie Wonder. Those are a few people I can think of now.

Petra Zeitz: Which guitars do you mainly play?

Chris Whitley: What I play a lot is literally a steel guitar, but it's called a steel-body guitar. I play a lot of electric guitars and I play synthesizer guitar. One of the songs on my first record I wrote on a synth-guitar. I also play the national steel guitars because they are the most pure in a simple way. They say a lot about me. The biggest problem for me being completely egocentric is that people think where I'm coming from is being like that guitar. The references to the national steel guitar are always Delta blues or Ry Cooder, traditional things. I'm really not that traditional. I'm not a purist who copies old music. I write songs and I don't try to do things that were done before.

Petra Zeitz: Has your songwriting developed out of your many experiences while traveling around, living in different places?

Chris Whitley: The fact that I travel a lot has to do with where I write from, it's not really what I'm writing about, but it's my vantage point. I never thought about it until I started being asked that question. Because I didn't grow up in one place, seven years is as long as I lived in any one place, and they were all places that were really quite far from each other. I don't have a home thing, somewhere I grew up and know a lot of people. The reasons why we moved a lot, the circumstances and what my parents did, all played a part in this development. My mother was a sculpturist and after my parents divorced, I lived with her and with my brother and sister in Mexico. She's an artist and we lived on the fringe of the normal world. Our world as a little family was not the normal scene and it definitely gave me some of that self-consciousness I have now.

Petra Zeitz: Being an artist yourself now, do you still feel different, like an outsider?

Chris Whitley: Yes, but now I have a license to be that way. In the art world people expect that you're that way. At the same time it's very weird, especially in entertainment. To a degree you're a freak show, an oddity, it's like: "Let's go see the weirdos!" In another way, people really need that because the consistency of our lives asks for that. I don't think of what I'm doing as art. I would love to think of it that way, but I don't. Art is a weird word to me. I like to believe that we live in a world of weirdos, I mean, it's not like there's a way that most people are; that is very consistent and boring. Most people have more strange histories than is ever really apparent.

Petra Zeitz: What made you want to leave the States and move to Belgium for a while?

Chris Whitley: It happened by chance. I was playing on the street in New York City and I met a guy who offered to manage me. He gave me a plane ticket and he knew all the big promoters in Belgium, so I went. It worked out for a little while and then it crumbled apart. I left there feeling really dejected. I left there and then went back and ended up staying. When I finally left again I was a different person. I got back to New York four years ago. My whole twenties were very weird; I wouldn't be 26 again for anything. I didn't know what I was doing.

Petra Zeitz: Suddenly you went from playing clubs to performing in huge arenas. How did you cope with this step?

Chris Whitley: All the things you do, like me playing in a little club in New York 12 years ago, or playing in a prison, or playing in places where there's retarded people,

everything you do gives you something. After enough years it all enmasses as experience. I'm on stages a lot and it's still always a struggle. I always try to get more out of myself. It's getting really nice now though, and for the first time I'm in a band I enjoy playing with. Before I enjoyed playing solo that much more, it was more expressive for me.

Petra Zeitz: Do you play with the same band you used for recording the album?

Chris Whitley: No, it's a different band, but in a way this is more like me than what's on the record. The band there was put together just for the recording. I really like the record and I feel like it's very much me but there are a few aspects that are missing, a certain edge that's only in the background. The album sounds too soft. I grew up with a lot of heavier music like blues rock, acid rock and that sort of thing, and it doesn't come across on the record as much as I wish it did. The songs are not depressing or sad, to me they are vital! To me they are direct expressions that aren't trying to sound cute or sweet. There's just this aspect of me which doesn't show enough on the record.

Petra Zeitz: Do you think this has to do with the production of it?

Chris Whitley: Yes, but it was not Malcolm Burn's fault as producer. For me, it was a very fast time and I also hadn't played with the band. I never played those songs or that style of music—the stuff I had been writing the most naturally since I started playing—with a band before. I couldn't imagine a lot of these things with a band, but we put them together with a band and it worked out OK. There just was this New Orleans thing which is a bit soft, very musical, but not aggressive. I really love New Orleans and I regard the musical culture there very highly, but it's not really my culture. The whole album was done in New Orleans and the production was a very fast thing. Three months before we started recording the record, I was working in a factory in New York. I met my publisher through Daniel Lanois, whom I had known for about a year, and two months after that I was making a record and I got a big advance payment. I was asking myself what was going on! Before that I had been working in this factory five days a week. My wife, my daughter and I were living in this basement apartment on a really shitty street. I was trying to write songs after work and I played them once a week in a little cafe—the same old stuff, nothing new, that I had been playing for 13 years.

Petra Zeitz: Is your first record "Living with the Law" a collection of your best material written over the years, or are they all new compositions?

Chris Whitley: At the time of recording the songs covered a three to four year period. I think "Big Sky Country" was about four years old, but some songs I wrote a bit later in New York City and some were even written in New Orleans.

Petra Zeitz: Where did you meet Daniel Lanois?

Chris Whitley: I was playing in a restaurant in New York and I met this photographer who offered to shoot some photographs of me. We went out to do some shots and she picked up Daniel who was a friend of hers and happened to be in town. We just played guitars together that day and we got along. I didn't know who he was or anything. He gave me his number and we played a bit more later that week. We kept in touch and I found out who he was. I visited him in Canada once at

Christmas and I went to see him in his studio in New Orleans a couple of times. The second time I went down there, I met my publisher. That's the whole story. Three months later I was making a record. It actually got finished in February 1991.

Petra Zeitz: Is this the first time in your life where you can live by making music?

Chris Whitley: Yes. Well actually I have lived off just making music before, but with very little money. It was always very difficult. I've gone through a lot of processes like "How many beats per minute are people dancing to?" I used to try to write that way. I used to record dance music, use computers and all that crap. It wasn't the most natural thing for me to do. "Living with the Law" is basically bass, drums and guitar.

Petra Zeitz: Was your record an immediate success?

Chris Whitley: It was pretty good. We toured, opening for Tom Petty, and we were received quite well everywhere. We did the Johnny Carson show and all the other big television shows. After the tour we went to Europe and Australia. I will start making my next record in the summer [1992].

Petra Zeitz: How did you feel the first time you had to perform in front of 20,000 people instead of 200?

Chris Whitley: It was fun! It's kind of frustrating being the opening band, mostly because you don't get to play very long, just about 35 minutes. But Tom Petty brought me on the tour because he liked my record and he was really good to us. We always had proper soundchecks and everything. Three months of doing that is still a lot of work for not a lot of playing, but the exposure is good.

Petra Zeitz: Do you regret that, once you're established enough, you might not be able to go back to playing the clubs?

Chris Whitley: No, I don't mind. You can always go back to the clubs. This last year has been crazy. I'm 31 and I've been playing a long time. If I'd been 21 and this thing had happened to me, I don't know how I would have responded. I think that my guidelines weren't so set and I was easily swayed. You get so influenced by people who pull you in different ways and tell you what to do and where to play.

INDEX

Music